I0803109

IMAGES
of America

KRUM

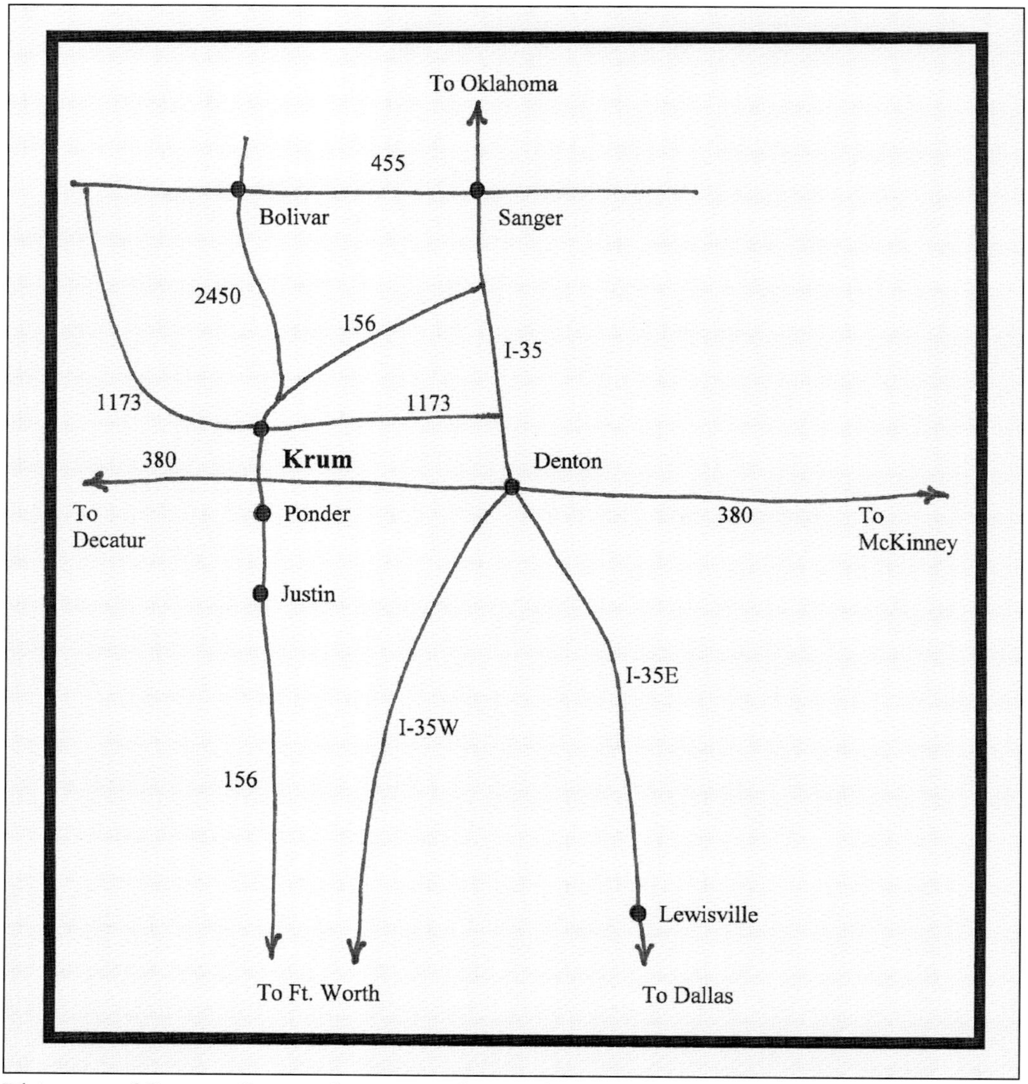

This map of Denton County focuses on the northwest portion of the county where Krum is located. Because of its position at the intersection of two state highways (156 and 1173), along with the presence of the Santa Fe Railway, Krum has become the banking and marketing center for this part of the county. (Courtesy of George U. Hubbard.)

On the Cover: This picture of the Krum Mill and Elevator Company symbolizes the role of wheat and grain as a source of Krum's early prosperity. The volume of wheat produced in the early 1900s kept this mill—along with two others—busy as the nation's leading shipping center, and the high quality of the wheat brought worldwide renown to Krum. The mill was a dominant feature of Krum's landscape until it was destroyed by fire in 1915. (Courtesy of Krum Historical Museum.)

IMAGES
of America

KRUM

Della Isbell Davis and
George U. Hubbard

ARCADIA
PUBLISHING

ISBN 978-0-7385-7991-7

Published by Arcadia Publishing
Charleston, South Carolina

Printed in the United States of America

Library of Congress Control Number: 2010940826

For all general information, please contact Arcadia Publishing:
Telephone 843-853-2070
Fax 843-853-0044
E-mail sales@arcadiapublishing.com
For customer service and orders:
Toll-Free 1-888-313-2665

Visit us on the Internet at www.arcadiapublishing.com

This book is dedicated to Kathryn Dodd, whose tireless efforts and countless hours have contributed greatly to getting the Krum Heritage Museum organized and functioning.

Contents

ACKNOWLEDGMENTS

The authors have received valuable help from several sources. All of the material in this book has been obtained from the Krum Society of Historic Preservation and its museum, the Krum Historical Museum, unless otherwise noted. The society and its officers have been most supportive in this project.

Even though Della Davis is one of the authors of this book, she needs to be acknowledged as Krum's historian. Since age 16, she has spent her life gathering photographs, memorabilia, and stories about Krum and its citizens. Della is primarily responsible for the establishment of the museum.

A number of individuals also need to be acknowledged. First and foremost is Kathryn Dodd, a board member of the Krum Society of Historic Preservation and a tireless worker in the museum. Kathryn has spent countless hours working with photographs and creating displays for the museum, and her work has been the basis for almost all of the pictures and information in this book.

Thanks also go to Donald Riley, who organized the society and made it into a functioning organization. Rod and Bonnie Barthold, John and Janice Callarman, Paul and Beverly Johnson, and Paul Monschke have all made valuable contributions of time and effort to the society and its museum, and therefore to this book.

INTRODUCTION

Krum is one of the jewels in the crown of north Texas towns and cities. Located 38 miles north of Fort Worth and 5 miles west of Denton, Krum sits at the intersection of State Highways 156 and 1173.

Historically, Krum's story began on March 13, 1857, when Texas governor E. M. Pease issued a 1,920-acre bounty grant of state land to the heirs of Charles Despallier. Despallier, an aide to Lt. Col. William B. Travis, had fought and died with Travis at the Alamo. The Despallier Grant, out of which the town site of Krum would be carved, was only a small part of the thousands of acres of state land that was available to homesteaders after Texas entered the union in 1845.

In December 1857, the administrator of the Despallier estate sold the grant at public auction from the courthouse steps in Houston, Texas. William R. Baker bought the entire tract for $40. It proved a good investment for Baker, as less than a year later he sold the land to Amelia Sterns of New York City for $4,800. Within three months, Stearns turned a neat profit by selling to a fellow citizen for $9,600. The land speculation shifted to Missouri nine years later, when John Morrison of St. Louis bought the tract for an undisclosed amount. Morrison then sold the land to A. W. Mead, also of St. Louis, for $2,000 in 1871. Mead broke up the tract and sold it in smaller parcels.

By 1876, a little settlement known as the Jackson community, named for land donor C. H. Jackson, sprang up on the hills across Hickory Creek, east of the present site of Jackson Cemetery. Because the pioneer families felt the need for a school and a place of worship, J. J. and Ava Barrett deeded 2.5 acres to the community to serve both purposes. Jackson deeded additional land to the community, and it was subsequently agreed that the north end of the plot would be used as a burial ground.

Krum's official beginning occurred in 1886, when L. L. Finley and G. M. Finley sold 2,000 acres to the Gulf, Colorado, and Santa Fe Railroad for a town site. The railroad established a depot in a boxcar about 2 miles north of the Jackson community and platted a town. It is believed that the town was named for A. R. Krum, one of the vice presidents of the Santa Fe Railroad. As a result of the railroad's actions, the entire Jackson community moved to the new site. This included physically moving the one-room schoolhouse and other buildings. Only the Jackson Cemetery remains in its original location.

The rich prairie soil of the region produced bountiful wheat harvests for which the community became famous. In the early 1900s, Krum was known as the largest wagon grain market in the United States. Over a million pounds of grain were shipped out in 1900, and it is said that the Chicago Board of Trade called every morning to ask about prices and volumes. The wheat grown in the area was of a superior quality, and it won prizes in many fairs, including grand prize in the 1904 St. Louis World's Fair. So superior was the wheat that it was eventually banned from competition at the State Fair of Texas in Dallas.

Krum's prosperity supported a hotel, 24 commercial businesses, two gins, two grain elevators, and one up-to-date flour mill. Its low, rolling hills provided beauty as well as fertility. At one time, Krum felt justified in advertising itself (on city letterhead) as the "Garden Spot of Denton County."

It was the citizens of Krum as well as the natural resources that gave the town its rich heritage. An example can be seen in the fire of 1907 that destroyed all the business establishments on the north side of McCart Street. When customers in McClister's Dry Goods Store learned that the store was about to be engulfed by flames, Floyd Curtsinger took charge: "Now don't you fellows get excited," he said, "but get busy and carry out these goods. Carry them carefully and you can save all the goods in this house." As he talked, he was taking shoes off the shelves and placing them on the counter. When the counter was loaded, the customers carried it out. They removed all the merchandise and even carried out the front doors. Similar acts were taking place in the other stores as well.

The weather brought other memorable situations. February 1899 was especially cold, with temperatures below zero. A Mrs. Brandenburger drove into town from Plainview in her cart to shop in R. C. Scripture's General Store. She was so cold upon arrival that she could not move, and several men had to carry her from her cart into the store. After warming a while, she collected her groceries, got into her cart, and returned home.

After a good rainstorm, a little branch running east of the railroad tracks fills with water. It is known locally as the "River of Jordan." On one occasion, two gentlemen of unsteady gait were wending their way home. Coming to the running stream, one said, "I think I'll baptize myself in the River of Jordan." He jumped in and had to be pulled out—a little more sober and wise. That is the way Krum's River of Jordan got its name.

Although agriculture was the early source of Krum's prosperity, the citizens were not lacking in "the finer things of life." Krum had literary groups and a debating society, and it supported a theater. There were fraternal organizations and ladies' auxiliaries. Sewing circles, quilting bees, ball games, and picnics added to the sociability and unity of the residents.

Today (2011) Krum is thriving and prosperous. The Santa Fe Railroad tracks, which run north and south, serve as a dividing line between "old Krum" and the newer residential additions on the eastern edge of town. Many new businesses have established themselves to serve these newer areas.

One

The Town

Krum is a wonderful place to live. Outstanding schools along with parks and playgrounds help make it a good place to raise a family. A well-stocked library and a weekly newspaper connect the citizens with the world, and a newly opened historical museum reminds residents of their heritage. Although the mills and gins are now gone, Krum still serves northwest Denton County in agriculture as well as in banking, public safety services, public education, and restaurants.

Krum's major claim to fame, however, is its people who are proud to tell the world that they live there. Without television, and with limited means of transportation, Krum's early residents found ways to socialize. The Literary Society provided opportunities for debates and dialogues, and there was an active needlework club and a Parent-Teacher Association. There was also a Masonic Lodge and a Woodmen Circle Lodge. Monthly activities, such as dinners, outings, and bazaars, were the norm in Krum's churches, and baseball games were held regularly.

On November 16, 1954, Krum became an incorporated city when citizens voted 75 to 13 in favor of incorporation. The following January, Francis W. "Pin" Fowler was elected mayor. After incorporation, many things were accomplished: The city took over the streetlights, paying for the electricity with tax money; additional streetlights were added; a city dump was purchased; and regular garbage collection began. Next, streets were paved around the school and all three churches. Krum became a progressive city.

In addition to their natural camaraderie, the people of Krum are enthusiastic supporters of their school basketball teams, which have been outstanding over the years. Both the boys' and the girls' high school teams have had their glory years, which include five state championships for the boys and one state tournament appearance for the girls. Krum now has a high school football team that will begin varsity competition in the fall of 2011.

Many descendents of the original settlers still reside in Krum—why go anywhere else? New families are also arriving continuously to fill the housing developments that have sprung up since the beginning of the 1990s.

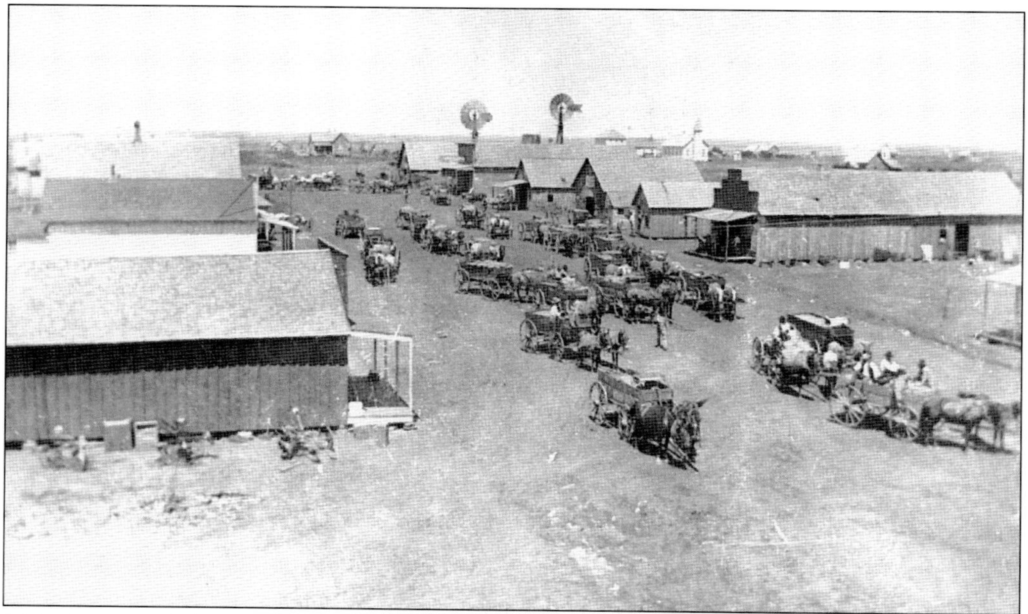

This photograph shows a busy northwest view of McCart Street in 1900. Brick buildings had not yet been "discovered" in Krum.

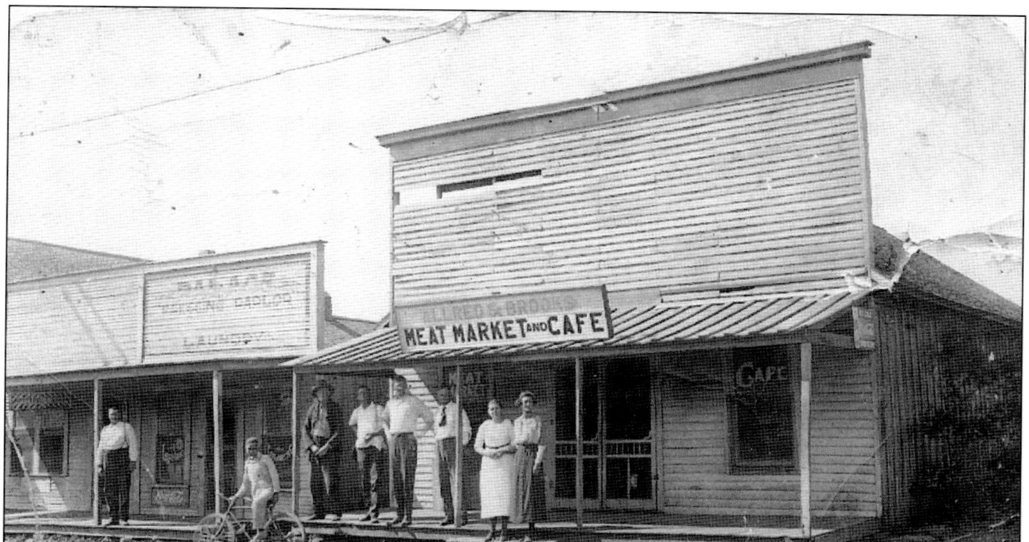

The first business establishments in Krum were wooden structures. Pictured in this *c.* 1915 image of the south side of McCart Street are, from left to right, Ned Gullett, J. O. McClister, Mark McFall, Bill Thomas, Basie Smith, Whit Renfro, Gladys Thomas, and unidentified. In 1906, a great fire destroyed every business on the north side of McCart Street.

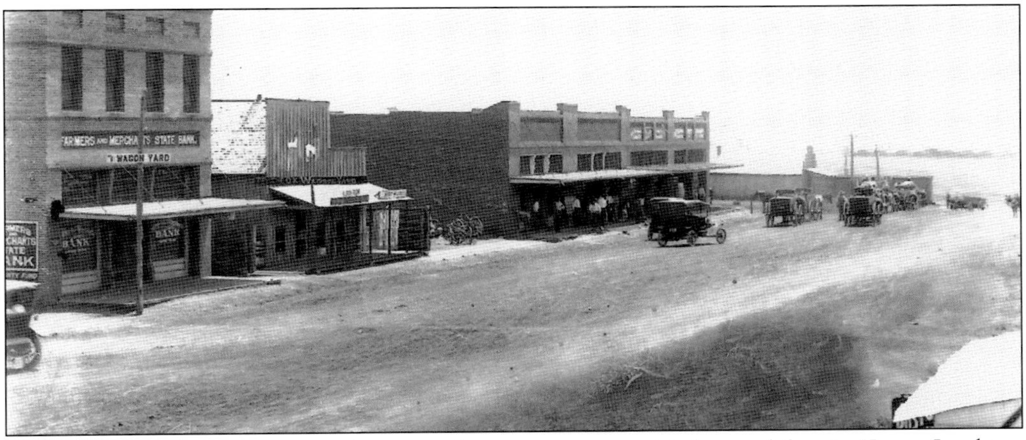

McCart Street, running east and west, is the main commercial thoroughfare in Krum. Looking to the northeast, this view dated in the 1920s shows the Farmers and Merchants State Bank at the intersection of McCart and First Streets. Immediately past the bank are brick buildings that contain the Silas Koiner Pharmacy and the McClister/Wilkins Dry Goods Store.

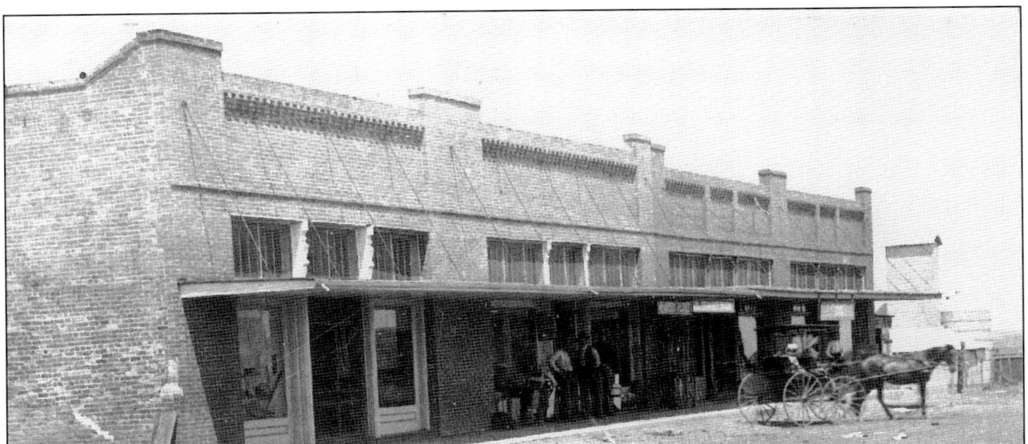

Looking to the northeast, a closer view of the pharmacy and dry goods store is obtained. These buildings were erected in 1909, and they are still in use as business and city offices and a restaurant.

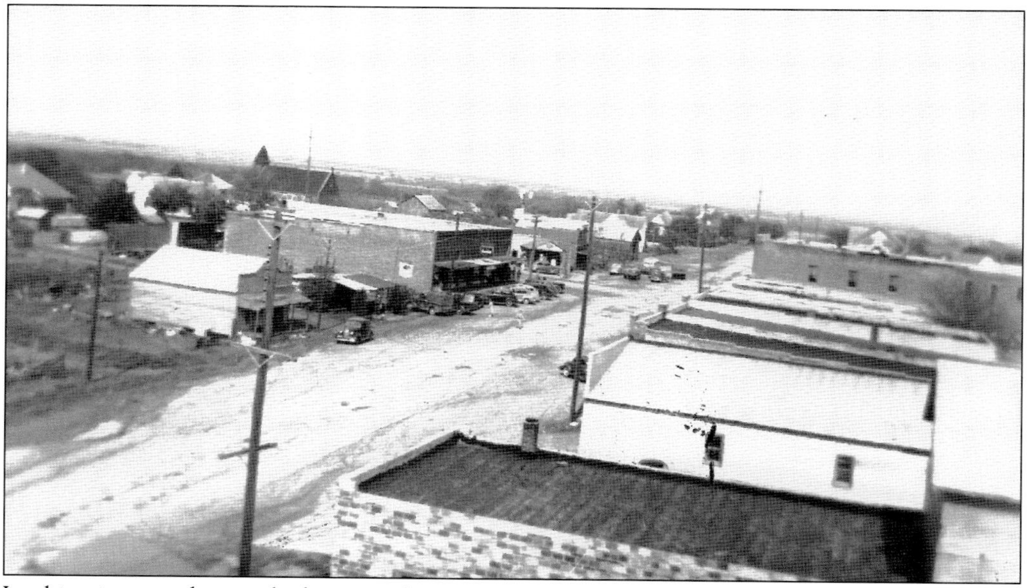

Looking in a southwesterly direction from R. L. Cole's grain elevator, McCart Street looked like this about 1940. The large brick building sits at the intersection of McCart and First Streets.

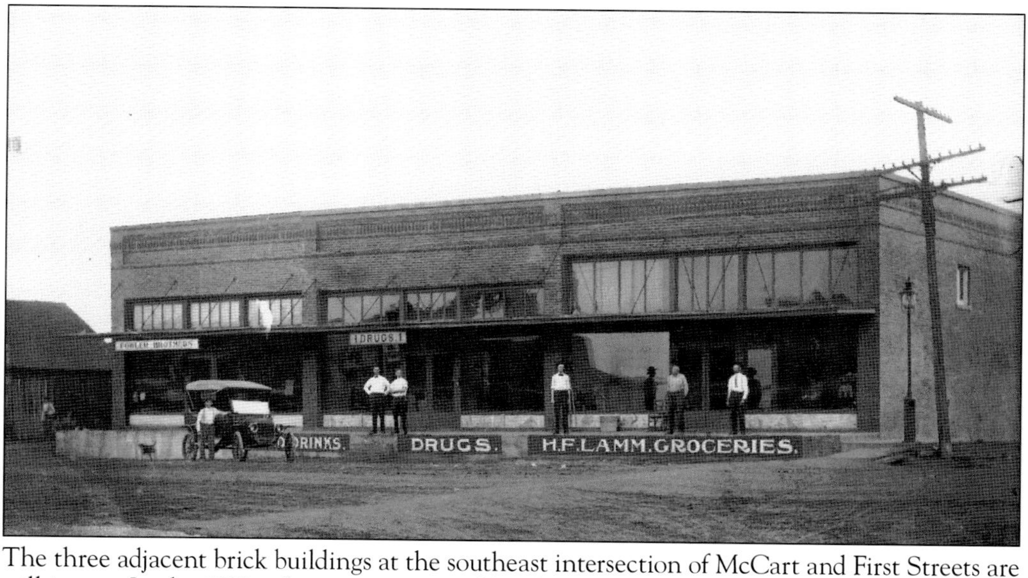

The three adjacent brick buildings at the southeast intersection of McCart and First Streets are still in use. In the 1910s, they were occupied by, from left to right, the C. R. Fowler Hardware Store, the Will Collier Drug Store, and the H. F. Lamm Grocery Store. The building on the left is currently occupied by Ms. Carolyn's Attic, and the Krum Diner is now where the Lamm store was located.

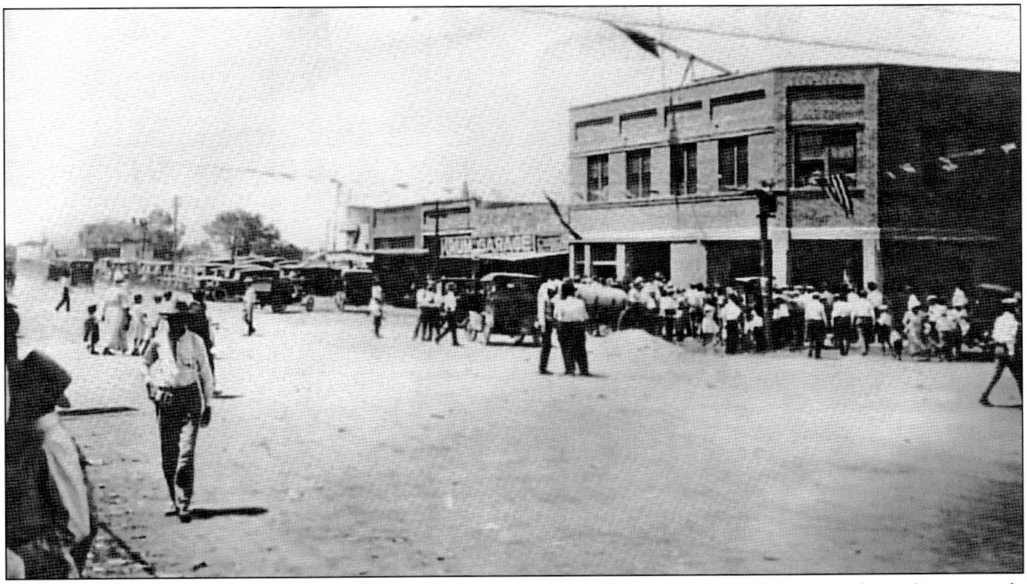

Looking to the northwest from the intersection of McCart and First Streets, this photograph shows additional business establishments in 1924. A crowd is gathered for the grand opening of the Muncy Building, which was built as a Ford dealership. The building now houses an attorney's office, a flower shop, and an auction house.

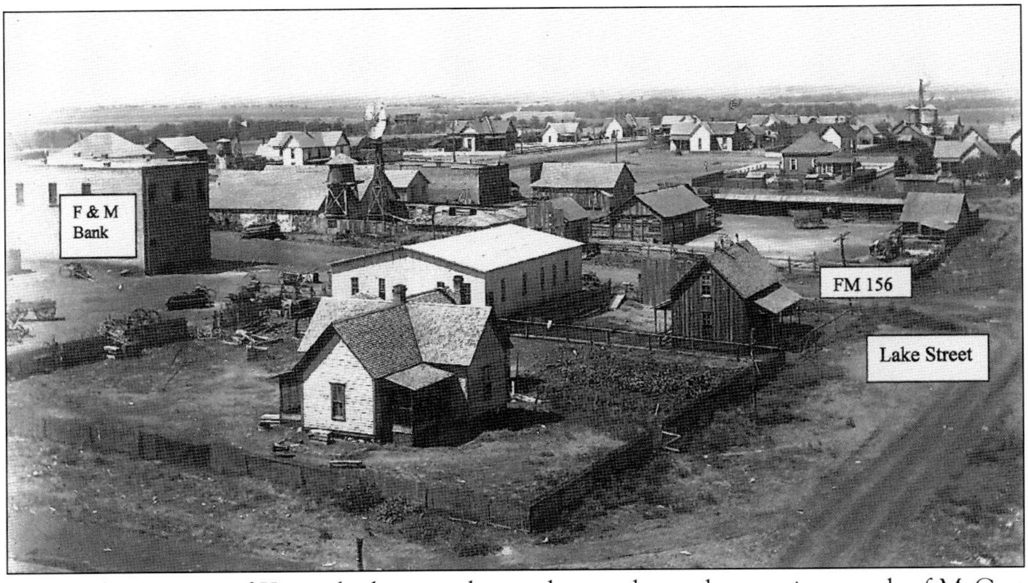

This bird's-eye view of Krum, looking to the southwest, shows the area just north of McCart Street as it appeared in the early 1900s.

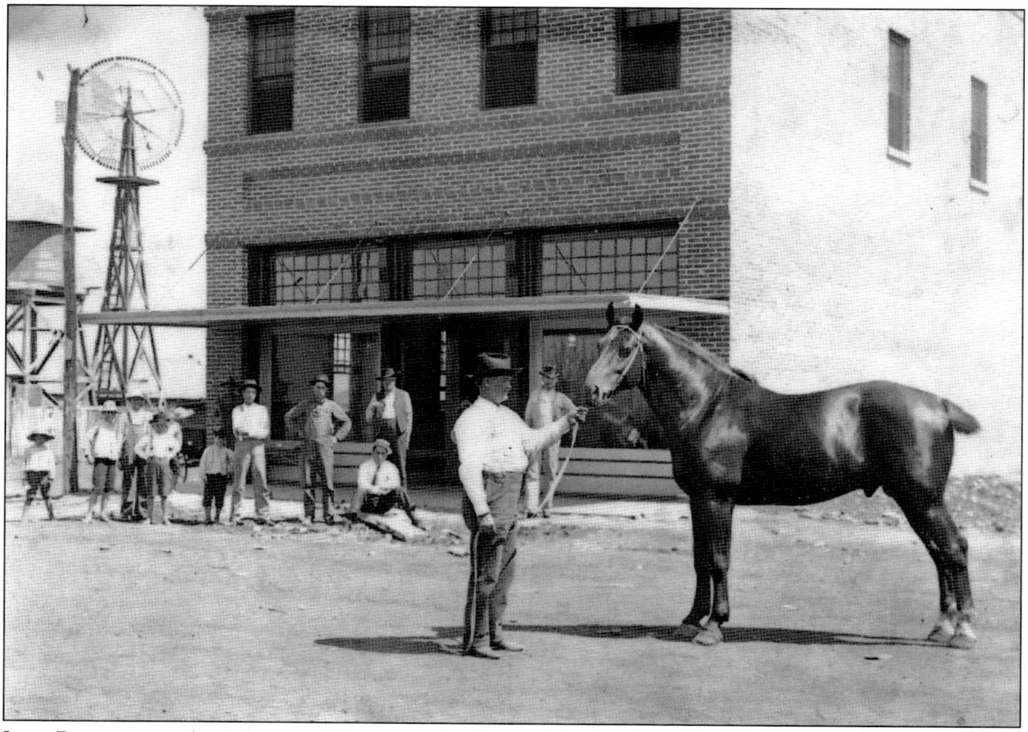

June Benton stands with one of his horses in front of the bank building on McCart Street. Benton owned a livery stable (not shown) to the right of the bank.

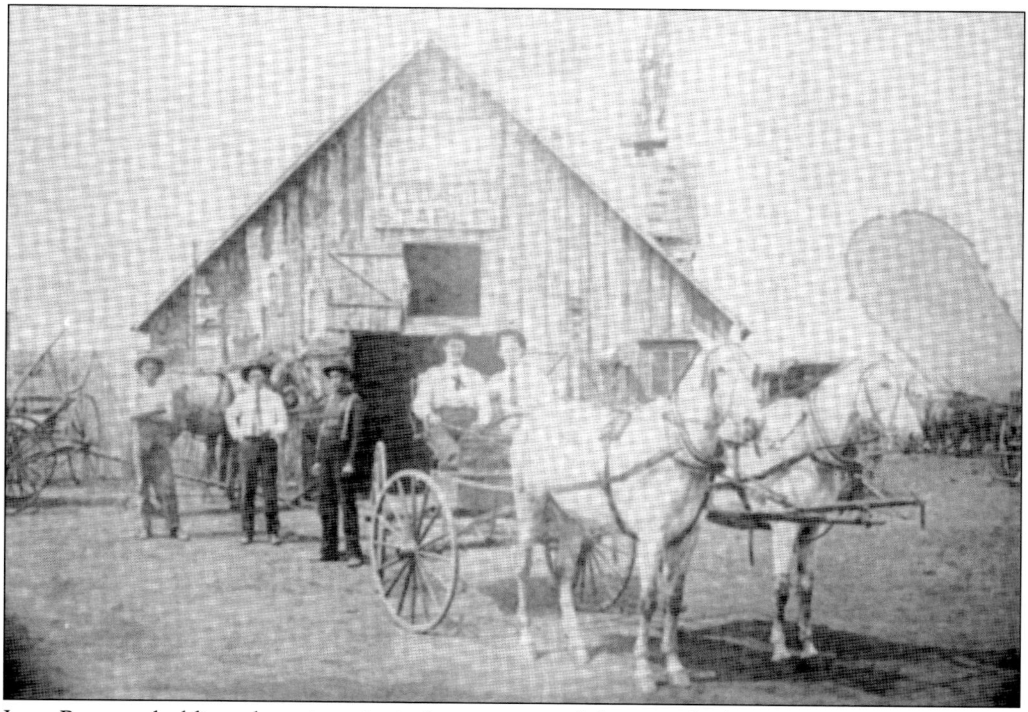

June Benton, holding the reins, sits in his wagon with his matched team in front of his livery stable on McCart Street.

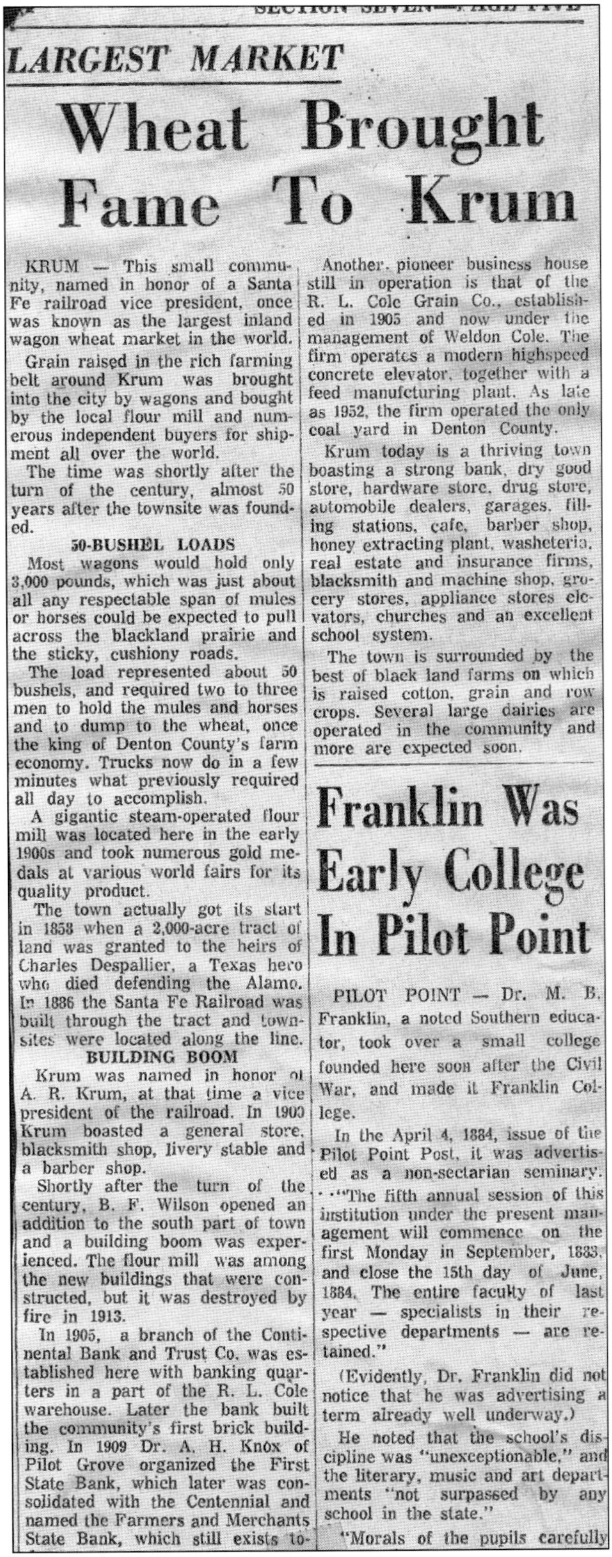

LARGEST MARKET

Wheat Brought Fame To Krum

KRUM — This small community, named in honor of a Santa Fe railroad vice president, once was known as the largest inland wagon wheat market in the world.

Grain raised in the rich farming belt around Krum was brought into the city by wagons and bought by the local flour mill and numerous independent buyers for shipment all over the world.

The time was shortly after the turn of the century, almost 50 years after the townsite was founded.

50-BUSHEL LOADS

Most wagons would hold only 3,000 pounds, which was just about all any respectable span of mules or horses could be expected to pull across the blackland prairie and the sticky, cushiony roads.

The load represented about 50 bushels, and required two to three men to hold the mules and horses and to dump to the wheat, once the king of Denton County's farm economy. Trucks now do in a few minutes what previously required all day to accomplish.

A gigantic steam-operated flour mill was located here in the early 1900s and took numerous gold medals at various world fairs for its quality product.

The town actually got its start in 1853 when a 2,000-acre tract of land was granted to the heirs of Charles Despallier, a Texas hero who died defending the Alamo. In 1886 the Santa Fe Railroad was built through the tract and townsites were located along the line.

BUILDING BOOM

Krum was named in honor of A. R. Krum, at that time a vice president of the railroad. In 1900 Krum boasted a general store, blacksmith shop, livery stable and a barber shop.

Shortly after the turn of the century, B. F. Wilson opened an addition to the south part of town and a building boom was experienced. The flour mill was among the new buildings that were constructed, but it was destroyed by fire in 1913.

In 1905, a branch of the Continental Bank and Trust Co. was established here with banking quarters in a part of the R. L. Cole warehouse. Later the bank built the community's first brick building. In 1909 Dr. A. H. Knox of Pilot Grove organized the First State Bank, which later was consolidated with the Centennial and named the Farmers and Merchants State Bank, which still exists to-

Another pioneer business house still in operation is that of the R. L. Cole Grain Co., established in 1905 and now under the management of Weldon Cole. The firm operates a modern highspeed concrete elevator, together with a feed manufcturing plant. As late as 1952, the firm operated the only coal yard in Denton County.

Krum today is a thriving town boasting a strong bank, dry good store, hardware store, drug store, automobile dealers, garages, filling stations, cafe, barber shop, honey extracting plant, washeteria, real estate and insurance firms, blacksmith and machine shop, grocery stores, appliance stores elevators, churches and an excellent school system.

The town is surrounded by the best of black land farms on which is raised cotton, grain and row crops. Several large dairies are operated in the community and more are expected soon.

Franklin Was Early College In Pilot Point

PILOT POINT — Dr. M. B. Franklin, a noted Southern educator, took over a small college founded here soon after the Civil War, and made it Franklin College.

In the April 4, 1884, issue of the Pilot Point Post, it was advertised as a non-sectarian seminary.

"The fifth annual session of this institution under the present management will commence on the first Monday in September, 1883, and close the 15th day of June, 1884. The entire faculty of last year — specialists in their respective departments — are retained."

(Evidently, Dr. Franklin did not notice that he was advertising a term already well underway.)

He noted that the school's discipline was "unexceptionable," and the literary, music and art departments "not surpassed by any school in the state."

"Morals of the pupils carefully

Krum's role as a large-scale producer of excellent wheat attracted national and international fame as evidenced by this article in the *Dallas Morning News* on February 3, 1957.

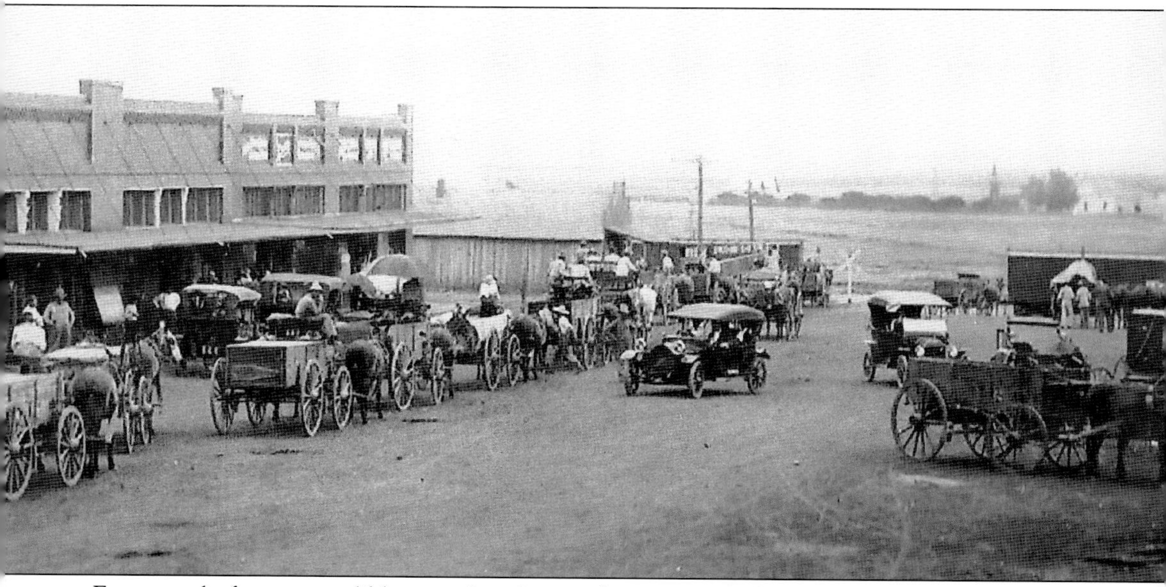

Every week, farmers could be seen lined up with wagons of wheat waiting for their turn at the public scale. A typical wagonload of wheat would measure about 50 bushels and weigh about 3,000 pounds. The area around Krum was renowned for both the quality and quantity of its wheat. The year 1900 was a banner year in which over a million pounds of grain were shipped from Krum. Krum's wheat won prizes in fairs throughout the nation, including grand prize at the St. Louis World's Fair in 1904.

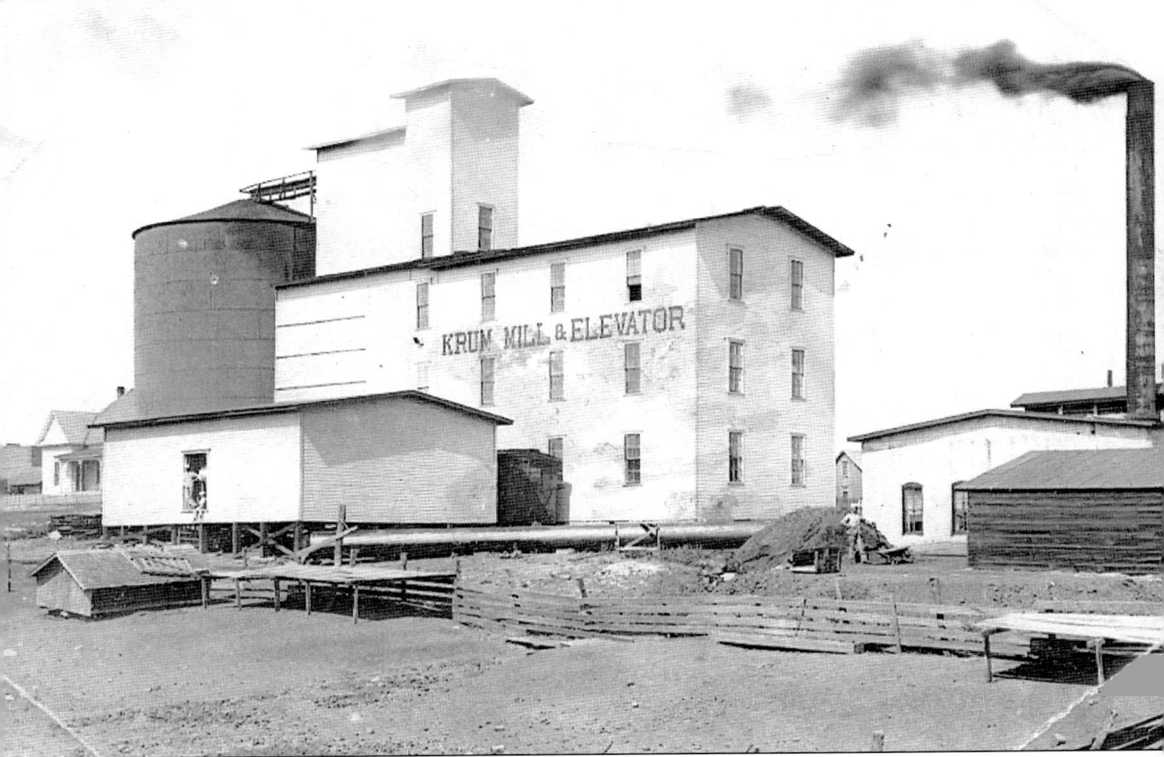

In the spring of 1901, Ed F. Lamm, brother of Harve Lamm, came to Krum and persuaded the farmers in the area to organize a stock company for the purpose of establishing a flour mill "where your wheat is grown." The Krum Mill and Elevator Company was formed. Lamm subscribed 50 percent of the stock, and the rest was sold to local farmers and businessmen. A gigantic steam mill was bought in Wynnewood, Indian Territory, then dismantled and brought to Krum. Its capacity was 150 barrels of flour per day, which later increased to 200 barrels. The capacity of the elevators was 30,000 bushels and later increased to 65,000. The mill went into production in August 1901, and soon 10 carloads of Rainbow, Red Ribbon, and Lily brands of flour were being shipped every week to as far away as San Angelo. In 1908, Lamm sold the mill to S. A. Blewett, who operated it until it was destroyed by fire in 1915. At one time there were three such mills in Krum.

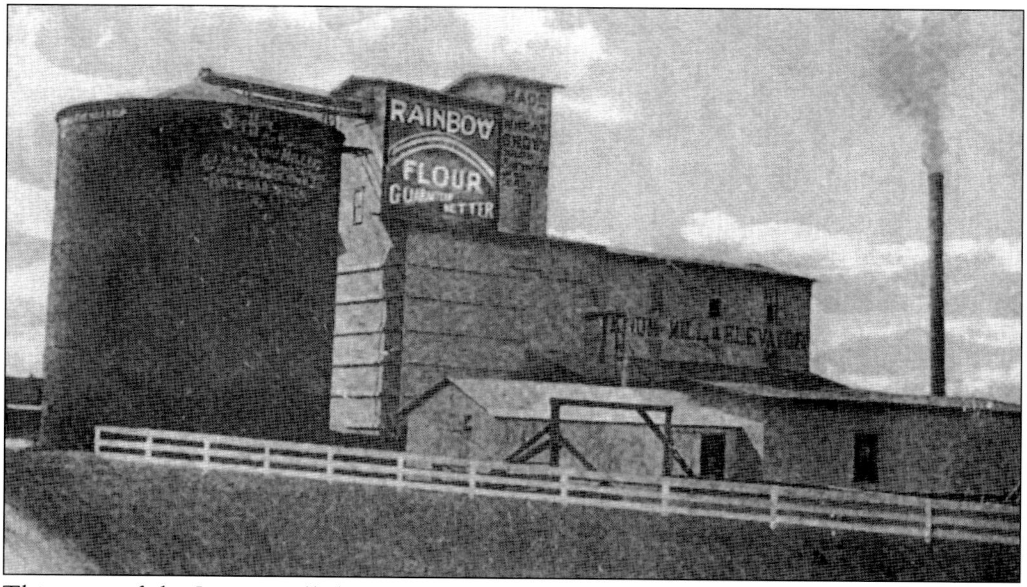

This view of the Lamm mill shows the large advertisement for Rainbow Flour, the facility's primary product.

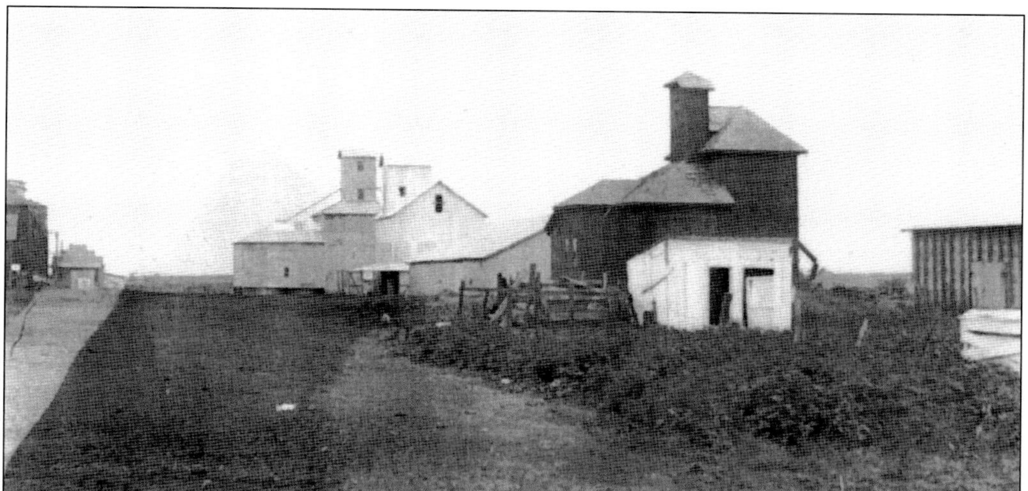

The Burrough's Elevator is the light-colored building in the background, and the Bewley Elevator is the dark-colored building in the foreground. Enough wheat was produced in the area to keep the mills busy.

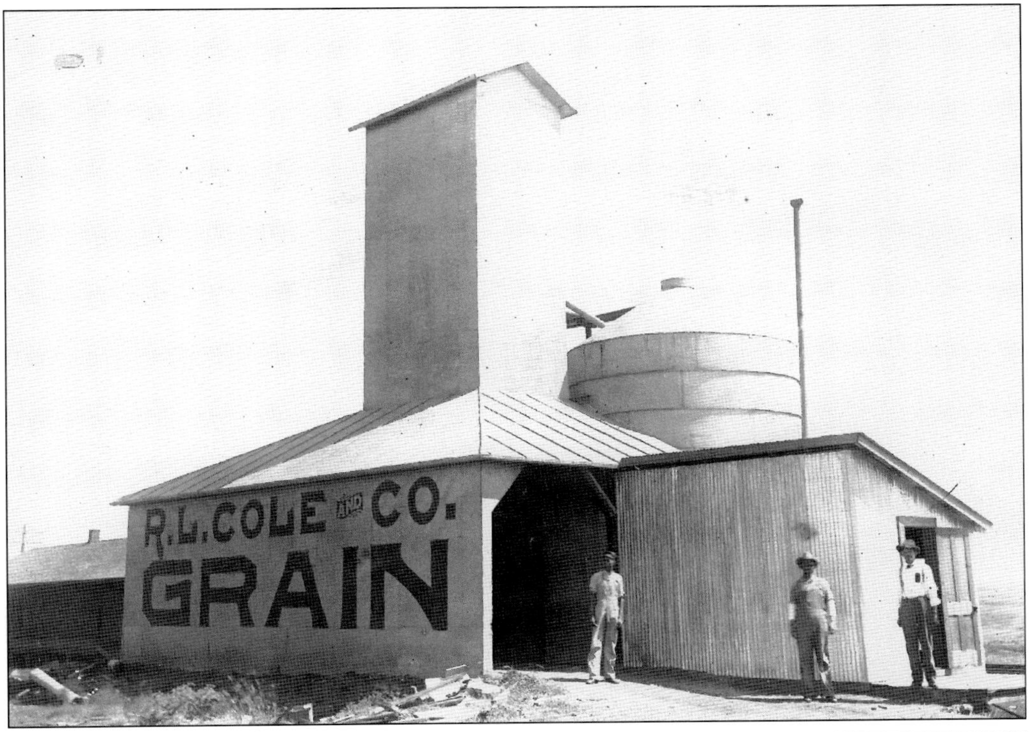

R. L. Cole is shown at far right in front of his first grain elevator. His brother-in-law, Walter Finley, stands in the center, and an unidentified person is at left. The concrete elevator was built in the 1920s, and the mill itself was on a lot to the west.

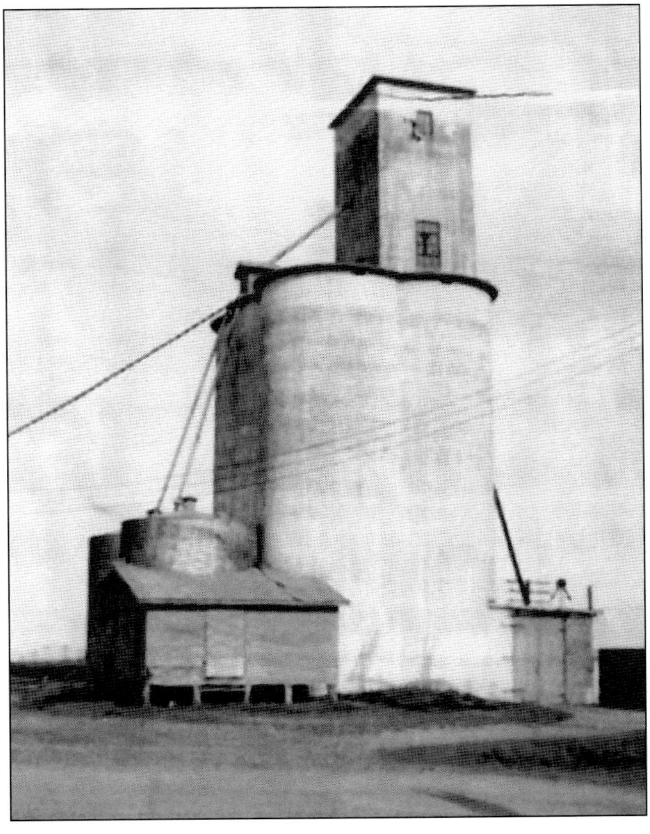

At its height, Krum boasted three flour mills. The R. L. Cole mill, which operated from 1905 to 1956, still exists. The concrete elevator currently serves as private living quarters for a local family.

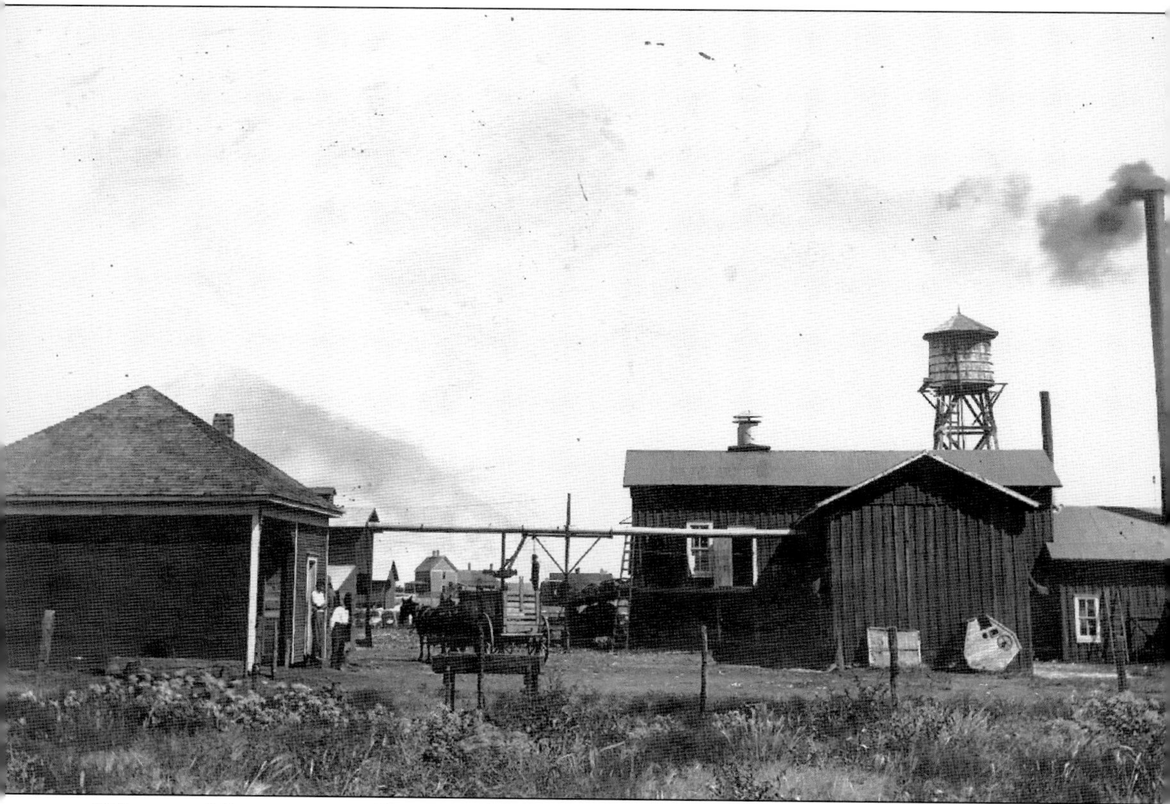

Wheat and flour were not Krum's only commodities. Meat and cotton were also produced here. The Knox cotton gin was one of two gins built in 1909. Constructed by Dr. A. H. Knox and later managed by his son, Cecil, the gin operated until 1950, when, after the death of Dr. Knox, L. R. Richey dismantled it and moved it to another location. In the 1920s, two more gins were opened. Around 1920, J. B. Henderson put in gin number three. In 1924, three partners—from left to right, Will Koiner, Lee Koiner, and W. E. Cox—built the Koiner Gin Company. Joe Voth installed the machinery and stayed on to operate it. Lee Koiner was the engineer, and Earl Cox was the manager.

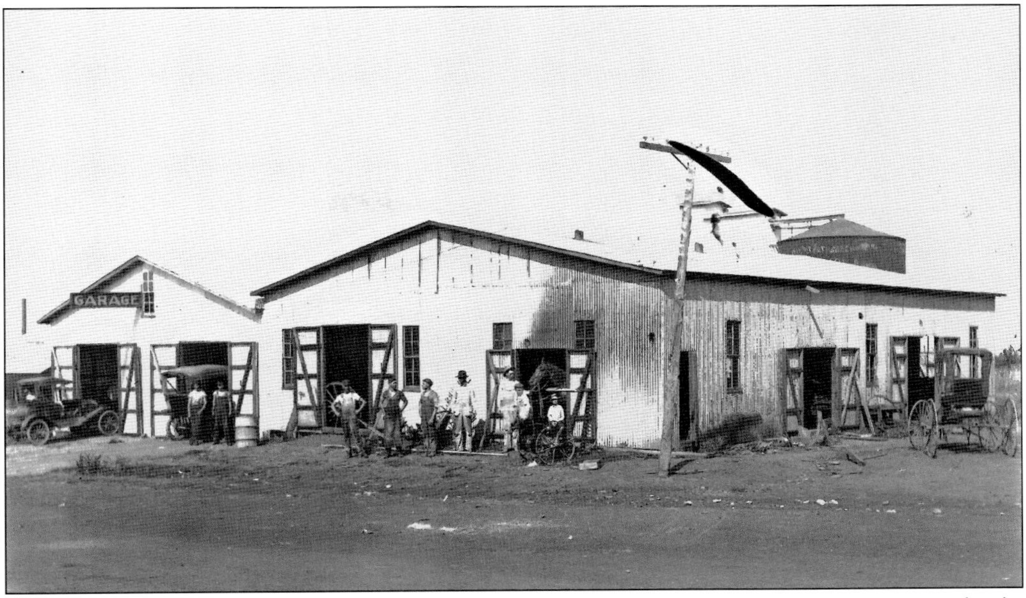

Blacksmith shops were needed for shoeing horses, sharpening plowshares, repairing wagon wheels, and providing an anvil for cowboys to shoot at on the Fourth of July. R. R. Turner established Krum's first blacksmith shop in 1888. In 1900, C. C. Hornsby established a second shop (above) equipped with three forges, one full-time horseshoer, a woodman, and two helpers. A. W. "Watt" Jones moved to Krum in 1912 and bought the Hornsby business. The Watkins Garage, owned by Herman Watkins, is at left.

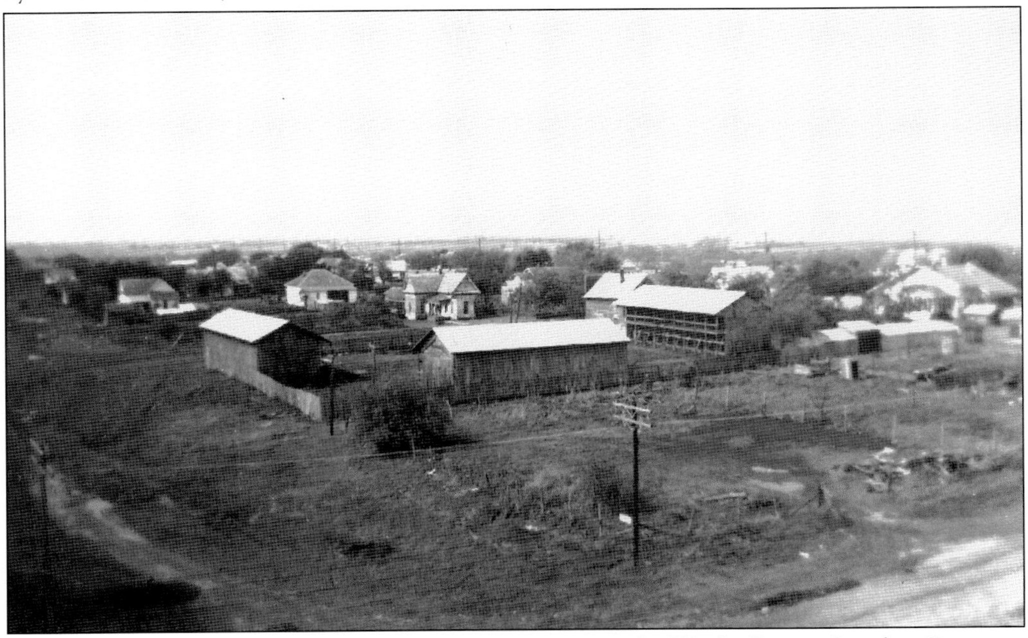

Arthur Jackson established a lumberyard in Krum in 1891. The Waples-Painter Lumber Company acquired it in 1910. In 1912, the Lyon-Gray Lumber Company established a second lumberyard in town. Then the Foxworth-Galbraith Lumber Company bought both yards (Waples-Painter in 1924 and Lyons-Gray in 1934) and consolidated them. Nelson Dyer bought the consolidated yard in 1950 and leased it to Jimmie and Bill Ginnings, who operated it until Bill's death.

KRUM BRANDS

S — Buddy & Skip Barnett
Krum, C., LH.

C — Robert W. Cochran
Krum, C., LH.

XB — C. L. Briscoe
Krum, C., LH.

Ē — Eddie Evans
Krum, C., Behind LSH

C — C. E. Faviman
Krum, C., RSH.

P — J. D. Holland
Krum, C., RH.

HB — J. D. Holland
Krum, C., RSH.

RM — Ray McGee
Krum, C., RH.

T̄L — Lorene Judkins
Krum, C., High on LH.

◇m — Ralph Miller
Krum, C., Rh.

M-M — Earl Merritt
Krum, C., LSL

JP — Jack Parkey
Krum, C., RH.

DP — Donald Paddock
Krum, C.H., LH.

3M — T. D. Richards
Krum, C.H., LH.

S — James D. Schertz
Krum, L., LH.

L — Johnnie A. Schertz
Krum, C., LH.

S — Dale Schluter
Krum, C., R.Cage

N — Neal Schluter
Krum, C., LH.

S — T. Frank Stem
Krum, C., LH.

E — Earnest E. Stocker
Krum, C., LH.

K — Kevin K. Stocker
Krum, C., LH.

Raising cattle was as important an agricultural function as growing wheat and other grains. Each cattle rancher had his unique brand so that cows mixed together on an open range could be identified and gathered at roundup time. These brands were active in the 1960s.

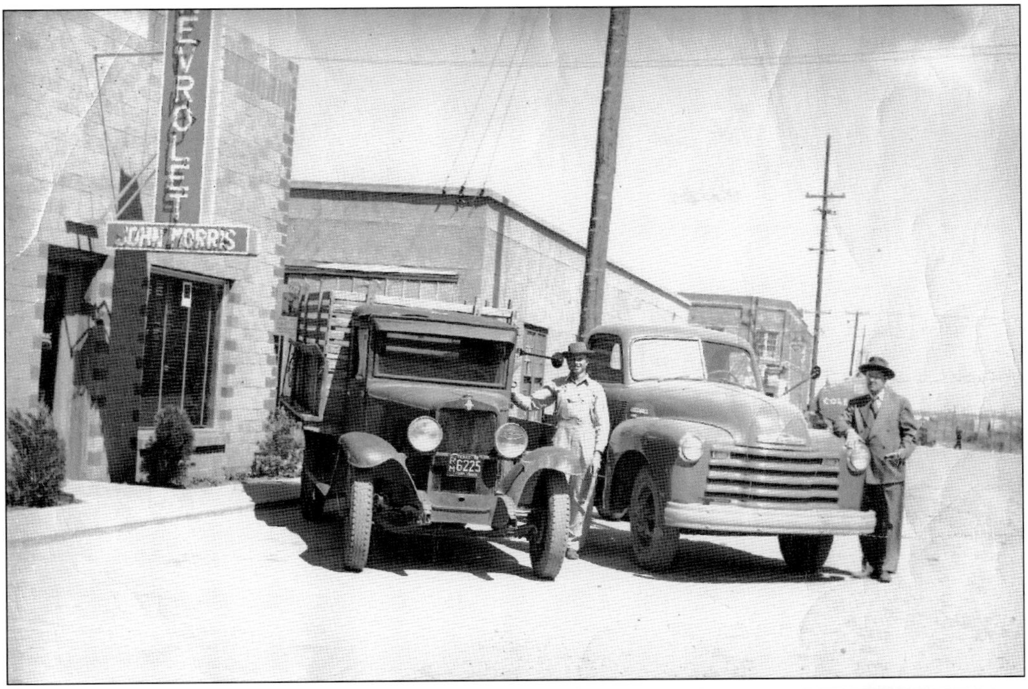

Herbert Barthold (left) stands with the truck he is trading in for the newer model (right) beside John Morris, owner of Morris Chevrolet. Morris had sold Barthold the original vehicle 20 years earlier.

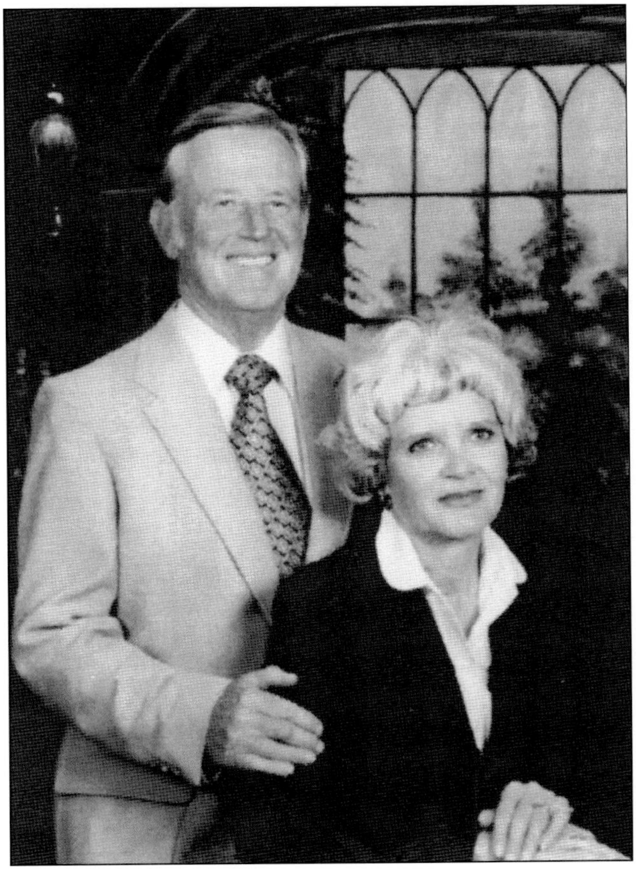

When John Morris died in 1973, George Piott, who had been with the company since 1951, bought the business. George and his wife, Verda, operated the Chevrolet agency for over 10 years.

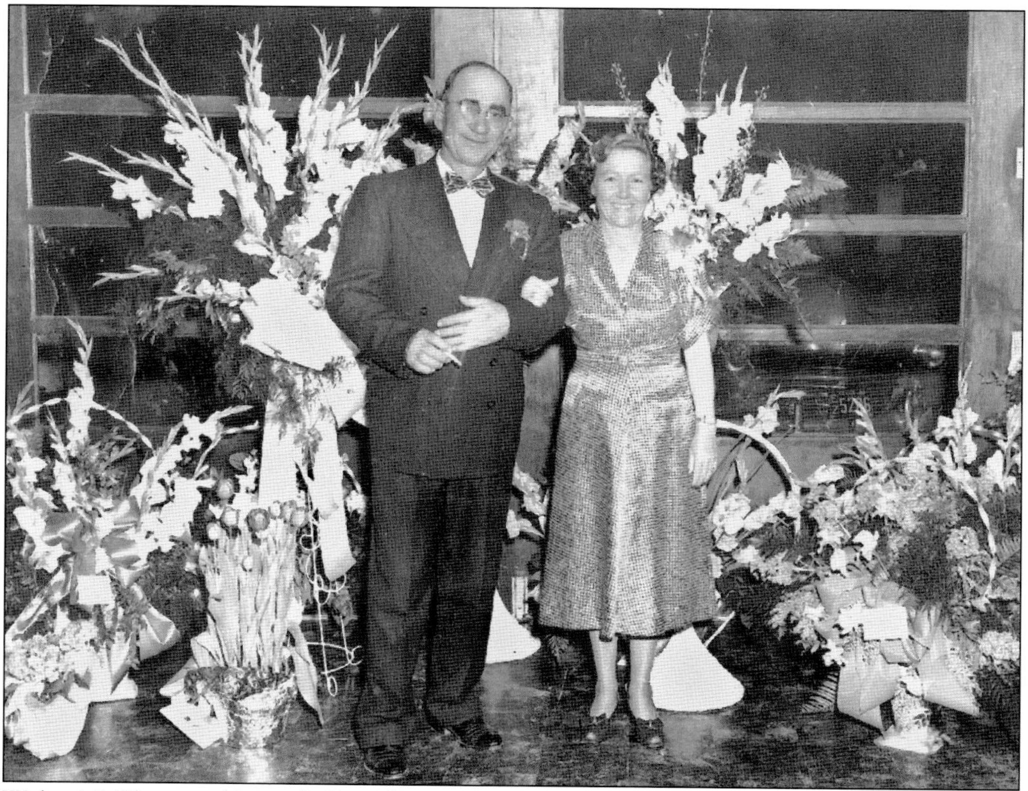

Walter McClister and his wife, Dorothy, opened a Chrysler-Plymouth dealership in the old Muncy Building in 1940. They enlarged the building in 1949 to accommodate a showroom and a parts department. Here they are celebrating the grand opening of the enlarged business.

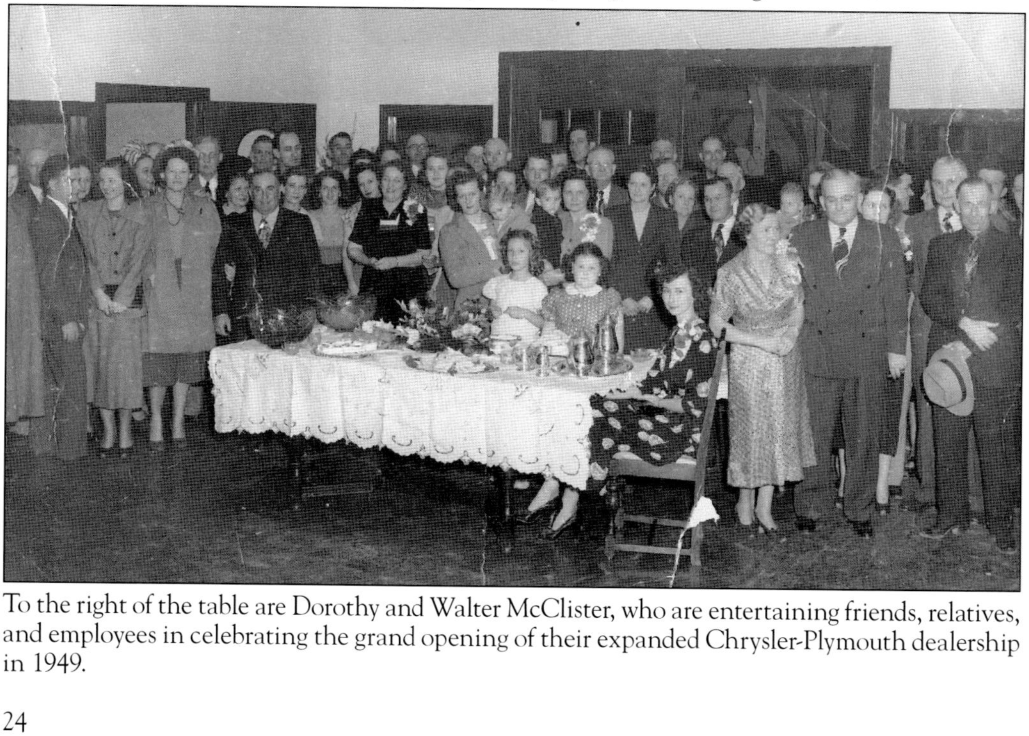

To the right of the table are Dorothy and Walter McClister, who are entertaining friends, relatives, and employees in celebrating the grand opening of their expanded Chrysler-Plymouth dealership in 1949.

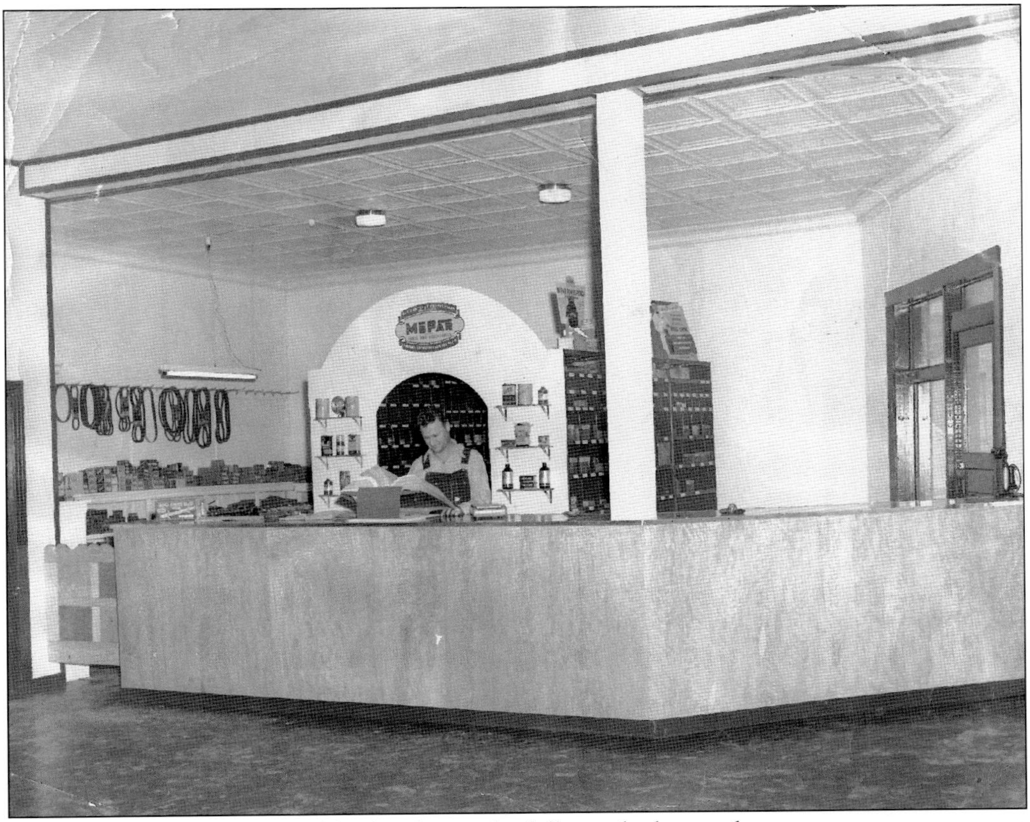

Walter McClister's remodeled facility featured a fully stocked parts department as a component of the 1949 expansion of his Chrysler-Plymouth agency. Waymon Miller, the parts clerk, is seen behind the service counter.

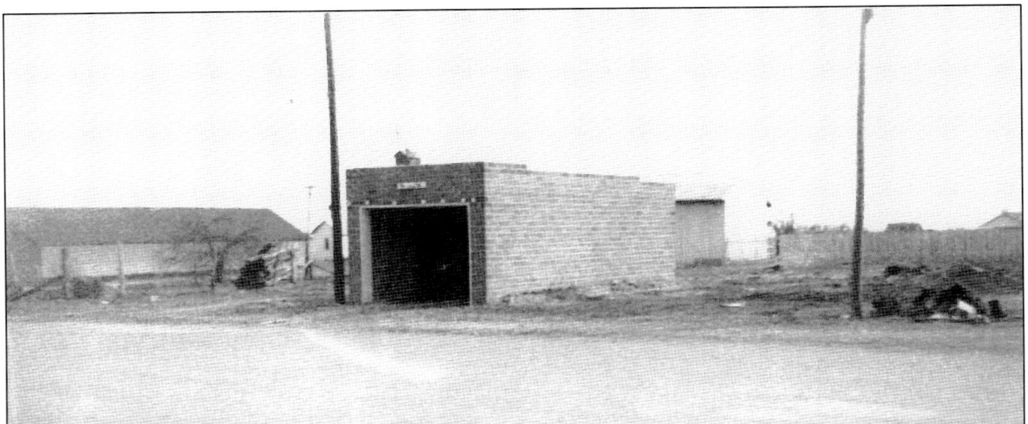

John Morris built this building in 1947 for Krum's first fire truck, and he donated the building as a gift to the town. The building later housed Krum's first library, then a beauty parlor, and it currently houses the police department.

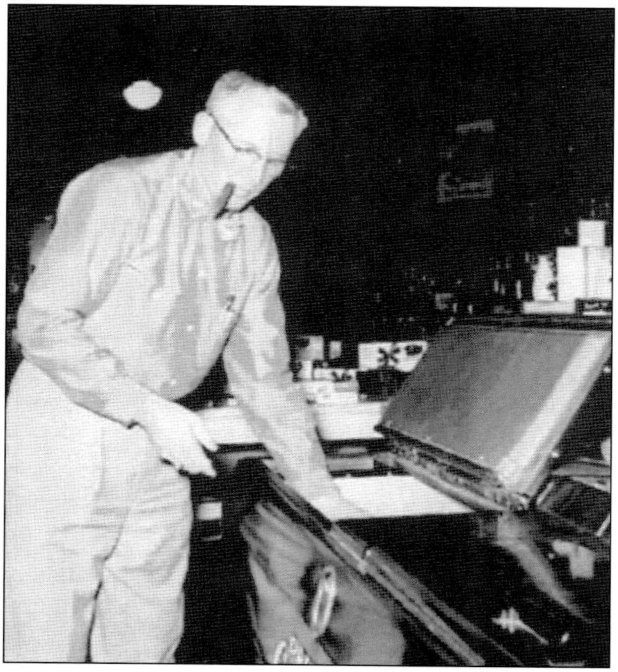

Wilkins' Drug Store, owned by Earl Wilkins, occupied a prominent location on McCart Street between First Street and the railroad tracks. Wilkins makes sure that cold soda pop was available to his customers. He took pride in being well stocked and in providing for the needs of his clientele.

Bess Cofer and Bennie Enis are enjoying the magazines in Wilkins' Drug Store and perhaps just each other's company.

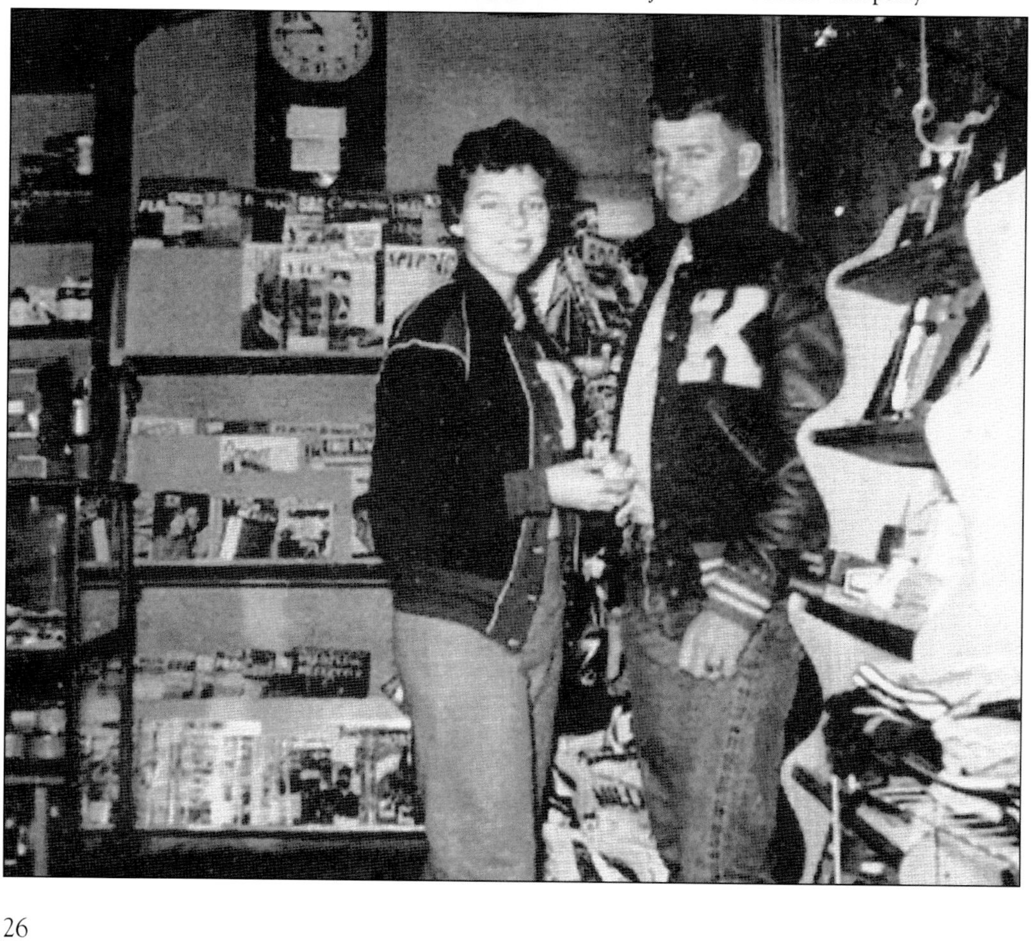

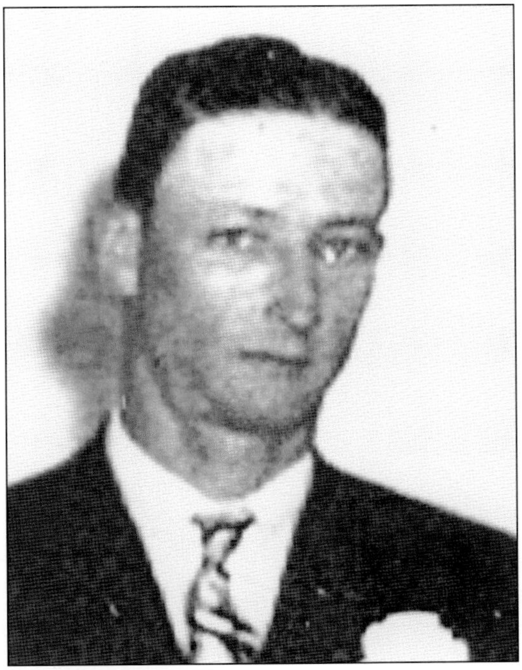

From Krum's incorporation in 1954 to 2011, eight people have served as mayor. Francis W. "Pin" Fowler (right) was Krum's first mayor. Krum's current (2011) mayor is Terri Wilson (below).

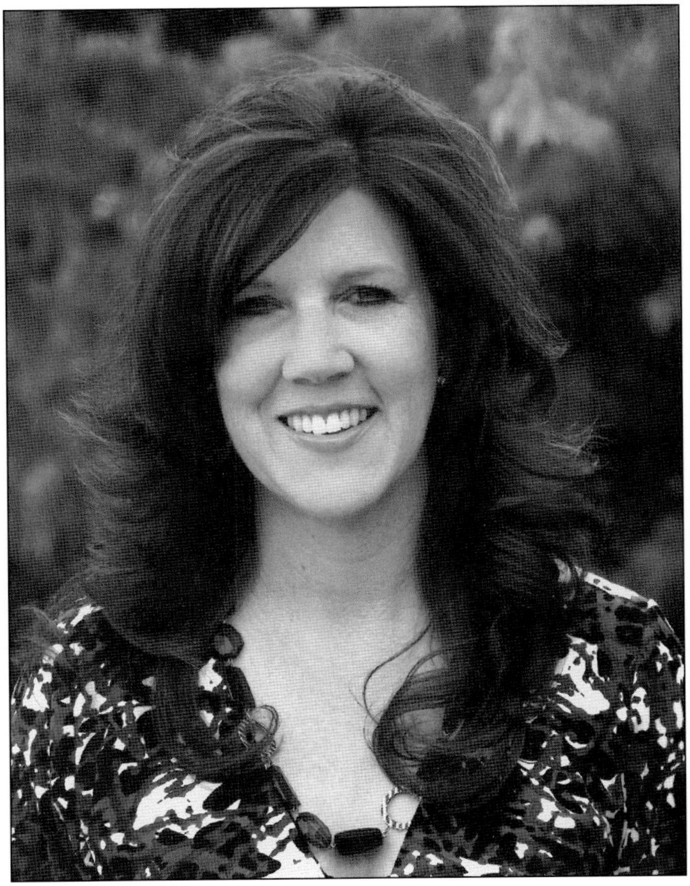

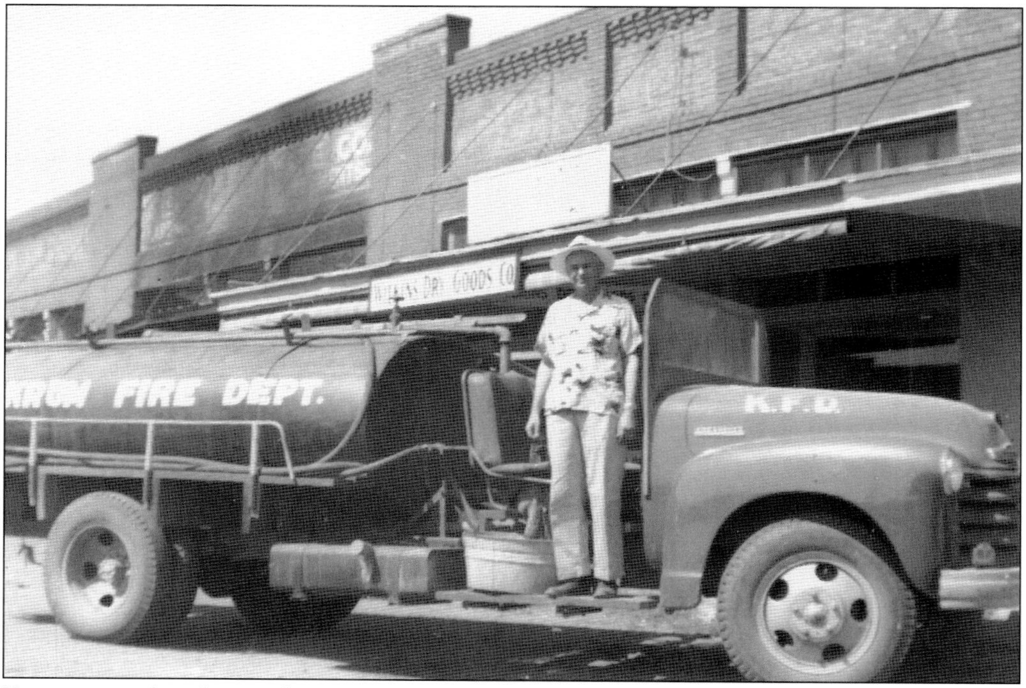

Krum got its first fire truck in 1947. The Allen Butane Company donated a tank, and citizens passed the hat to purchase a secondhand truck chassis. Weldon Cole stands on the running board of the truck.

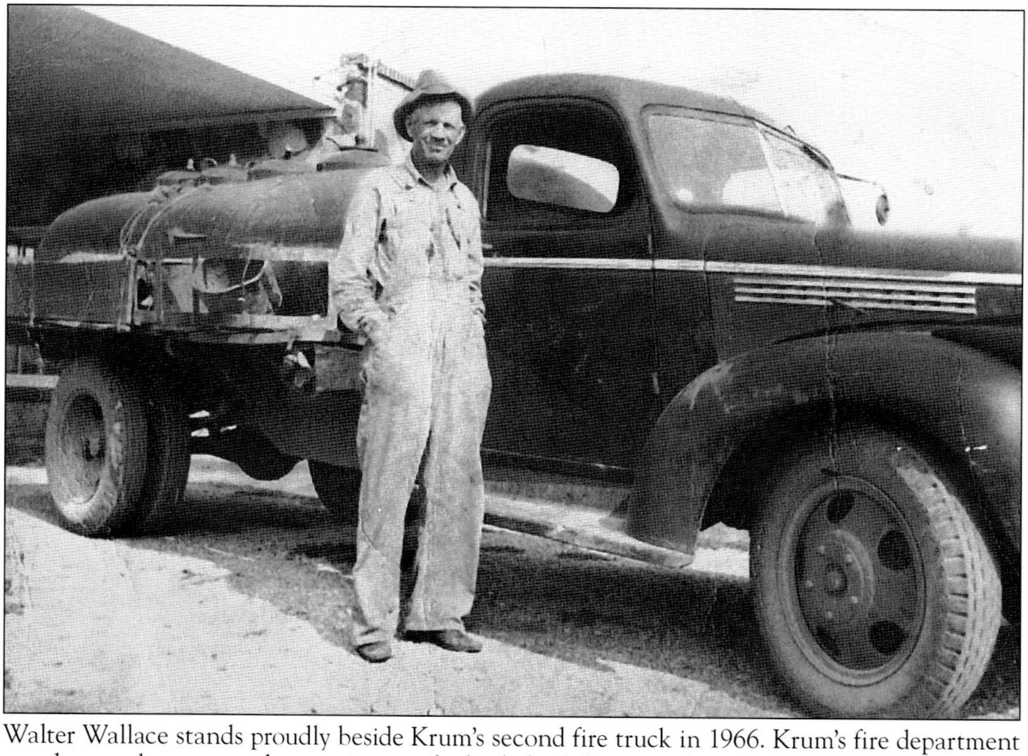

Walter Wallace stands proudly beside Krum's second fire truck in 1966. Krum's fire department now has modern, up-to-date equipment for both firefighting and emergency medical services.

KRUM FIRE DEPARTMENT PRESENTS

H. M. RUSSELL & SONS COMPANY

Denton, Texas

TURBO REFRIGERATION

1515 Shady Oaks Drive — Denton

PILOT POINT LIVESTOCK EXCHANGE

Hudspeth Commission Company - 686-2234
Mohon Commission Company - 686-2240
Sale Every Saturday - 11 a. m.

DENTON CONCRETE COMPANY

409 E. Sycamore - Denton

CHAS. MORRIS PONTIAC - BUICK

See The Beautiful New 1967 Models

Denton, Texas

T n T Eggs

TRUITT-THOMAS EGG FARM

Denton, Texas

LEWISVILLE NATIONAL BANK

Building For Your Community

Lewisville, Texas

COMPS MISSION BEVERAGE COMPANY

Denton, Texas

FARMERS & RANCHERS LIVESTOCK COMMISSION

Sale Each Wednesday 10 a. m.

Denton, Texas

COUNTRY MUSIC SHOW

Oct. 27th

The Krum Fire Department supplements its tax revenues by frequent moneymaking ventures. These activities, which include barbecues, car rallies, dinners, and so forth, not only help feed the fire department's coffers, but they also contribute significantly to unity and pride among Krum's citizens.

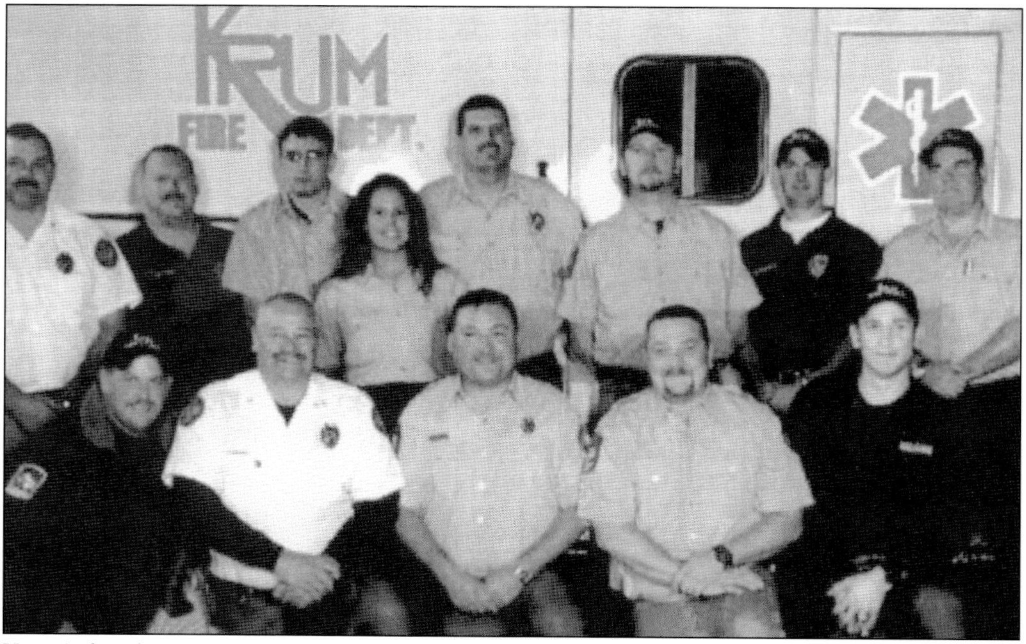

Krum's fire department, consisting of both full-time employees and volunteers, is well trained in both firefighting and emergency medical procedures. Pictured in this 2004 photograph are, from left to right, (first row) Chris Boor, Ronnie Johnson, Joe Galicia, Calvin Bland, and Wade Woody; (second row) Troy Mills, David Fletcher, Brent Jonas, Victoria Valerio, Paul Head, Brad Sebastian, Corey Gregory, and Randy Caswell.

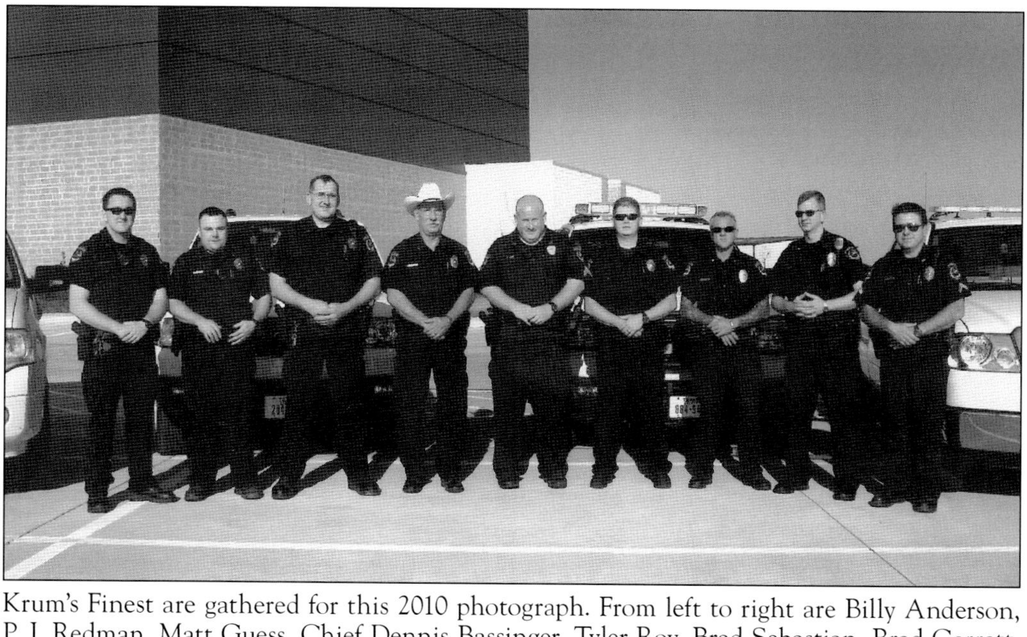

Krum's Finest are gathered for this 2010 photograph. From left to right are Billy Anderson, P. J. Redman, Matt Guess, Chief Dennis Bassinger, Tyler Roy, Brad Sebastian, Brad Garrett, Terry Hargis, and Mike Strand.

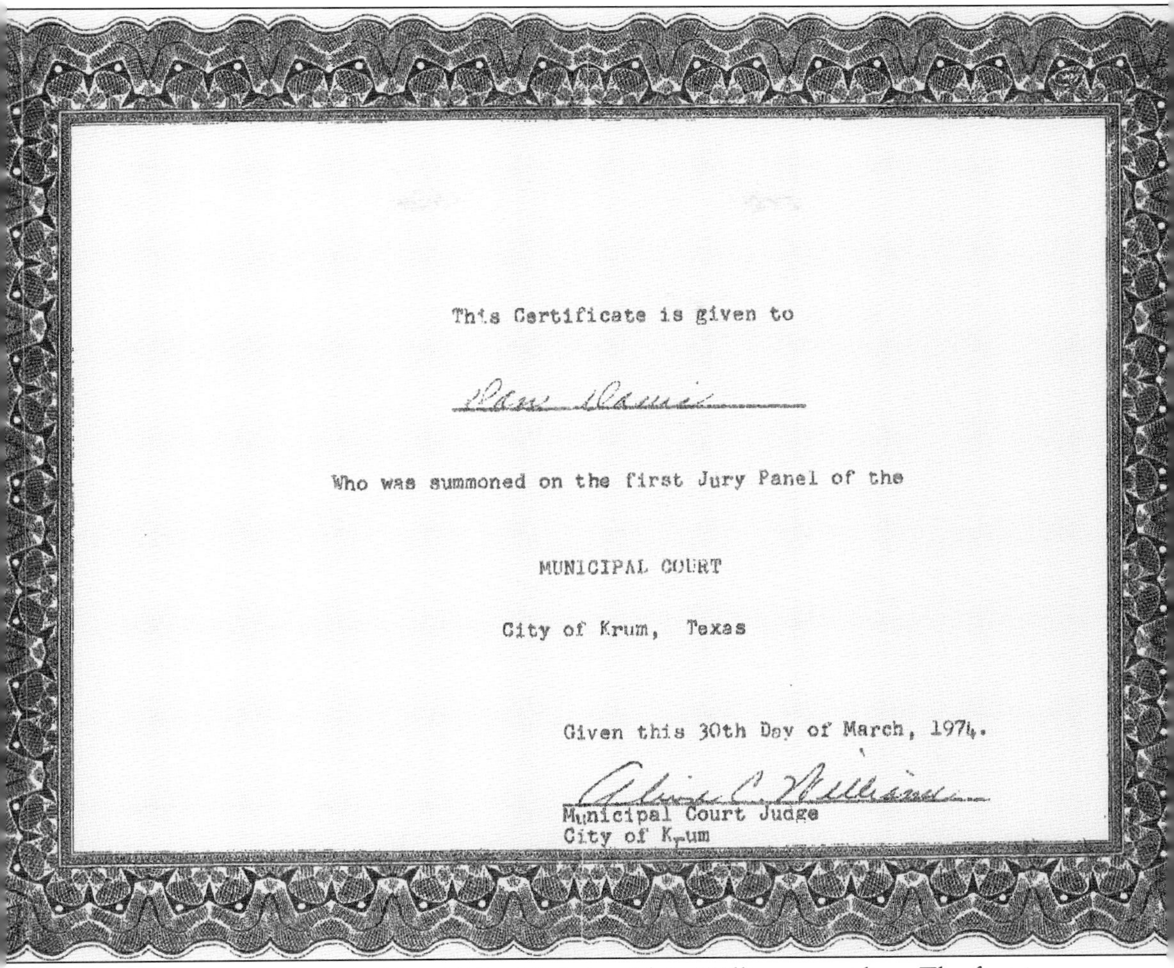

This Certificate is given to

Who was summoned on the first Jury Panel of the

MUNICIPAL COURT

City of Krum, Texas

Given this 30th Day of March, 1974.

Municipal Court Judge
City of Krum

Krum's first jury trial was held in 1974 with Judge Alvin Williams presiding. The first jurors were Don Davis, Dale Gant, Gus Guerra, Bennie Enis, Harold Hamm, Melba Kimberlyn, Dean Padgett, Larry Lamonica, and Tracy Collom. This certificate was in commemoration of service on the first municipal jury in Krum.

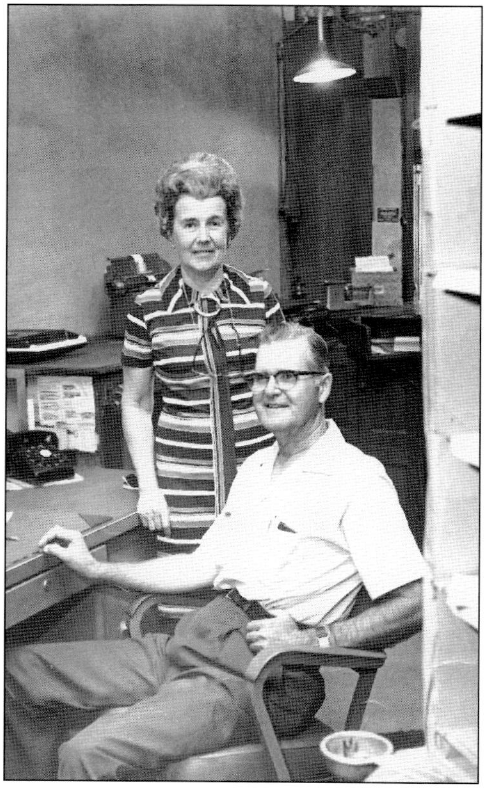

As the first appointees under civil service law, Pauline and Morris Ferrell served as postmasters almost continuously from 1935 to 1972. Before 1935, the winning political party appointed postmasters after each presidential election. S. D. Chadwell acted as Krum's first postmaster from 1888 until an official appointment came for L. L. Finley to serve in that position.

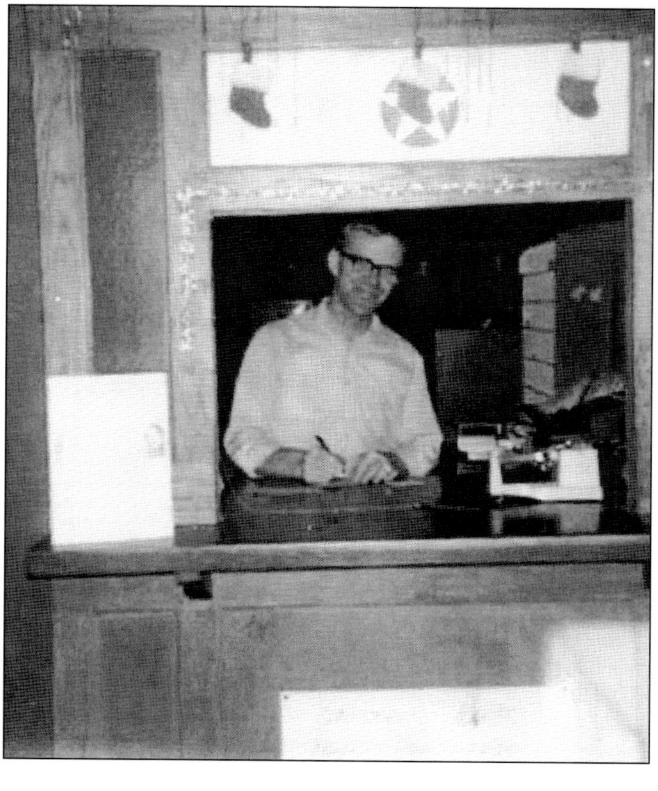

Tracy Collom followed the Ferrells as Krum's postmaster in 1972. Here Collom stands ready to assist customers in the new postal facility built in 1976. Krum's post office was established in 1888 in L. L. Finley's General Store. Shortly thereafter it moved into a frame building next door, where it remained until 1910, when it moved into the vacated Continental Bank building. Several more moves ensued until 1976, when the post office relocated to a new business center built by Jack Mitchell on Lake Street, across from the original high school.

Beginning in 1900, several weekly newspapers were published in Krum. The *Krum Banner* thrived for the longest period, from 1922 to 1929. It was operated by Mary Baily Wallace, who headed the Baily Publishing Company.

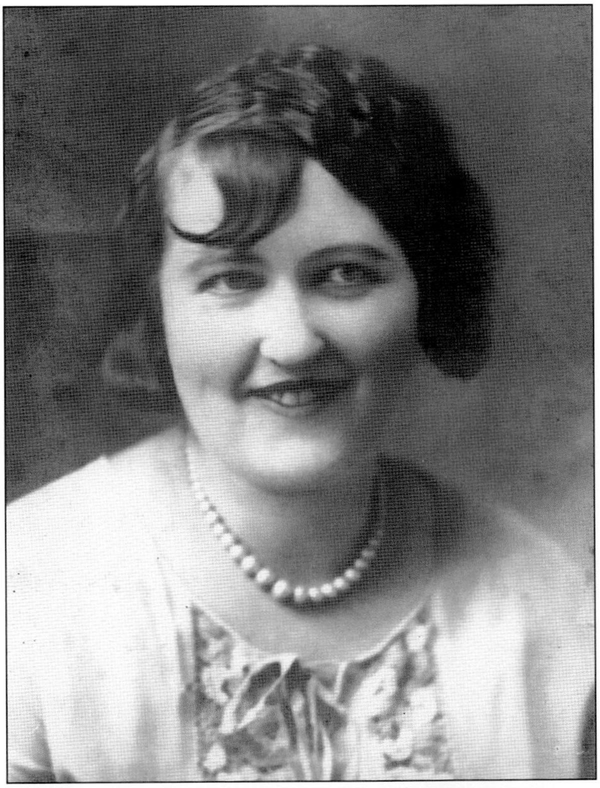

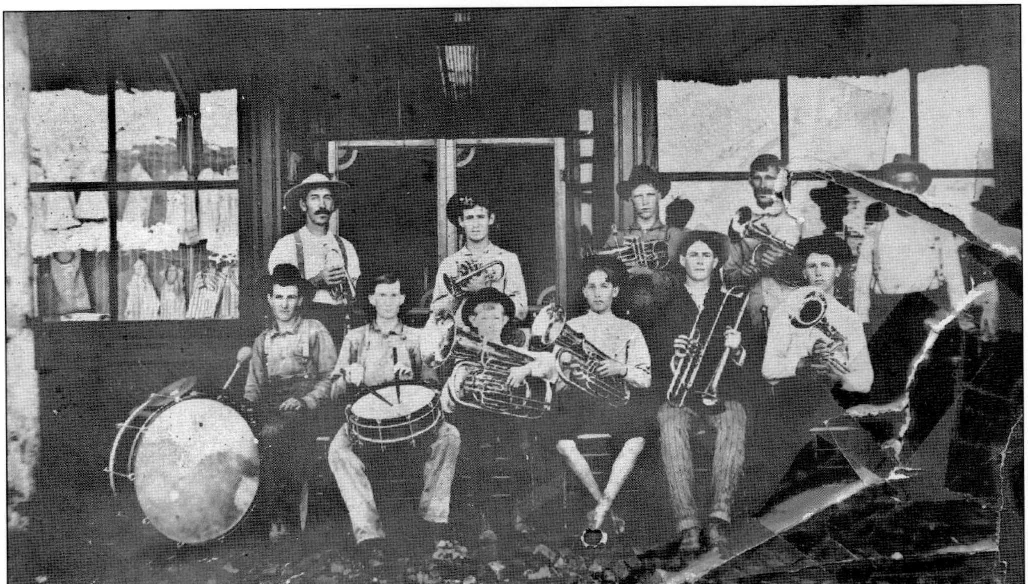

One of Krum's entertainment attractions was its brass band under the direction of W. F. Clevenger. On a bandstand erected at the intersection of McCart and First Streets, the group gave a concert every Tuesday night. Among the band members are A. F. "Rusty" Lindley and his brother, Tom, both on drums; O. J. Chism, bass; W. F. Clevenger, baritone; Paul Gose, lead coronet; and Jimmy Wright, trombone. Five of the eleven band members shown are unidentified.

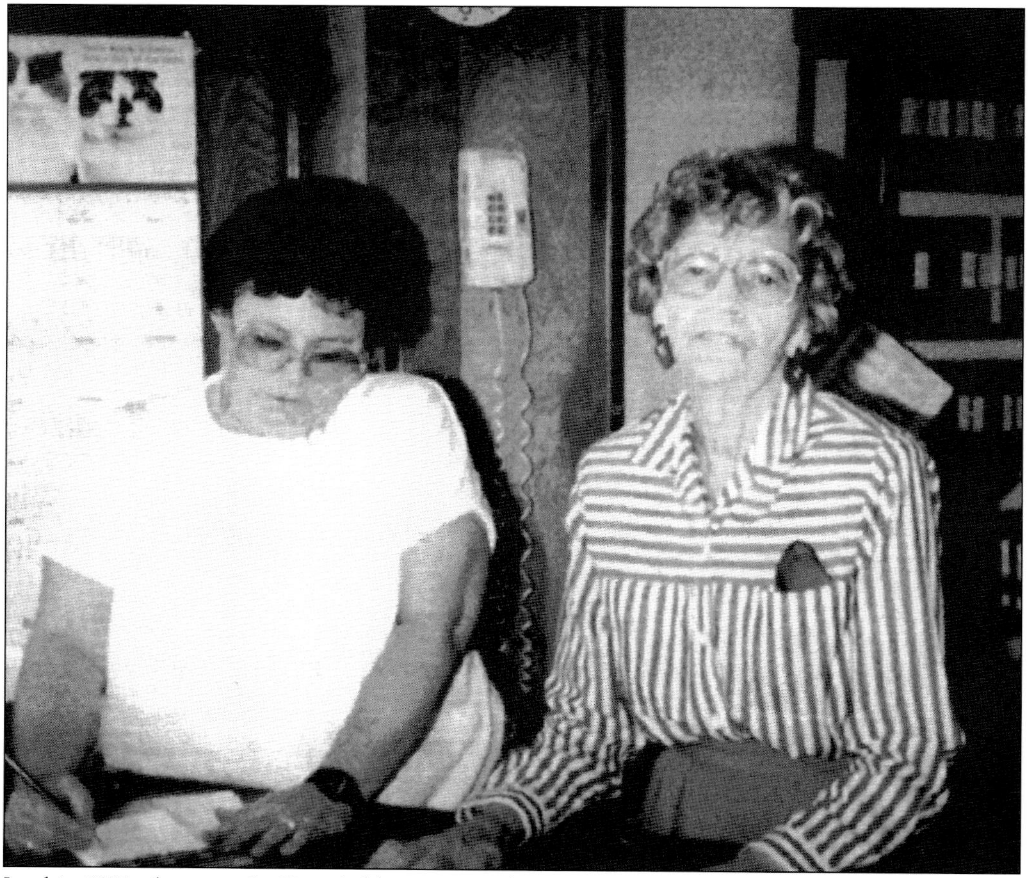

In this 1981 photograph, Krum's librarian, Katherin Boyer, jots notes on a pad while librarian aide Blanche Dodd stands by.

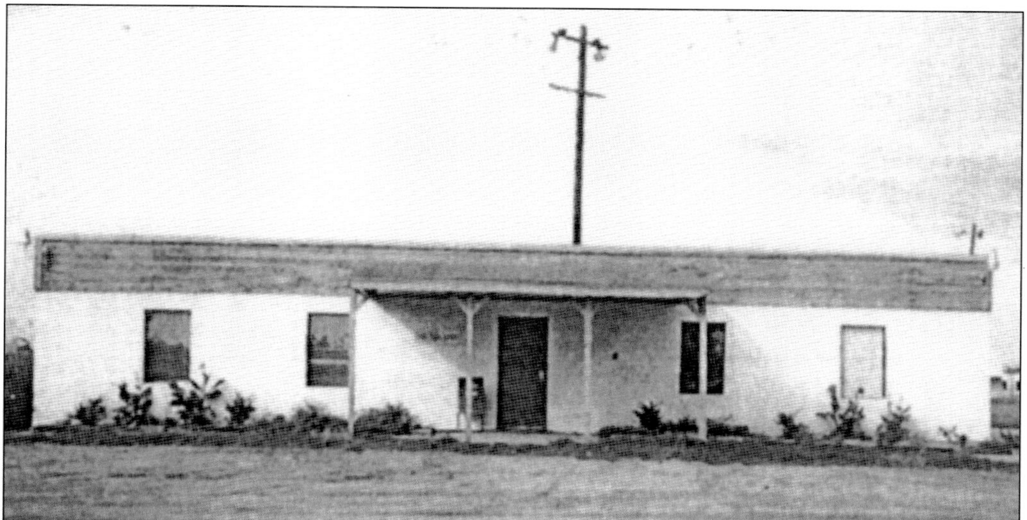

This building, former home of the Krum Young Citizens Club, is the fourth location for Krum's public library. After several renovations, the library is still located here.

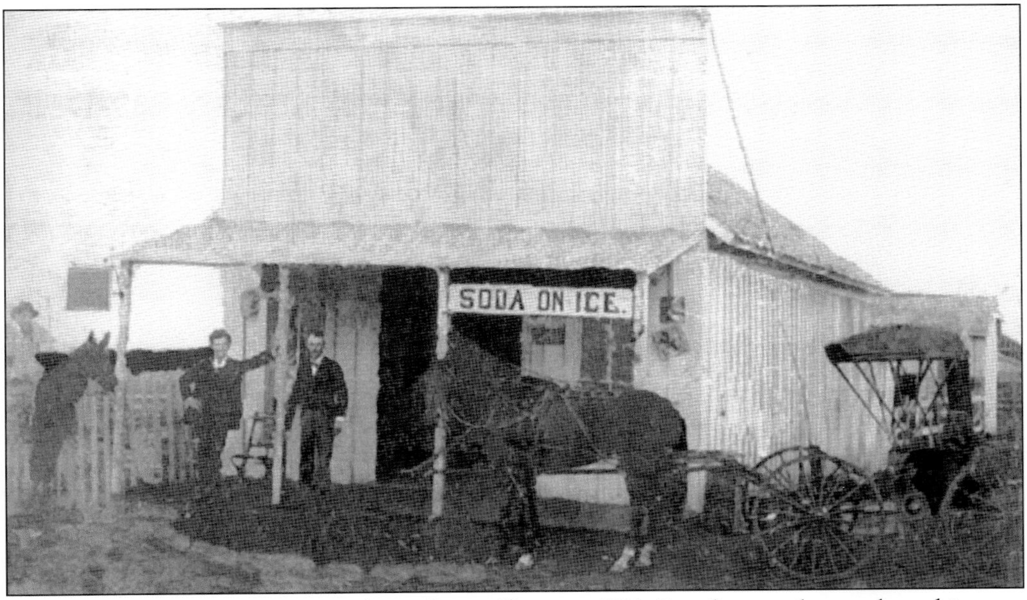

Dr. Wallace G. Kimbrough opened an office in Krum in 1891. Standing on the porch are his sons, Wallace (left) and Walter (right), who joined their father in his medical practice after completing Vanderbilt Medical School. The younger Dr. Wallace later moved his practice to Denton.

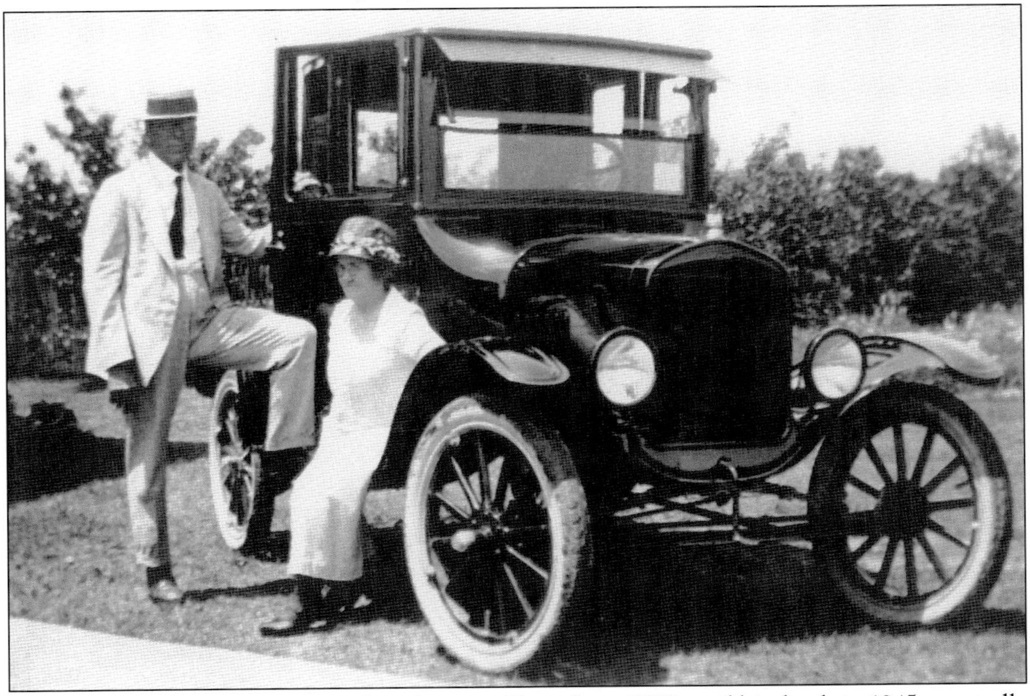

Dr. James Caughey Gose practiced medicine in Krum from 1898 until his death in 1945, reputedly delivering more than 5,000 babies. He never refused medical care to anyone regardless of the person's ability to pay. Upon his death, Gose had many jars of pickles and other preserved food that had been given to him in lieu of medical bills. Here he and his wife, Annie, pose with Krum's first car. On a trip to Decatur, an irate bull mistook the car for another bull, and the race was on. Finally, the bull got tired, and the car prevailed.

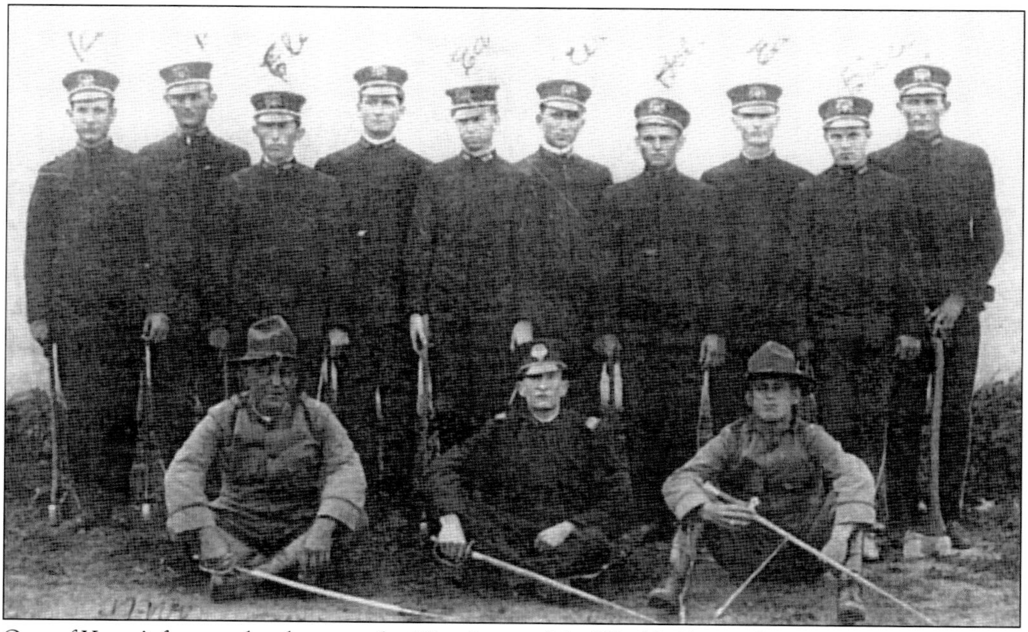

One of Krum's fraternal orders was the Woodmen of the World. Shown from left to right are (first row) W. F. Clevenger, Tom Lindley, and Paul Gose; (second row) Rusty Lindley, a Mr. Ball, Elden Gresham, R. E. Bryant, Edmon Muredy, Walter McClister, Ballard Eubanks, Edison Mounts, Edward Eubanks, and Kimball Briscoe.

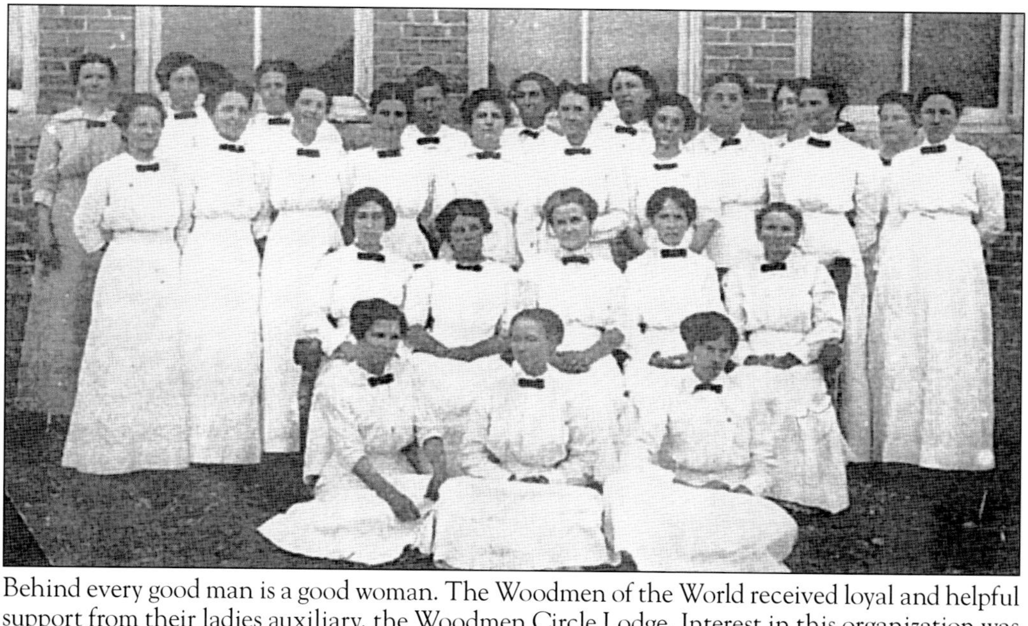

Behind every good man is a good woman. The Woodmen of the World received loyal and helpful support from their ladies auxiliary, the Woodmen Circle Lodge. Interest in this organization was at its height during the years of 1908 to 1916, when membership numbered between 20 and 30.

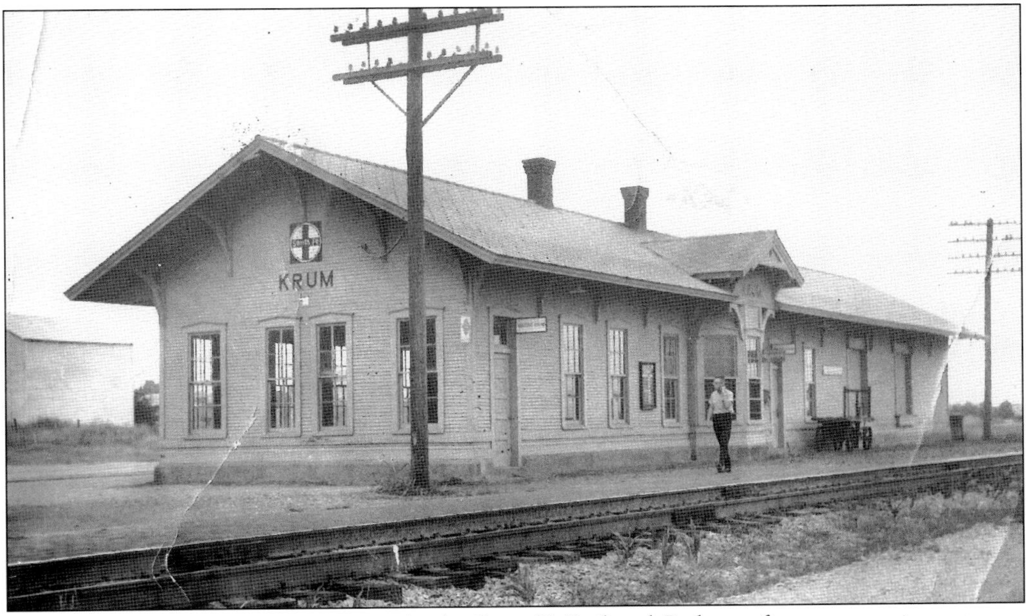

Krum was an important passenger stop for the Santa Fe Railroad. Perhaps of even greater importance, the railroad provided access to markets for Krum's agricultural production.

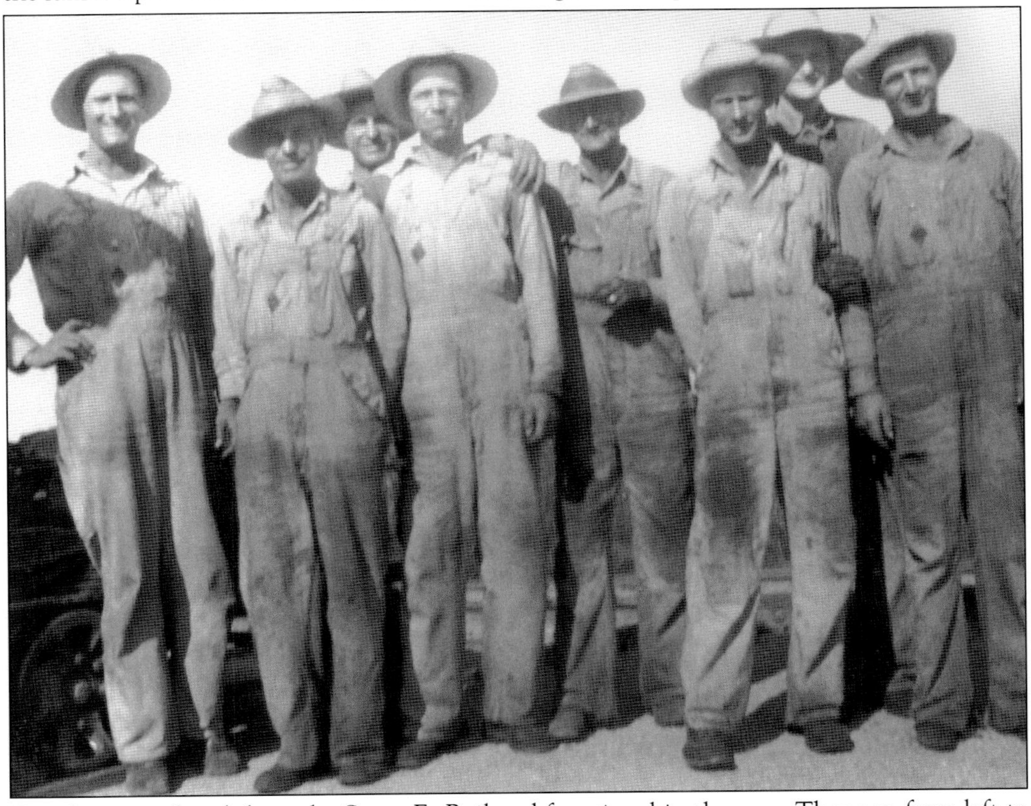

Krum's section hands kept the Santa Fe Railroad functional in the area. They are, from left to right, Charles Cline, Fletcher McBee, Hiram Henderson, LeRoy Simpkins, Major McBee, Lewis Standifer, Ralph Henderson, and John Carter.

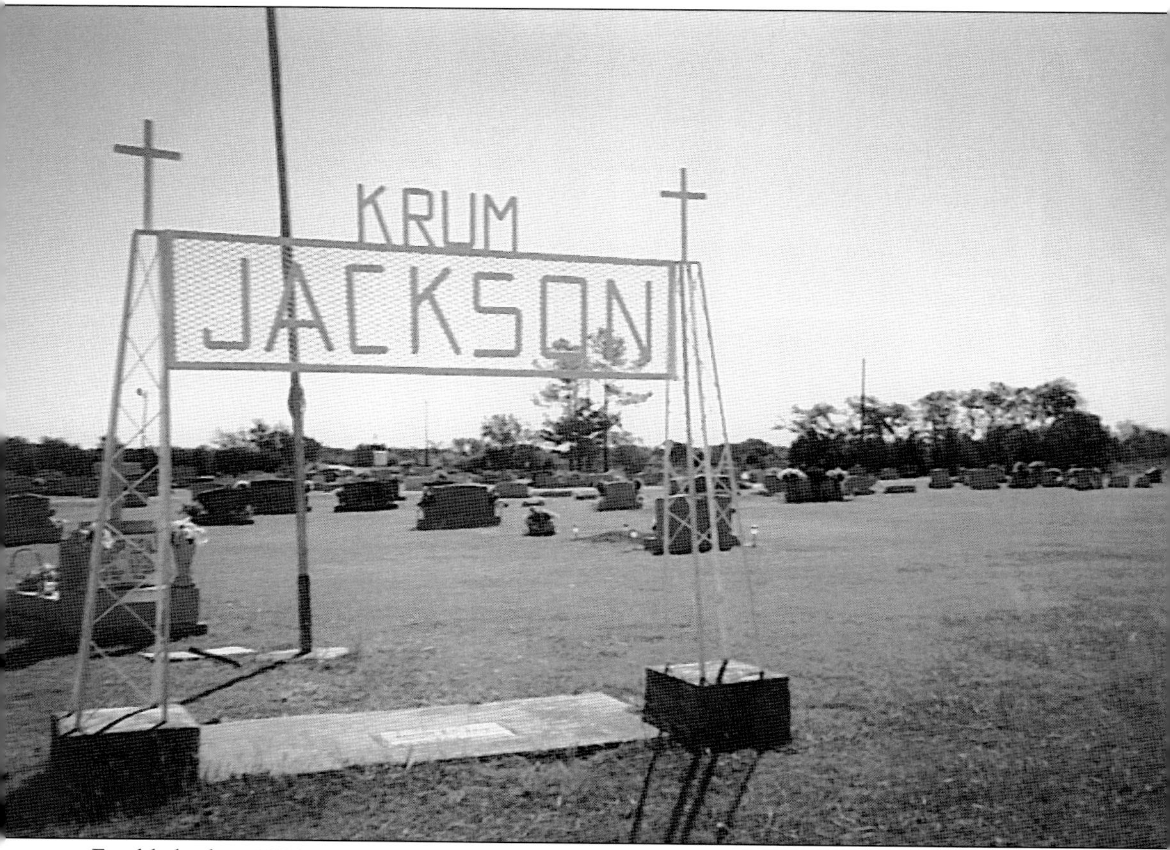

Established in 1876 as part of the original Jackson community, Krum's cemetery is still in its original location, about 2 miles south of present-day Krum. It is owned and maintained by the Jackson Cemetery Association, organized in 1895. Current members of the cemetery board are Ronnie Riley, president; Chris Cofer, secretary; Susan Dodd, treasurer; Joyce Johnson Sauter, record keeper; Melissa Davis, caretaker; Della Davis; Janice Callarman; Tommy Chapman; Terry Knight; Randy Knight; and Daron Enis. When a historical marker was dedicated at the Jackson Cemetery in 2004, Charlene Keefer spoke and related the following reminiscence: "Back in the very early days, if a woman was married to John Smith, she was listed as 'Mrs. John Smith.' The first marking of a grave space for a burial that I got to help Edward Barthold (the secretary) with was Faye Finley Dyer. We looked all around the area until I found a stone that said 'Gordon Dyer.' I asked if that was it. He said, 'Yes, and if she'd a went by her right name, we could have found her easier.' Of course, her right name was Mrs. Gordon Dyer."

Two

The Banks

Since the establishment of its first bank, Krum has served as the financial center of northwest Denton County. The history of banking in Krum had its beginning when J. W. Wilkinson, president of the Continental Bank and Trust Company of Fort Worth, established a branch of that bank in Krum in 1905. It occupied the first brick building in town.

Seeing Krum's potential as a finance center, Dr. A. H. Knox, who had been practicing medicine in Pilot Grove, Texas, sold his practice there and moved to Krum in 1909. Dr. Knox erected a two-story brick building at the northeast corner of the intersection of McCart and First Streets, and he opened the First State Bank in July of that year. In 1910, the two banks merged and became the Farmers and Merchants State Bank, occupying the building Knox had built. Wilkinson was elected president, although he was inactive in the bank's operation because of his banking duties in Fort Worth. Knox, now executive vice president, managed the Krum bank's operations until 1937, when he became its president. Byron Smith Sr. was named its cashier. The Continental Bank building was torn down after World War II.

John W. Porter bought controlling interest in the bank in 1970, and he was joined by J. T. Jones Jr. Porter became chairman of the board, and Jones became executive vice president. In 1972, Jones was elected president of the bank, but he resigned that position in the following year, and Porter served as interim president until Edwin Mullins was elected in 1974. Mullins was followed by Vaughn Andrus, who retired as president in 2005, when the institution was sold to the First United Bank of Ardmore, Oklahoma.

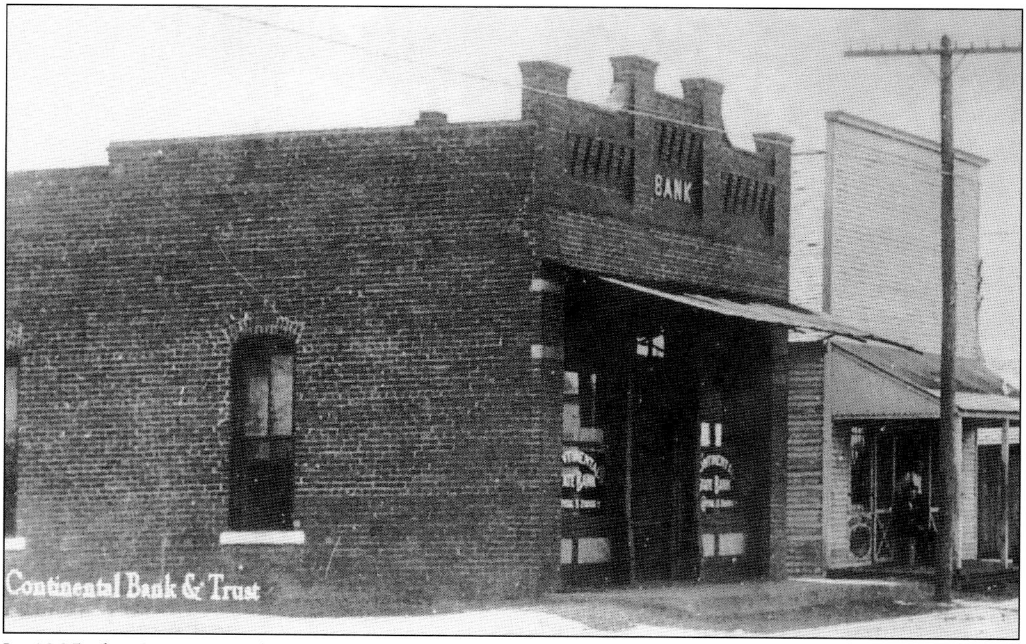

In 1905, the Continental Bank and Trust Company of Fort Worth established a branch in Krum. Housed in a one-story brick building, the Continental Bank served the wheat farmers and the other agricultural and business activities of the area. It was the first brick building in Krum.

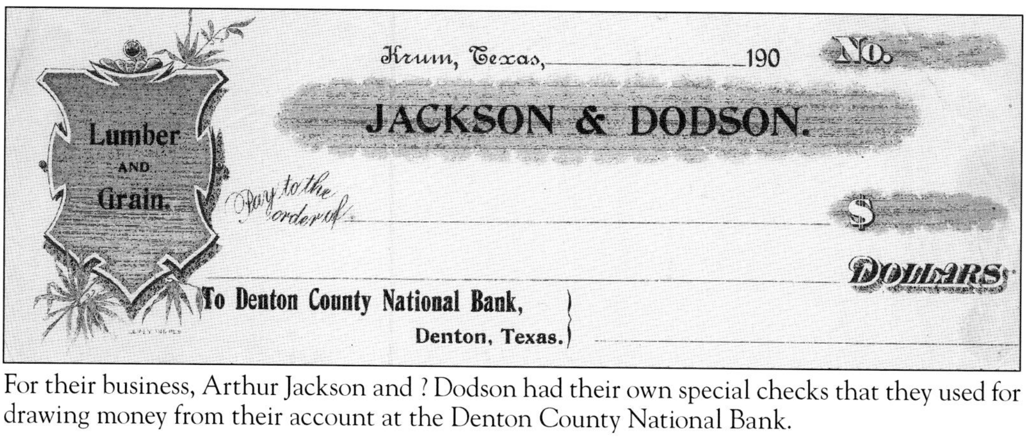

For their business, Arthur Jackson and ? Dodson had their own special checks that they used for drawing money from their account at the Denton County National Bank.

In 1909, Dr. A. H. Knox established Krum's second bank, the First State Bank, in a two-story brick building he built at the northeast corner of the intersection of McCart and First Streets. The following year, the two banks merged to become the Farmers and Merchants State Bank (F&M).

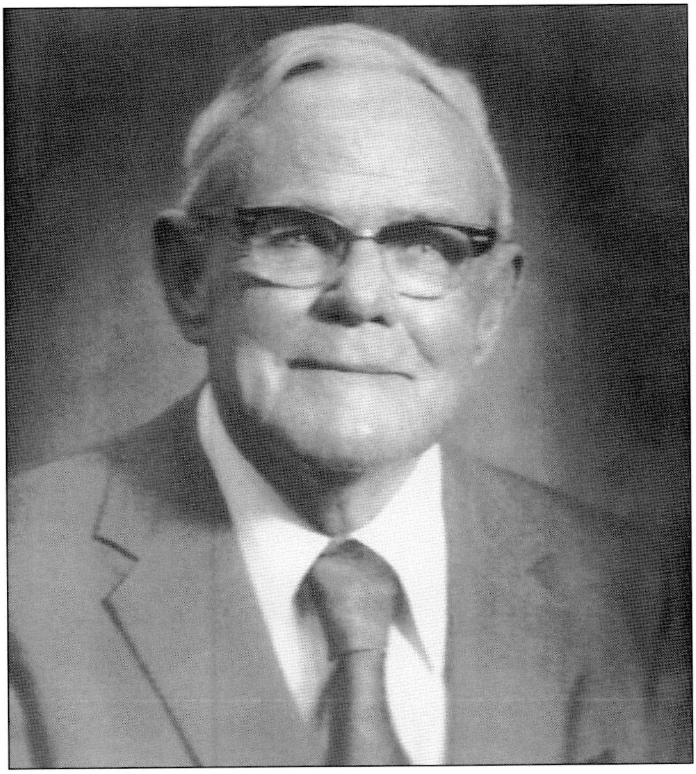

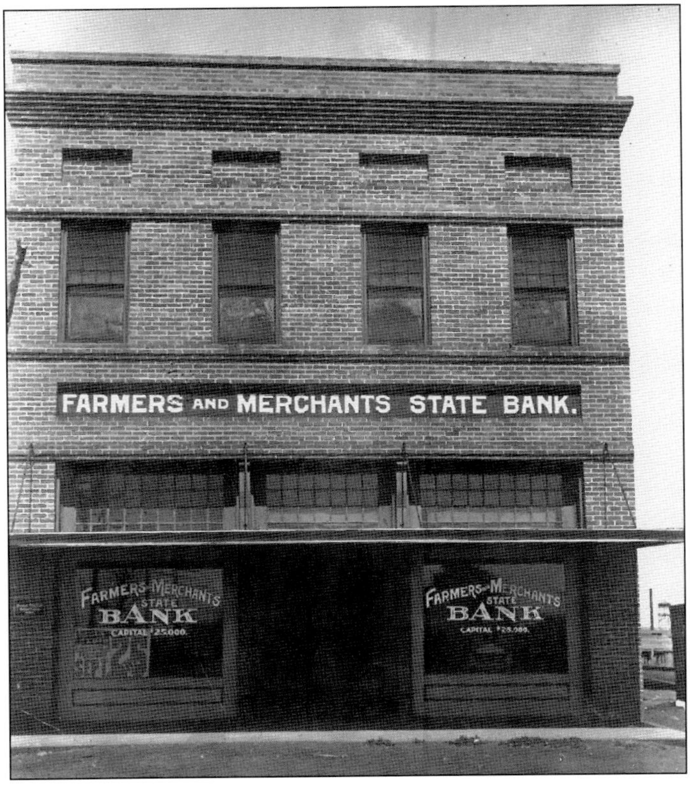

Dr. Knox built this two-story brick building for his First State Bank, which became the Farmers and Merchants State Bank in 1910. The building was in continual use as a bank until 2008. It now houses the Krum Heritage Museum.

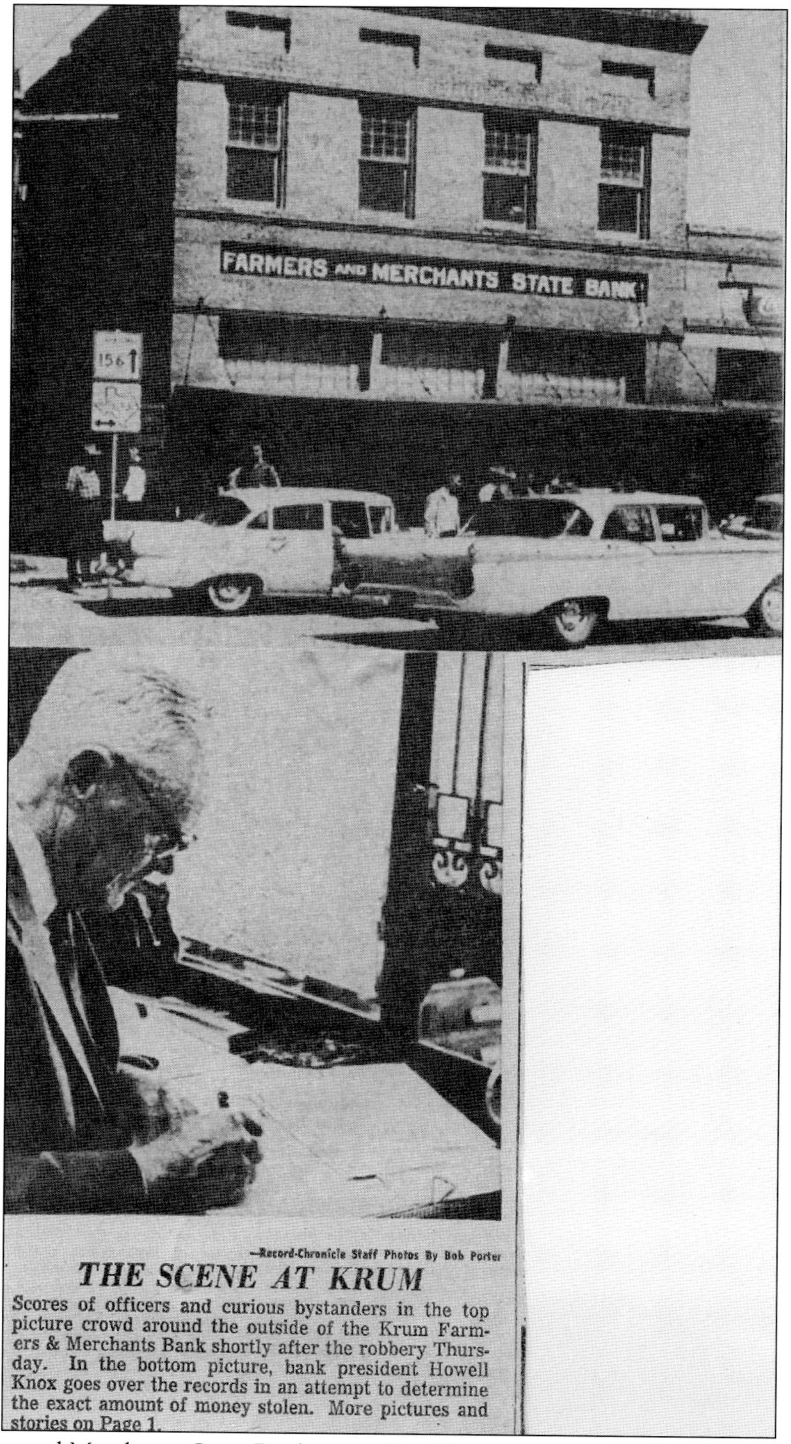

—Record-Chronicle Staff Photos By Bob Porter

THE SCENE AT KRUM

Scores of officers and curious bystanders in the top picture crowd around the outside of the Krum Farmers & Merchants Bank shortly after the robbery Thursday. In the bottom picture, bank president Howell Knox goes over the records in an attempt to determine the exact amount of money stolen. More pictures and stories on Page 1.

The Farmers and Merchants State Bank was robbed four times—in 1925, 1954, 1959, and 1970. In the first robbery, the thieves got $1,200 cash and were eventually caught. In the other three robberies, the FBI caught a lone bandit each time. The *Denton Record-Chronicle* reported the 1954 robbery in its pages.

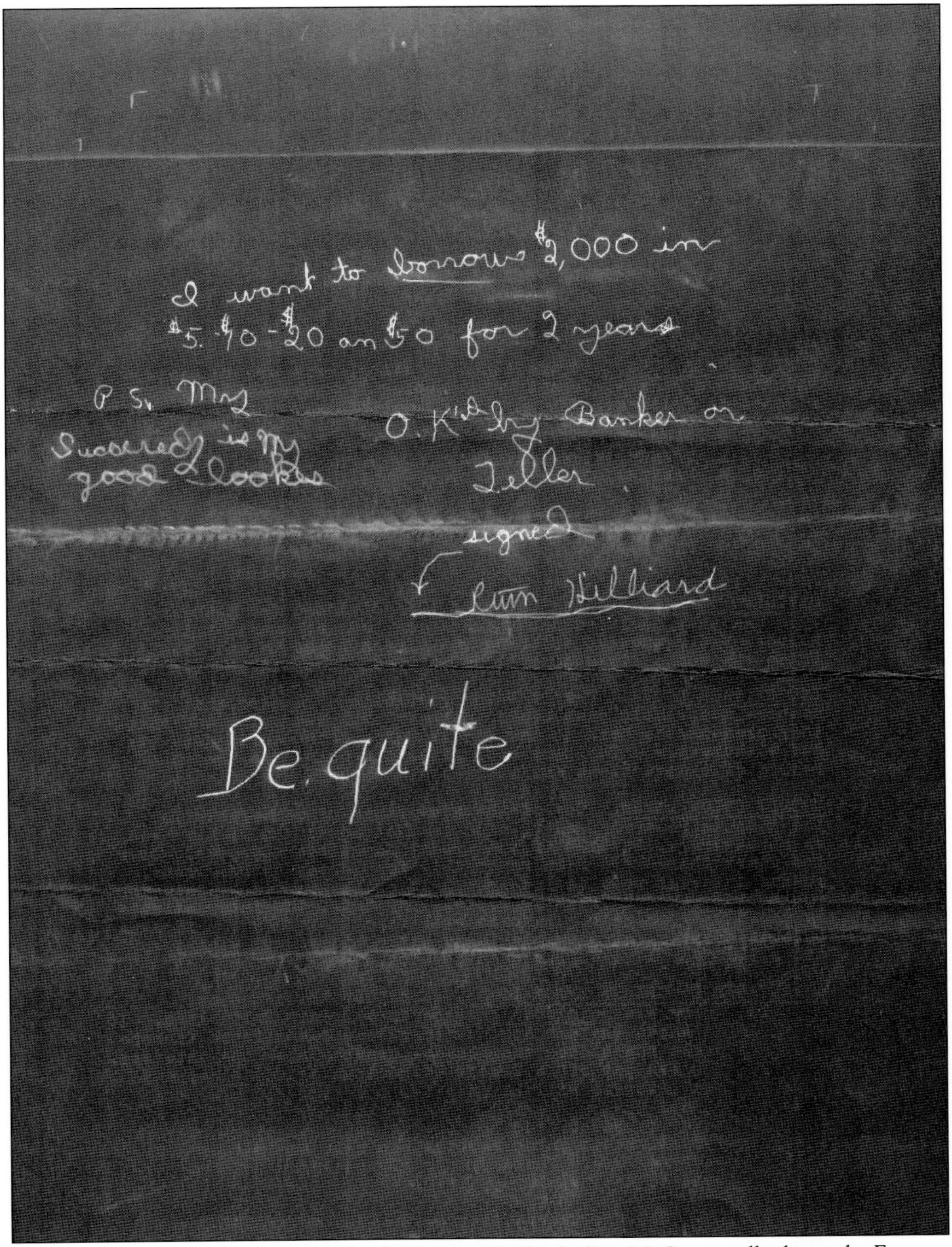

I want to borrow $2,000 in
$5.$10-$20 an $50 for 2 years

P.S. My
Success is my
good looks

O.K'd by Banker or
Teller
signed
Ruth Hilliard

Be.quite

In the robbery on March 20, 1959, blond, 19-year-old Charles Roy McCrory walked into the Farmers and Merchants State Bank and asked about a savings account. At the same time, he quietly handed the note seen here, which called for a loan of $2,000 in $5, $10, $20, and $50 bills for two years, to the teller, Ruth Hilliard. McCrory's "loan" amounted to $1,885. He was apprehended a few hours later in Grapevine and brought back to the Krum bank so that Hilliard and Margaret Schulter could identify him. According to McCrory, he attended school at Krum for a couple of years and chose the Krum bank to rob because it was in "a small town without much law."

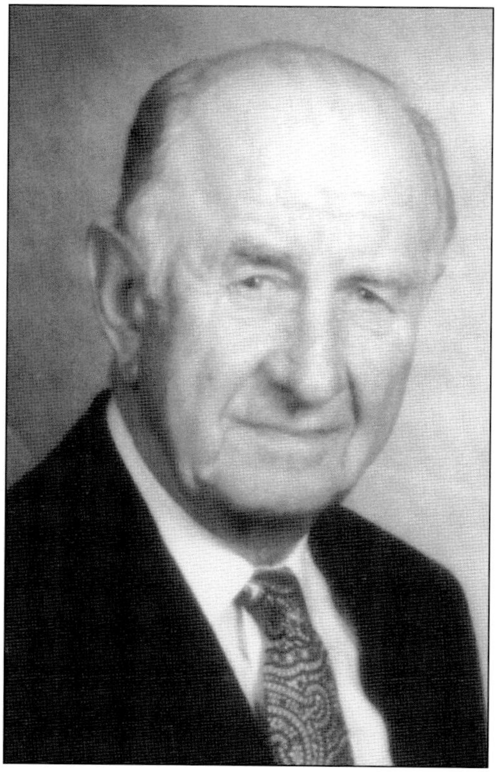

John W. Porter moved to Denton County in 1959 and immediately began buying land and businesses. In 1970, he bought controlling interest in the Farmers and Merchants State Bank. Although preferring to function in the background, Porter served as the bank's president from 1972 to 1974.

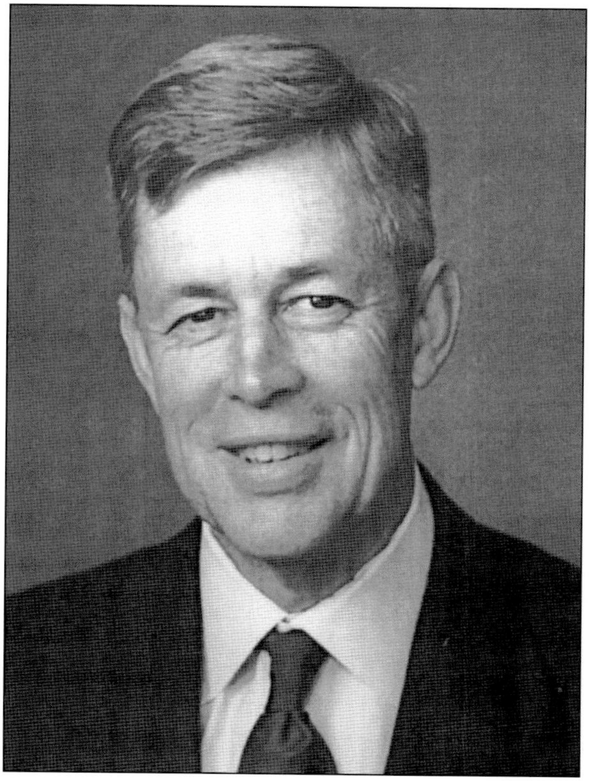

Vaughn Andrus was the last president of Krum's Farmers and Merchants State Bank. When Vaughn decided to retire in 2005, the bank was sold to First United Bank, which is based in Ardmore, Oklahoma.

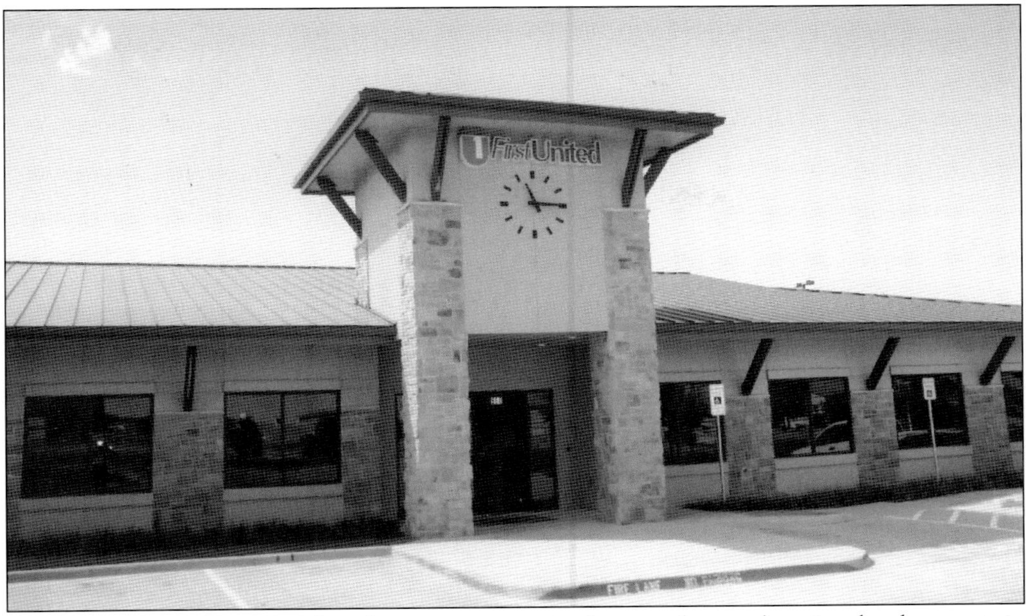

In order to continue its growth and to more conveniently serve the new housing developments in the eastern outskirts of Krum, First United Bank built a new facility at 960 East McCart Street in 2008.

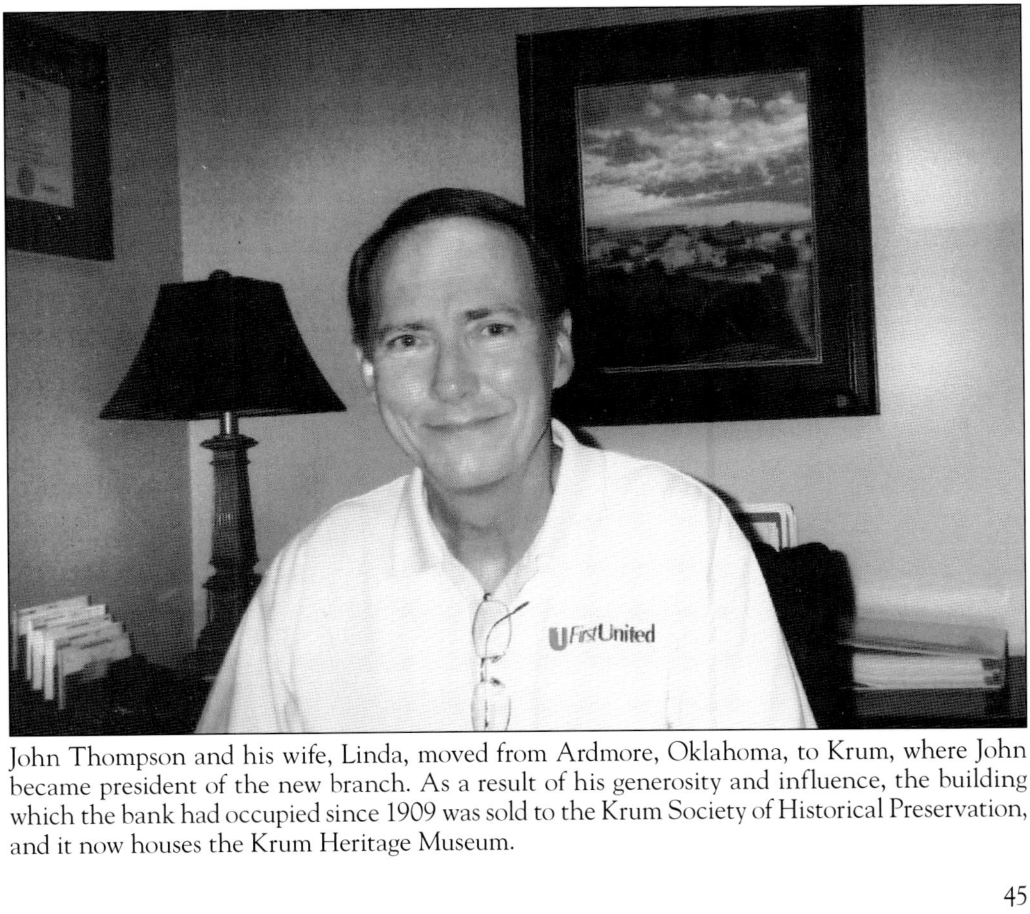

John Thompson and his wife, Linda, moved from Ardmore, Oklahoma, to Krum, where John became president of the new branch. As a result of his generosity and influence, the building which the bank had occupied since 1909 was sold to the Krum Society of Historical Preservation, and it now houses the Krum Heritage Museum.

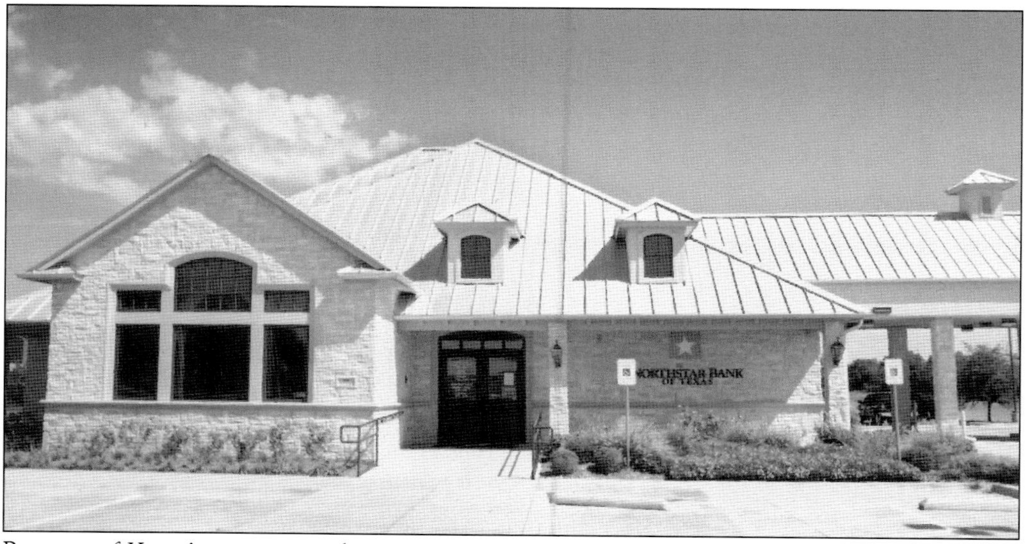

Because of Krum's recent population growth and its continued role as a financial center, the Northstar Bank established a branch in Krum in 2005. The Krum branch is located at 1101 East McCart Street, a convenient location for serving both the residents of "old town" Krum, plus those who reside in Krum's newer housing developments.

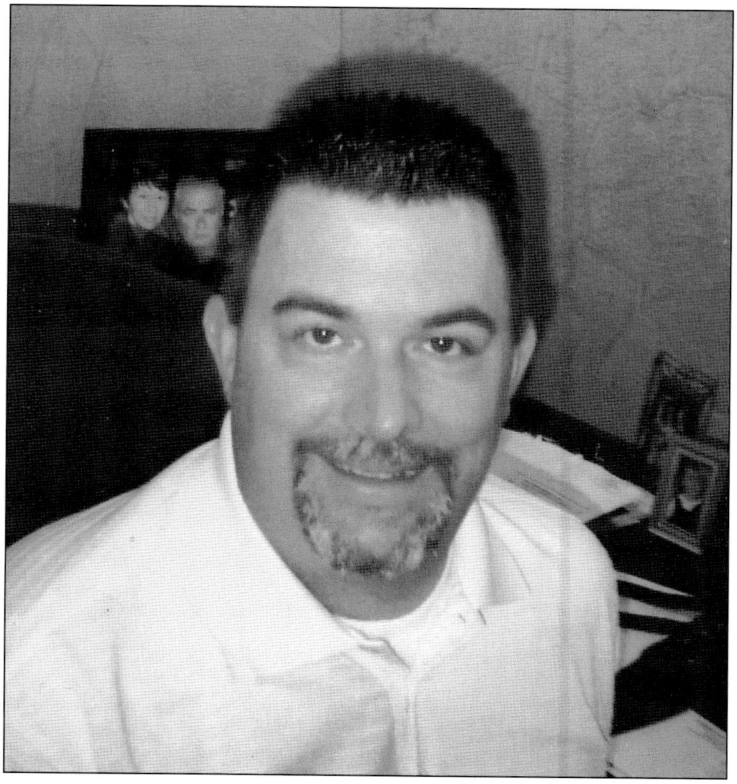

Since its inception in 2005, Krum's Northstar Bank has had two presidents (as of 2010). Margaret Copp served until her retirement in 2007, and Eric Borchardt (pictured) is the current president.

Three

The Schools

In 1976, the Krum Public Schools observed their 100th year of existence. Organized in 1876 by residents of the Jackson community, the first school met in a one-room schoolhouse sitting on 2.5 acres of land at the southeast end of the present Jackson Cemetery. The building, which was used as a schoolhouse and also as a meetinghouse, was moved to the town of Krum in 1891 and placed on the spot where Hattie Dyer Elementary School now stands.

By 1898, the school had outgrown its one-room quarters and used the Church of Christ meetinghouse for the primary grades for a few years. As all three teachers were graduates of normal schools, the faculty was educated above the average for rural schools in those days, and many students transferred to Krum from other districts to have the advantage of their instruction. Also, although most rural schools were in session for only three or four months a year, the Krum School session was for six months, and the parents paid for an additional month, giving the school a seven-month term.

In 1903, Krum's registered voters elected 49 to 1 switch to a free, tax-supported school system. Excellent facilities and faculty have followed. Bonds were voted in 1910 for a two-story brick building featuring six classrooms, an auditorium, and offices. It served well until being torn down in 1976. A one-story brick building, built in 1936, was then remodeled and air-conditioned in 1974 to become the new home of Krum High School.

The Krum Independent School District currently consists of a high school completed in 2004, a middle school, Blanch Dodd Intermediate School, Hattie Dyer Elementary School, and an Early Education Center.

Krum students have compiled enviable records academically and also athletically. Basketball has been Krum's major sport, with five state championships by the boys and one state championship appearance by the girls. The girls have won two state cross-country championships, with one for the boys. Football was incorporated into the program, with Class 2A varsity competition beginning in 2011.

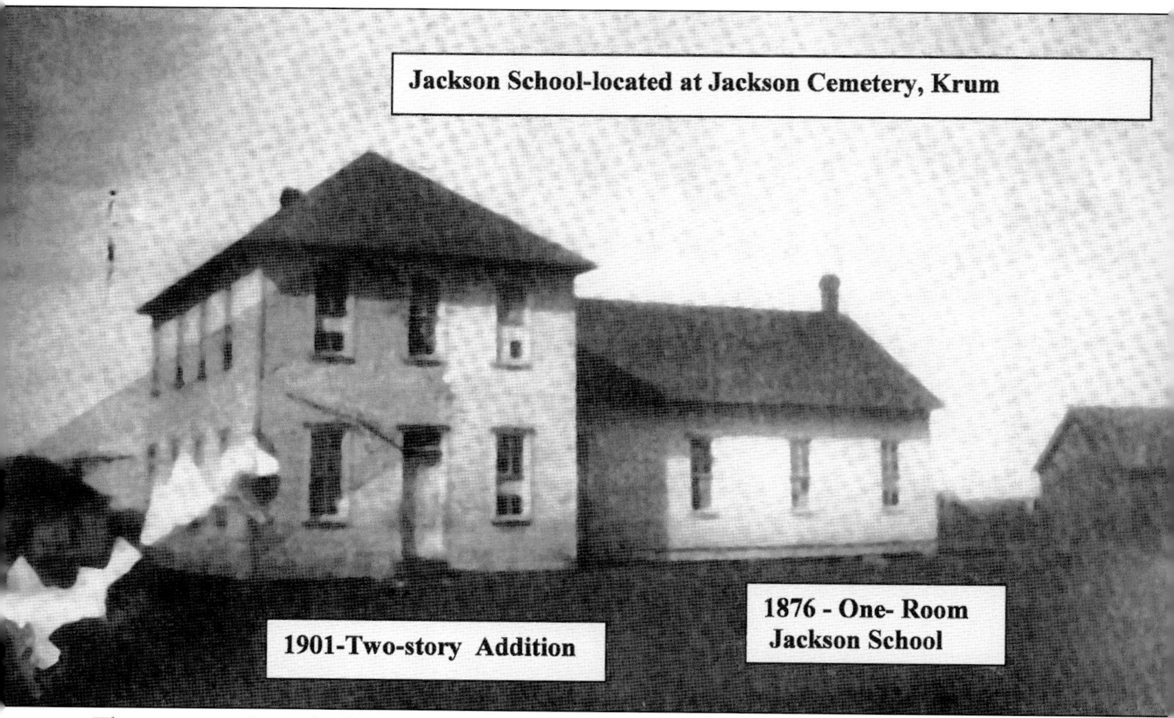

The one-story frame building is the original schoolhouse built in 1876 by the Jackson community. It was moved to Krum in 1891. The school soon outgrew its building, and the two-story addition was built in 1901. The structure was more than just a school building. It was also a social and religious center, the scene of social activities and civic meetings, and the home of the Baptist, Methodist, and Presbyterian Churches and the Church of Christ in their formative stages. There are still many fond memories of this building among Krum's senior citizens.

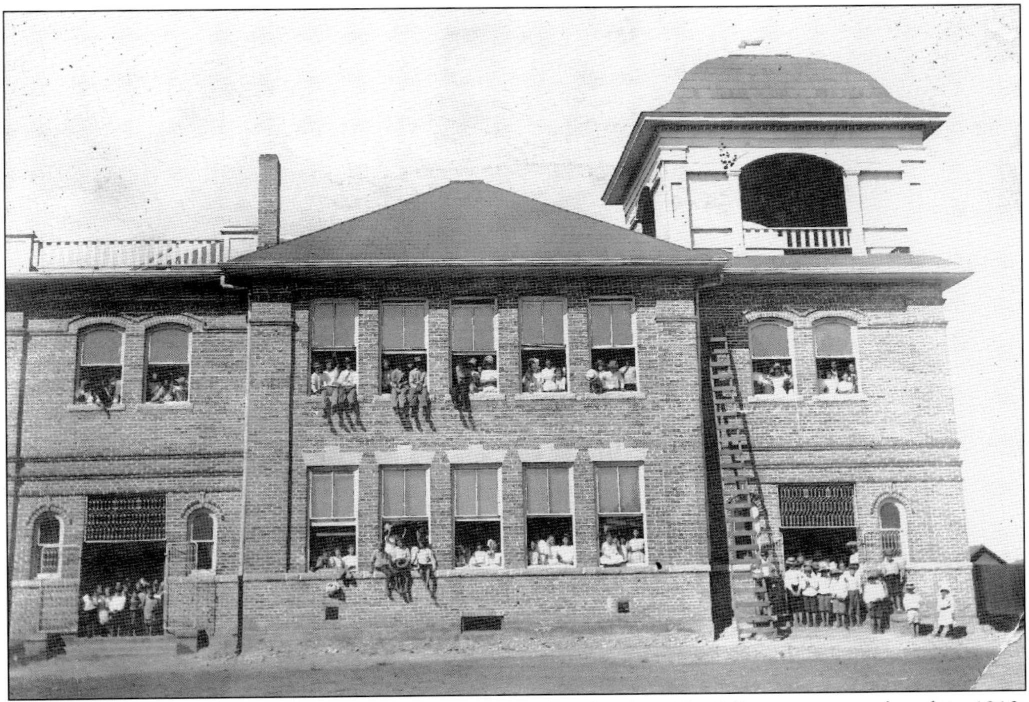

It was a proud day for Krum when a new two-story brick school building was completed in 1910. It appears that the new school had no shortage of students.

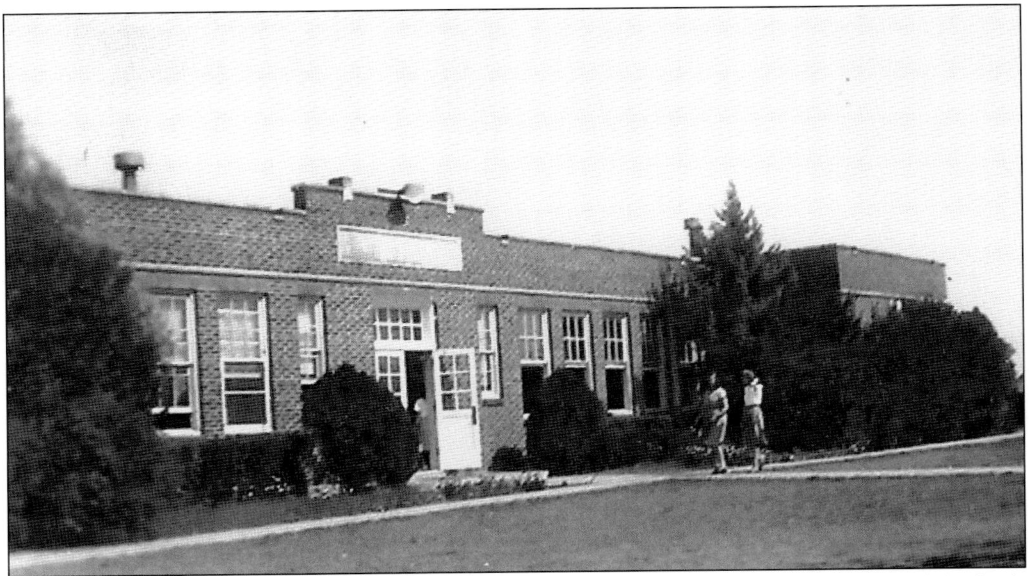

This building was erected in 1939 to house the high school. Enrollment had grown, and the high school had to be removed from the 1910 two-story structure.

Krum High

The old school stands alone,
So full of memories
As the walls began to fall

How the years went slipping by
It seemed like yesterday
And I was young again
And, the walls began to fall

The years have moved along so fast
And yet my memories so strong
As I watched with loving care
As the walls began to fall,

How you will be missed,
Good Ole "Krum High"

Della Davis
November 22, 2003

This poem, written tearfully by Della Davis as she watched the demolition of the school that was part of her life, expresses the sentiments of many who have fond memories of attending high school in Krum.

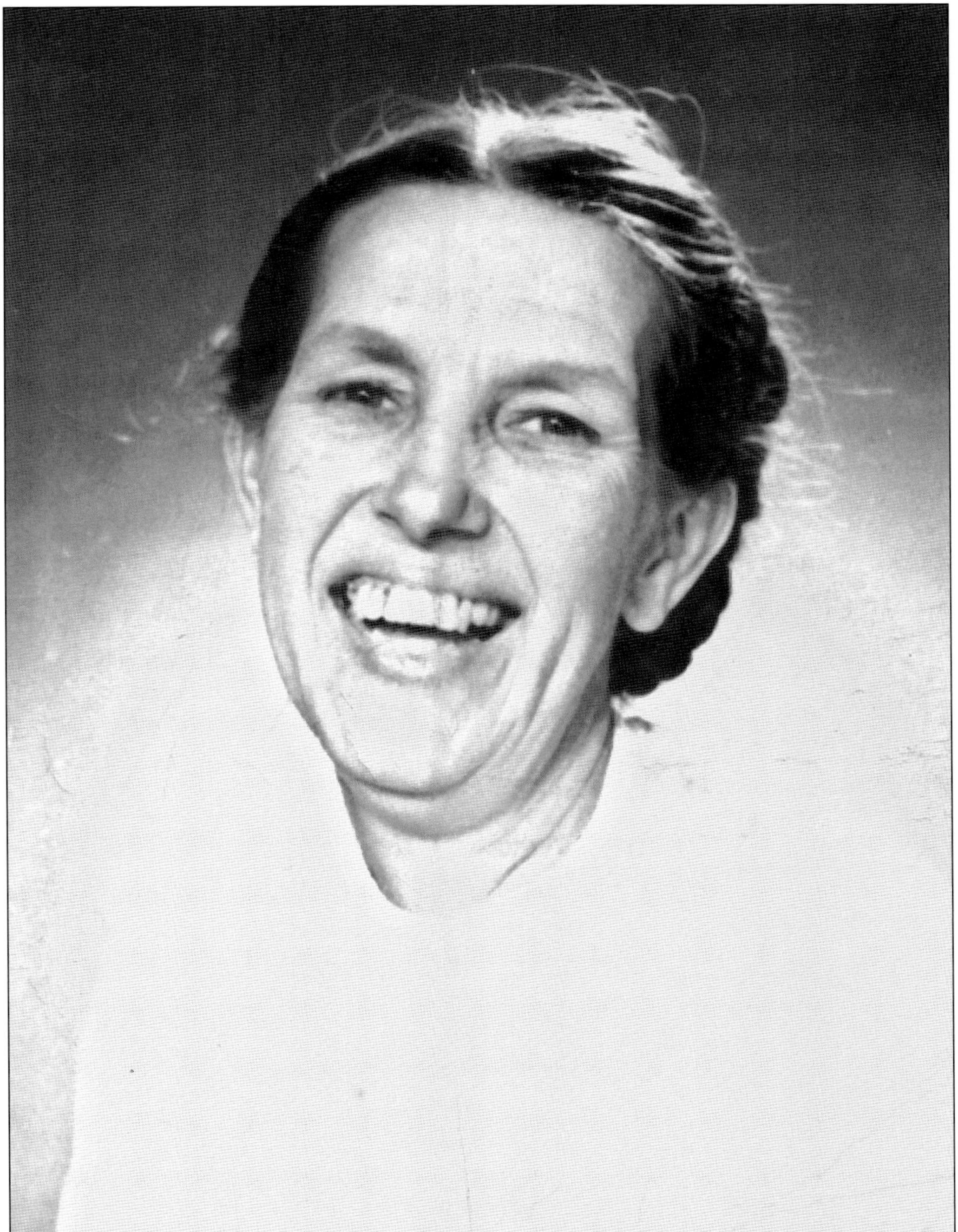

Hattie Dyer taught first and second grades at Krum School from 1940 to 1973. She instructed generations of Krum families. It was a sad day for the school and community of Krum when she retired in 1973. Dyer's retirement income was augmented by rentals and sales of property inherited from her deceased husband, Nelson. She also earned money delivering eggs to customers on a route she had established years earlier when she taught in Dallas County. A measure of the esteem in which Hattie Dyer was held is indicated by the fact that Krum's elementary school is now officially known as the Hattie Dyer Elementary School.

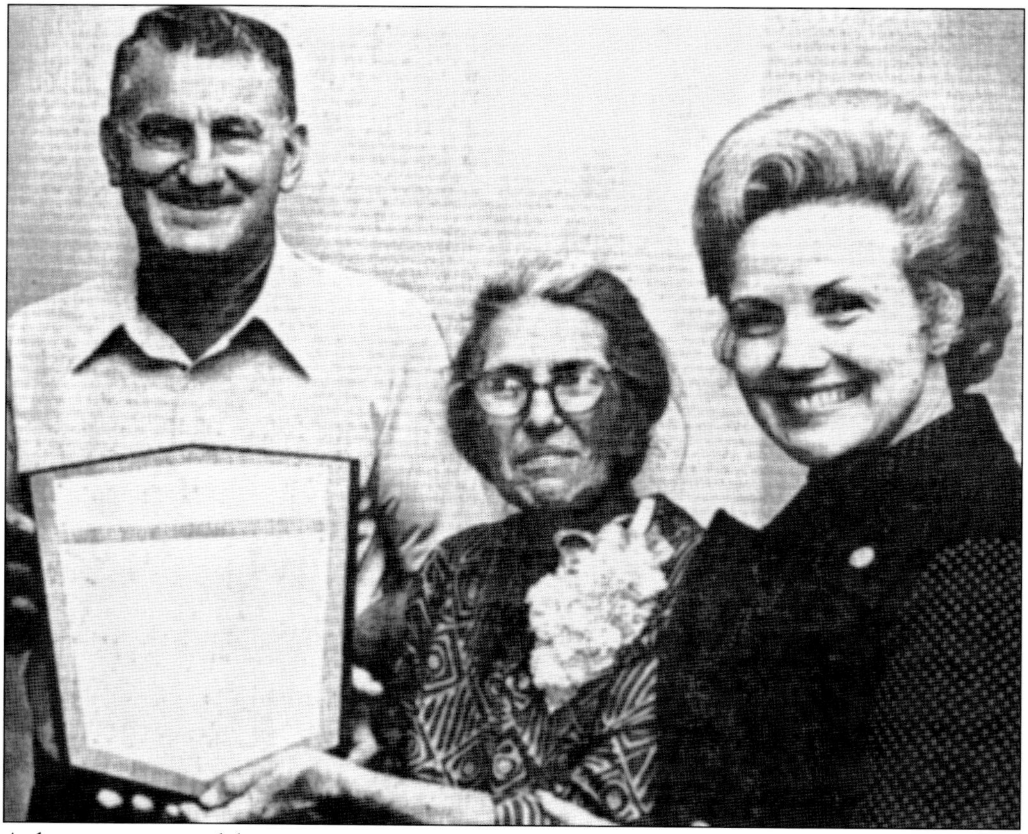

At her retirement celebration, Hattie Dyer holds a congratulatory plaque presented to her by Bob Irwin, school board president, while Dorothy McDaniel, a school board member, looks on. In addition, Mac Vincent, Krum School superintendent, presented Hattie with a scrapbook filled with letters from former first and second graders.

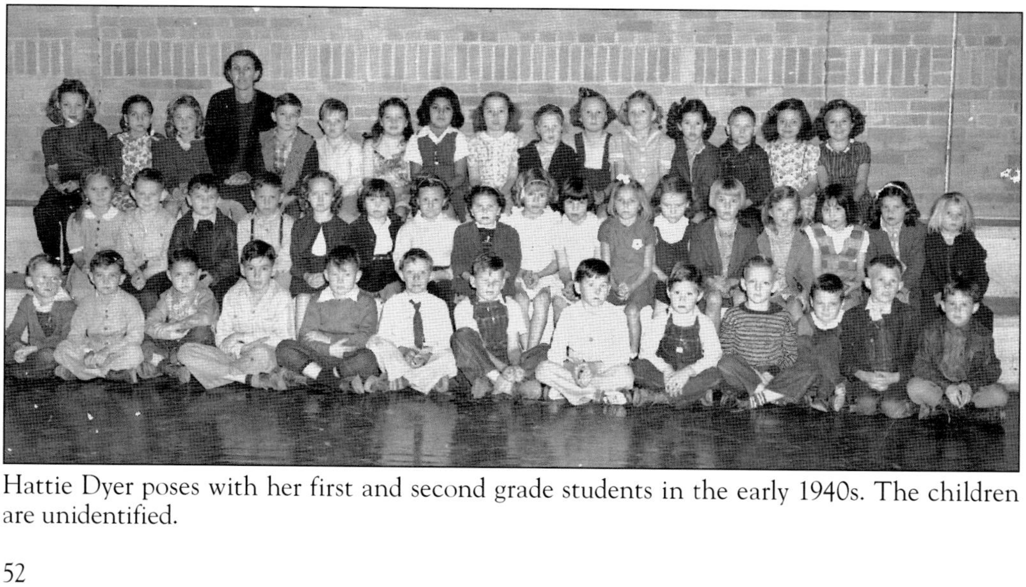

Hattie Dyer poses with her first and second grade students in the early 1940s. The children are unidentified.

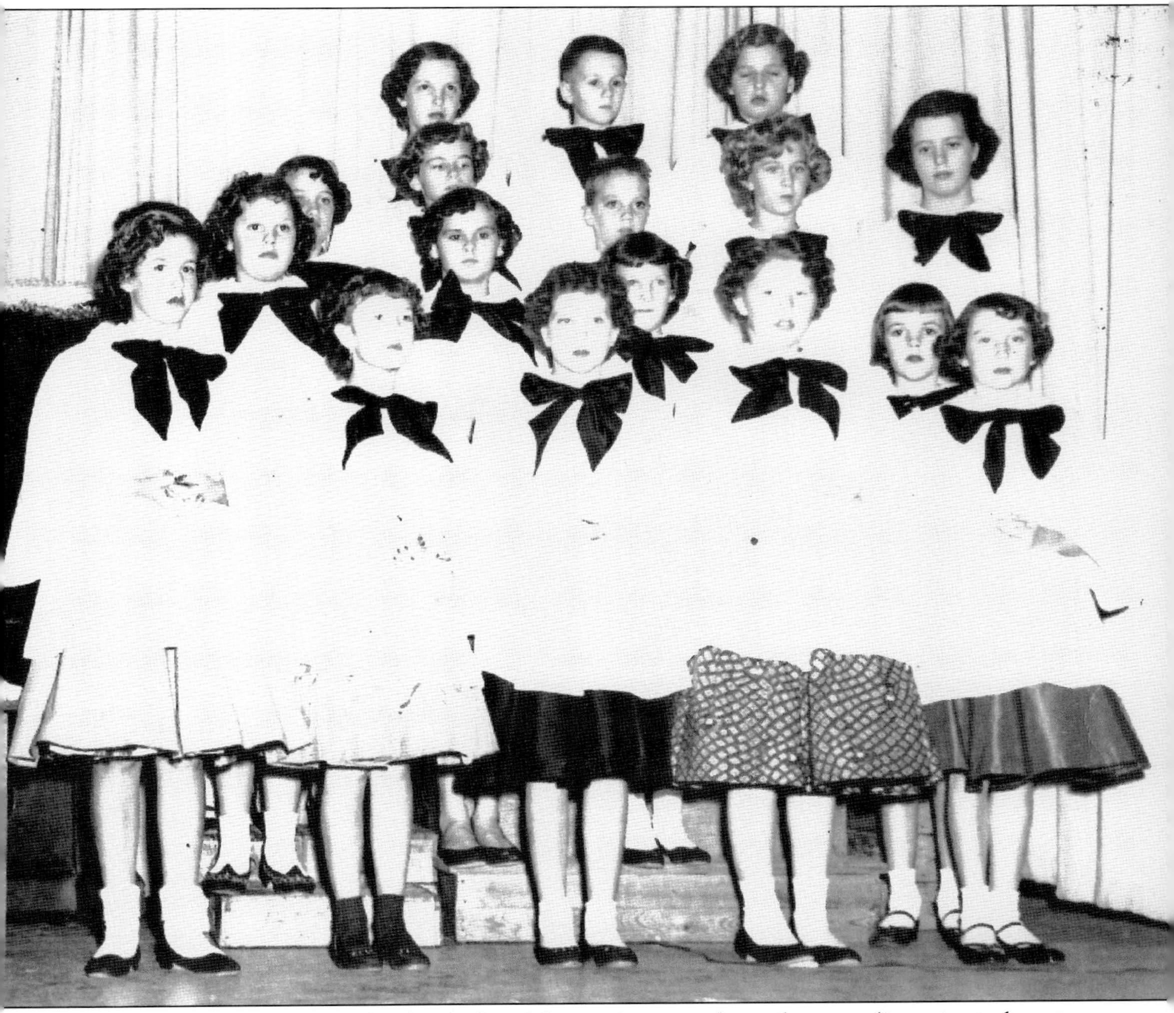

Mary M. Thrift's junior high school glee club members are dressed in angelic attire in keeping with the theme of their program. They are, from left to right, (first row) Betty Davis, Bonnie Sue Bunnell, Jane Barthold, Patricia Tindel, and Betty Boyd; (second row) Judy Carol Enis, Donna Kay Schluter, Carol Jean Kline, and Rheta Beth Barry; (third row) Charline Cline, Jean Tidbits, Don Dodd, Ethel Finley, and Martha Lamm; (fourth row) Linda Copp, Jary Copp, and Barbara Parkey.

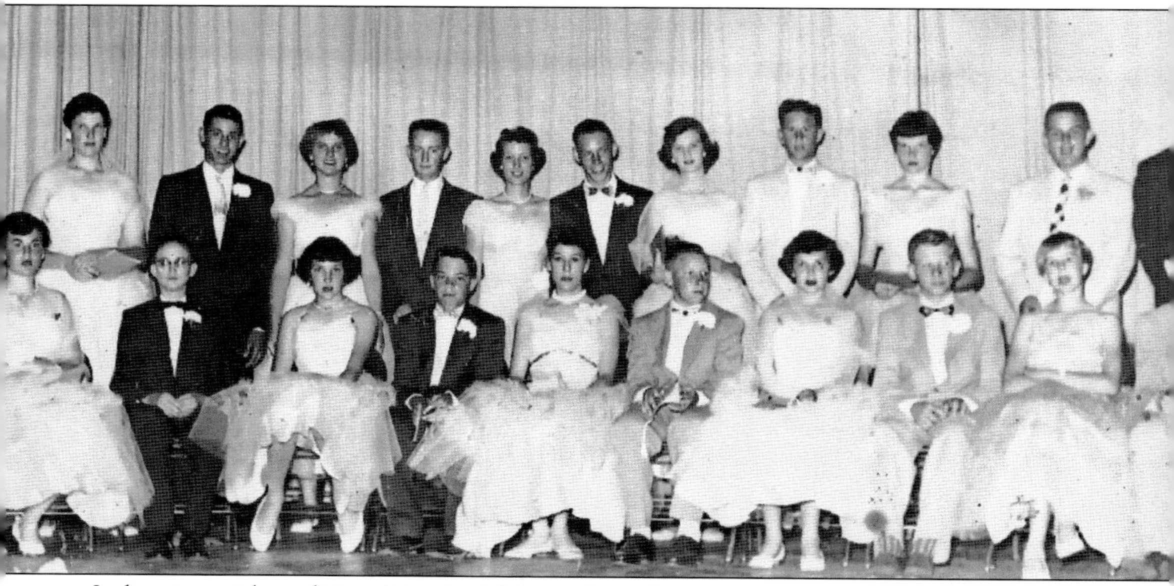

In keeping with tradition, Krum's eighth grade graduation ceremonies featured formality and elegance. In this photograph of 1955 graduates are, from left to right, (first row) Janet Hartin, Carroll Caddell, Joy Lou Masten, Dan Dodd, Janet Hensley, Freddy, Boenker, Jo Mack Moore, Fred Marrs, Charlotte Hensley, and Jon Newell; (second row) Sue Ann Harris, David McKinney, Gloria Cleary, Jerry Jackson, Glenda McKinney, Buddy Standifer, Denise Isbell, Dwayne Riney, Linda Yeatts, John Marshall, and faculty member George U. Peek.

Blanche Dodd and her daughter Kathryn stand at the entry to the Blanche Dodd Intermediate School, named in honor of one of Krum's outstanding citizens and community leaders.

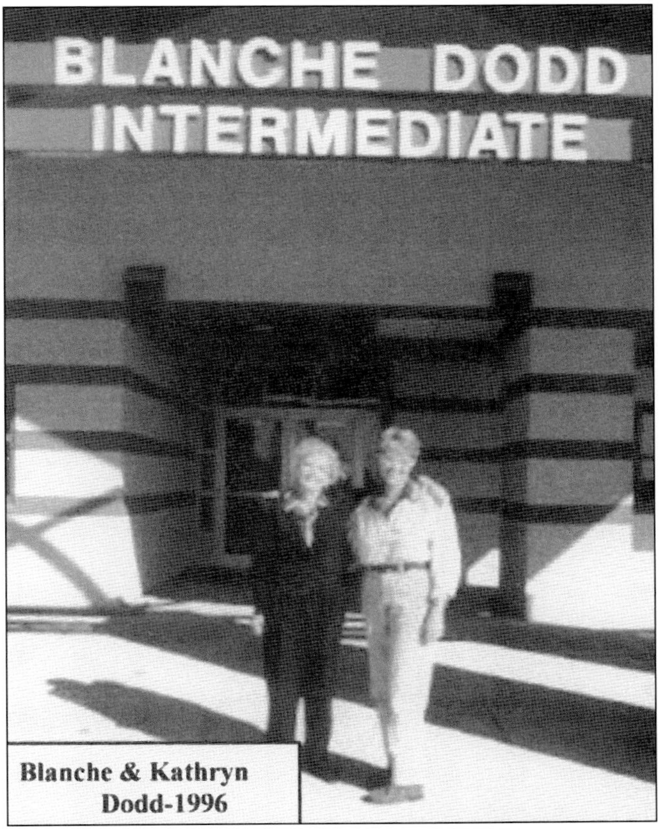

Wilson W. Davis and his wife, Robbie Lou, are a striking couple at a junior-senior banquet in the mid-1950s. As superintendent of schools, Davis also found time to teach mathematics and coach basketball. He had served previously as high school principal. Two other Krum educators—Bennie Enis and Troy Hamm—have also served as coach, principal, and superintendent.

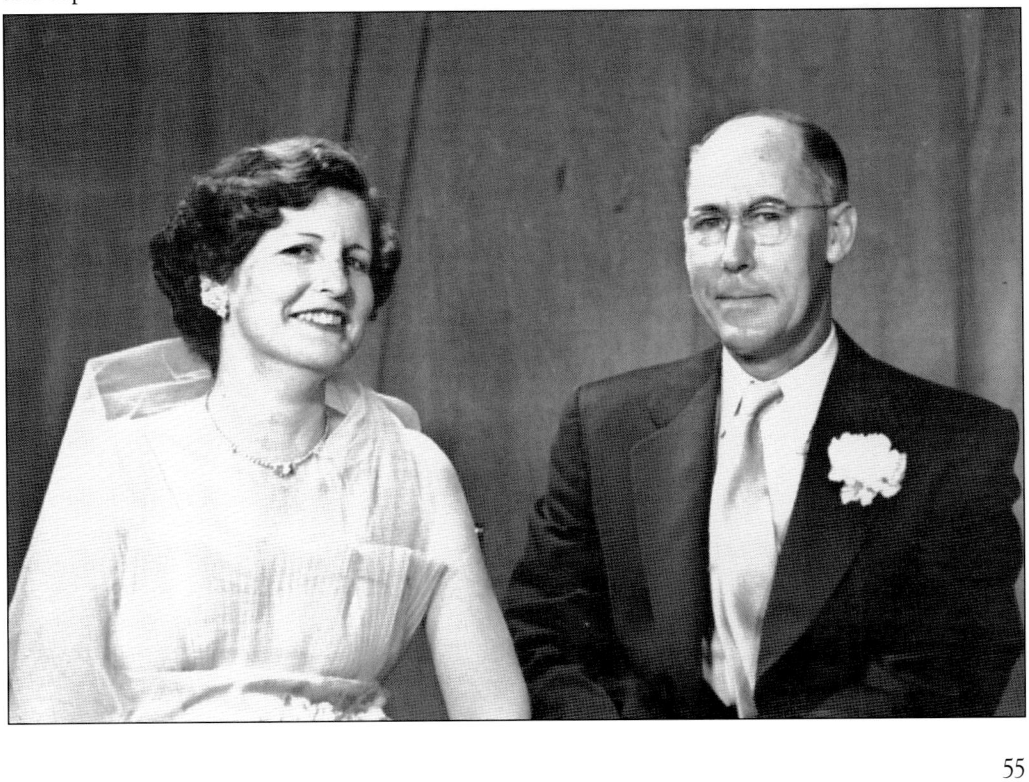

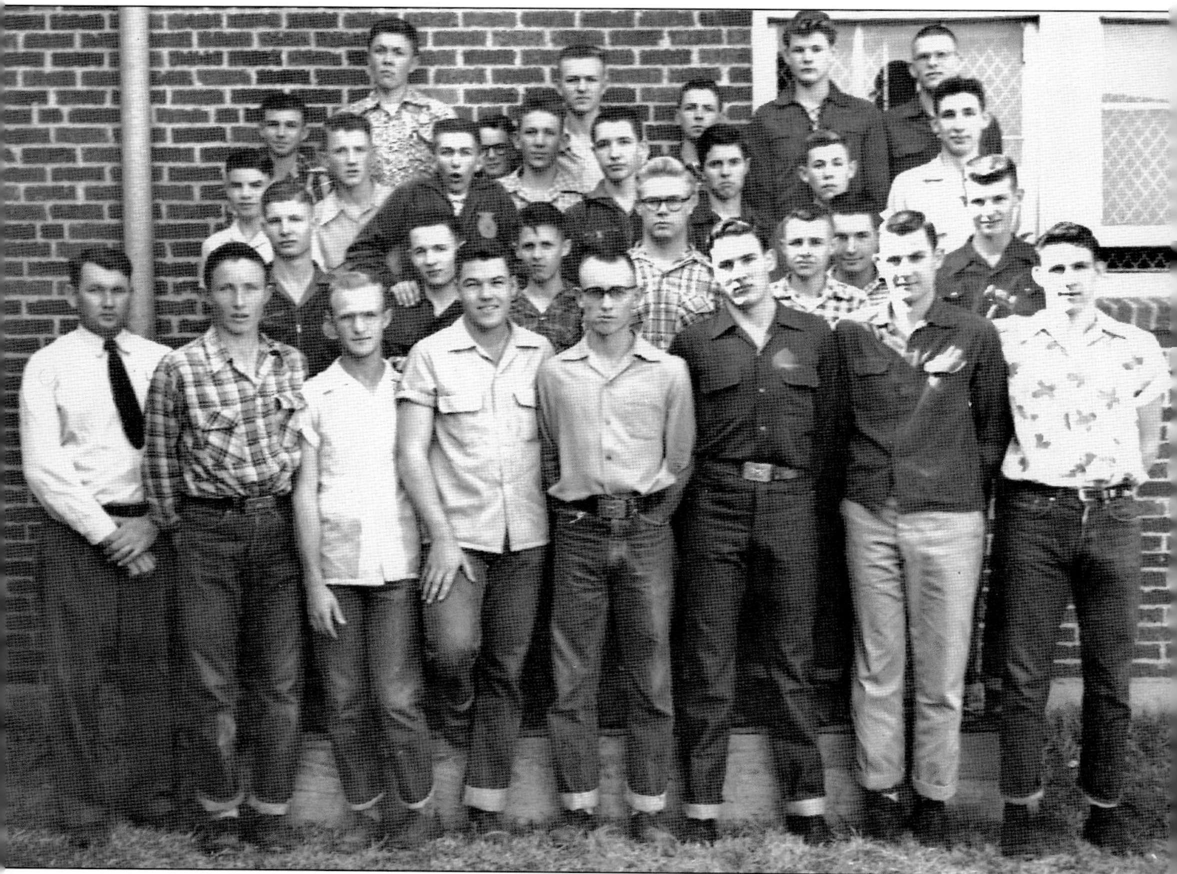

The Future Farmers of America organization has always been active in the Krum schools. Pictured in 1954 are, from left to right, (first row) teacher George Peek, Charles Standifer, Ben Finley, Fletcher McBee, Wendell Bartlett, Kenneth Hartin, Robert Wilburn, and Terry Masten; (second row) Stanley Caddell, H. L. Herring, Tom Buckley, Billy Don McCarty, Jack Cofer, Gerald Copp, and Larry Enis; (third row) Leonard Simpkins, Butch Murdock, Jimmy Hartin, George Boyd, Buddy McClure, Douglas Wells, Richard Hensley, and Billy Masten; (fourth row) Ballard Hopkins, Wayne Riley, Garland Holley, Milton Finley, Windy Fowler, Will Marshall, and Dale Schluter.

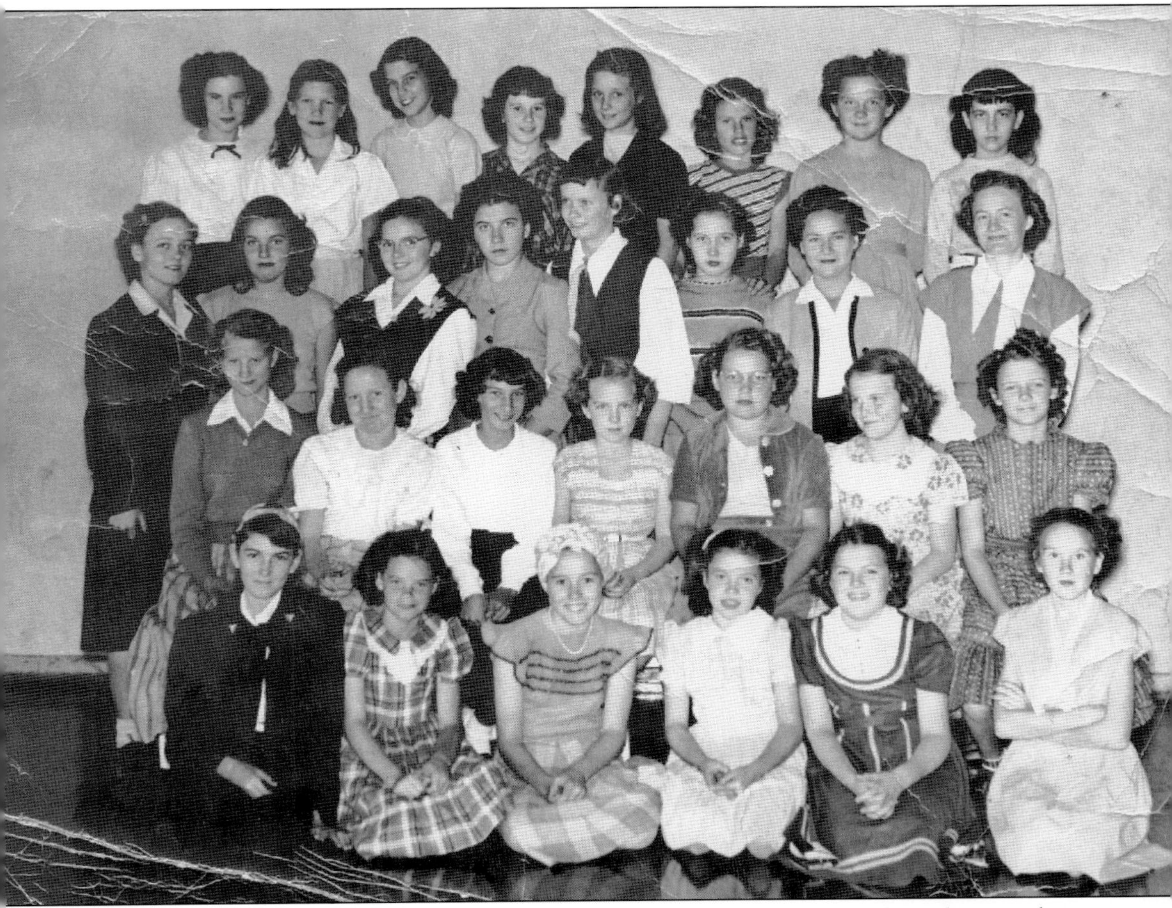

Student organizations at Krum High School were focused primarily on agriculture, homemaking, music, or theater. Pictured here are members of the girls' 4-H club in 1950. They are, from left to right, (first row) Margaret Davis, Betty Simpkins, Geneva Smith, Geneva Givens, Glada Harris, and Edith Greener; (second row) Barbara Isball, Delores Franks, Wilma Standifer, Dorothy Bartlett, Vanna Briscoe, Patsy Hudgins, and Nancy Knox; (third row) Marie Bartlett, Wanda Cofer, Marilyn Givens, Joyce Johnson, Yvonne McFarlin, Janette McClure, Dorothy Standifer, and music teacher Alene King; (fourth row) Bonnie Simpkins, Helen Hicks, Barbara Blocker, Janice Cole, Rena Riney, Betty Simpkins, Wilma Johnson, and Barbara Moore.

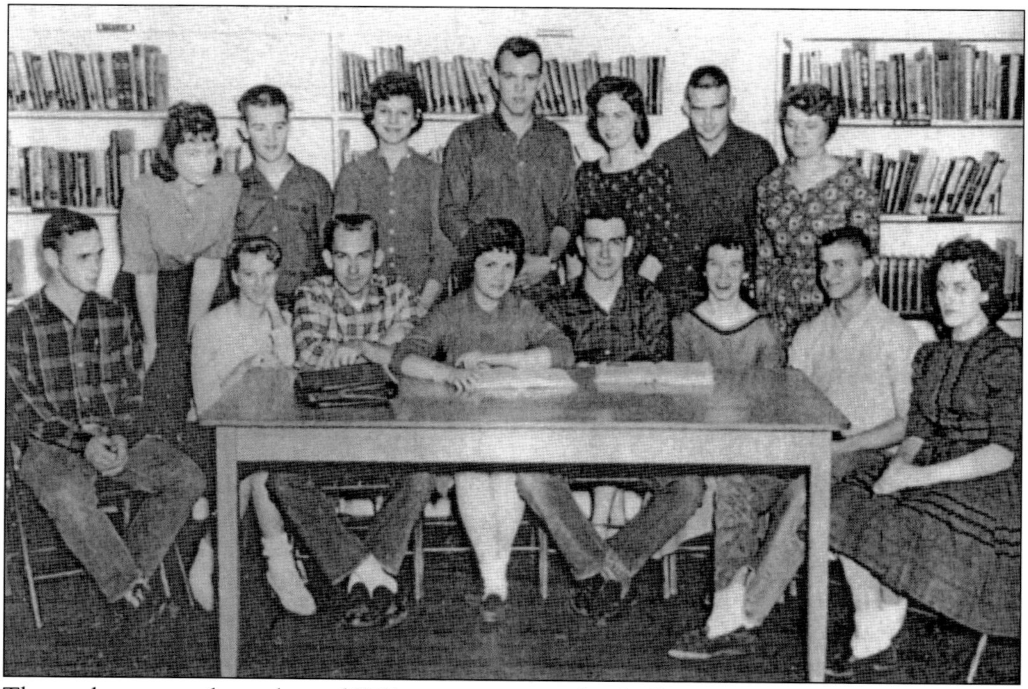

The student council members of 1961 were active in school affairs and took their responsibilities seriously. They are, from left to right, (first row) Wendell Standifer, Della Isbell, Charles Hare, Judy Enis, Wylie Koiner, Carol Klein, Ronnie Cullum, and Pat Martin; (second row) Charlene Cline, Jary Copp, Peggy Boenker, Jerry McKinney, Lou Ann Phillips, John Terrell, and Lillian Yeary.

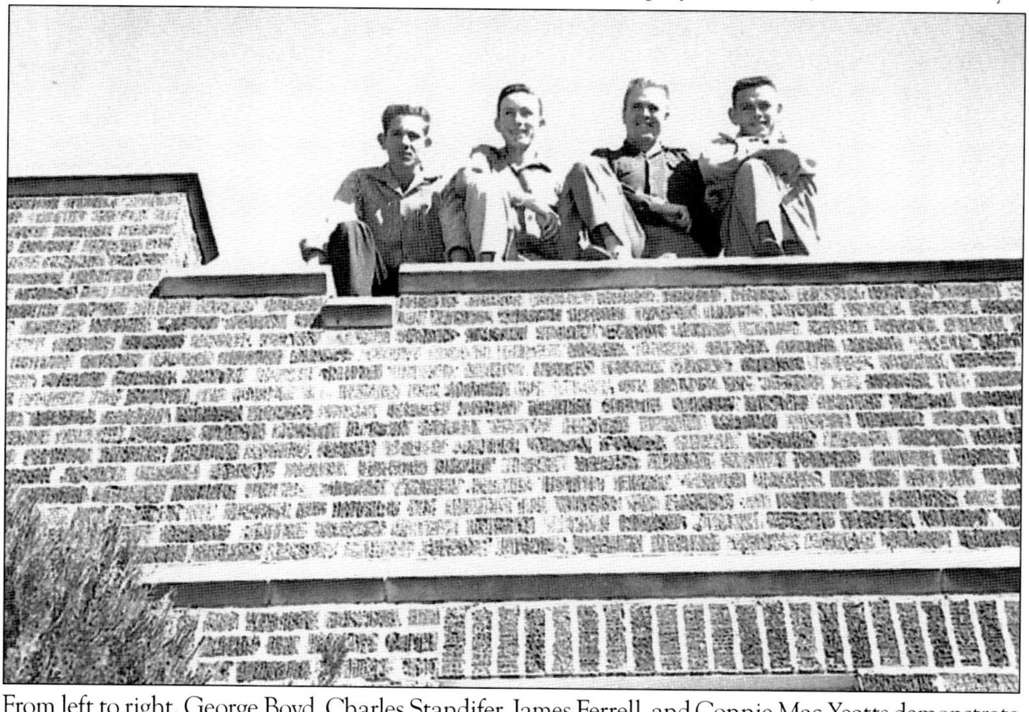

From left to right, George Boyd, Charles Standifer, James Ferrell, and Connie Mac Yeatts demonstrate their concept of "higher education" in this 1955 photograph.

Together

How can we make it better
    In this world today?
There are so many problems
    But there's got to be a way.
Murder, racism,
    Starvation, too
We all need to help
    And do what we can do.

I see the homeless man,
    Who has nothing to eat.
I see the little children
    Sleeping on the street.

Sometimes I stop and wonder
    Does anyone care?
In order to make a difference
    We have to make ourselves aware,
So right now look around you,
    And see what can be done;
And once we get this world cleaned up,
    The battle will be won.
I'm sure that there is something
    That each of us can do.
Together we can make it better,
    Together, me and you.

--- Kaye Cofer

One of the major characteristics among the citizens of Krum is their feeling of unity and togetherness. And one of the major objectives of schools is to produce citizens who can "make a positive difference" both locally and globally. Krum student Kaye Cofer captures both of these concepts in her poem "Together."

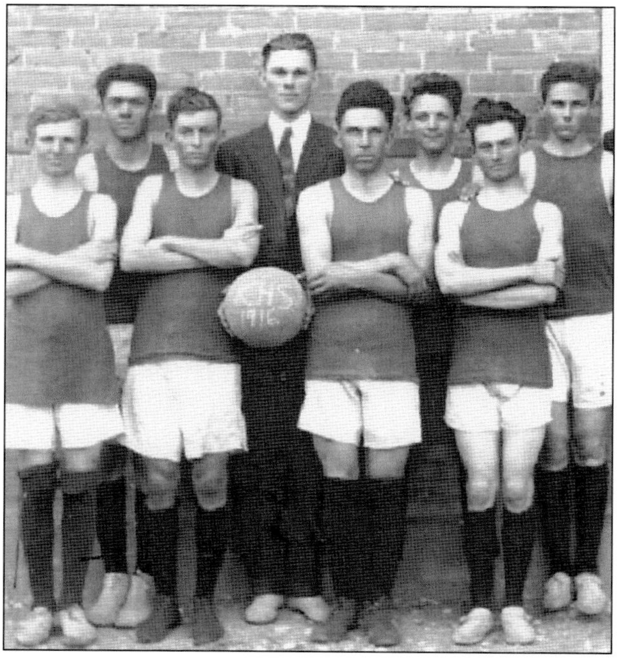

Basketball has been a popular school sport in Krum from the very beginning. Shown here is the 1916 team. Pictured from left to right are (first row) Homer Pruett, Guy Huffines, Bob McNabb, and Olin Nail; (second row) Loren Park, coach Jason Sanders, Cecil Knox, and Joe Russell.

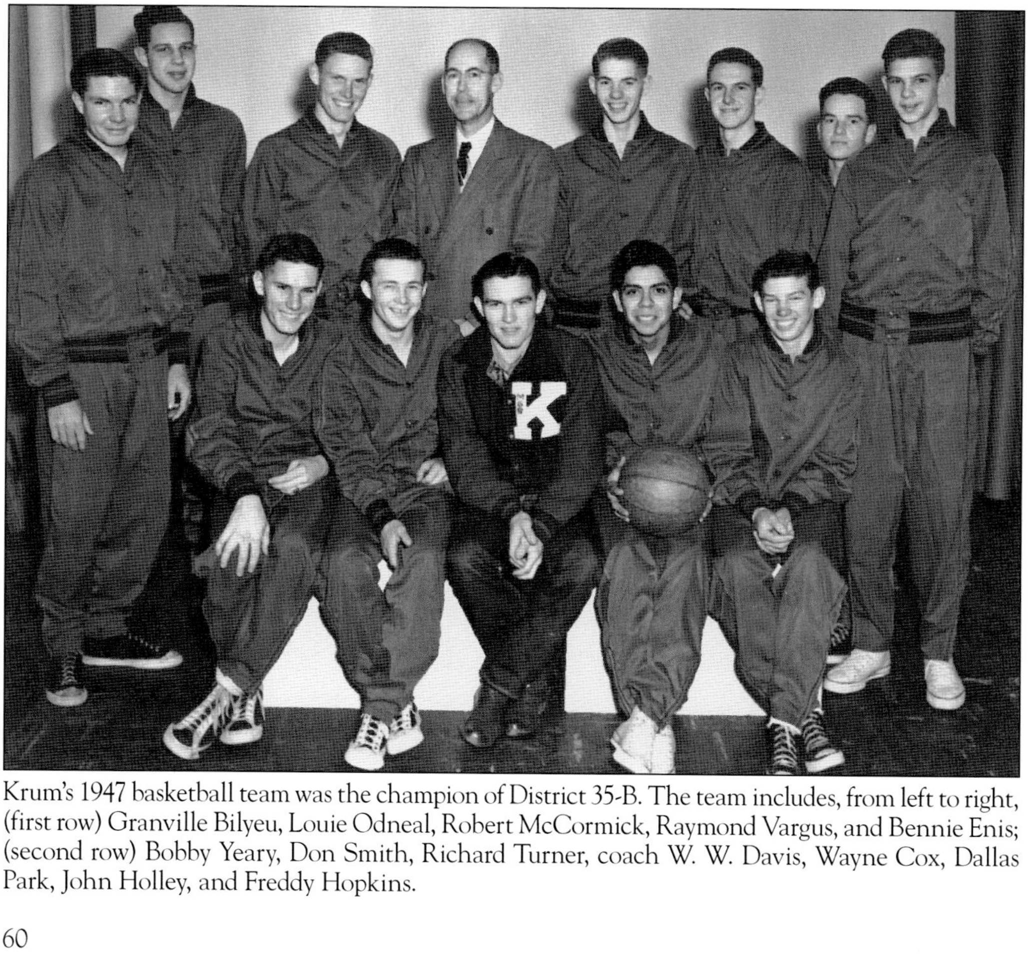

Krum's 1947 basketball team was the champion of District 35-B. The team includes, from left to right, (first row) Granville Bilyeu, Louie Odneal, Robert McCormick, Raymond Vargus, and Bennie Enis; (second row) Bobby Yeary, Don Smith, Richard Turner, coach W. W. Davis, Wayne Cox, Dallas Park, John Holley, and Freddy Hopkins.

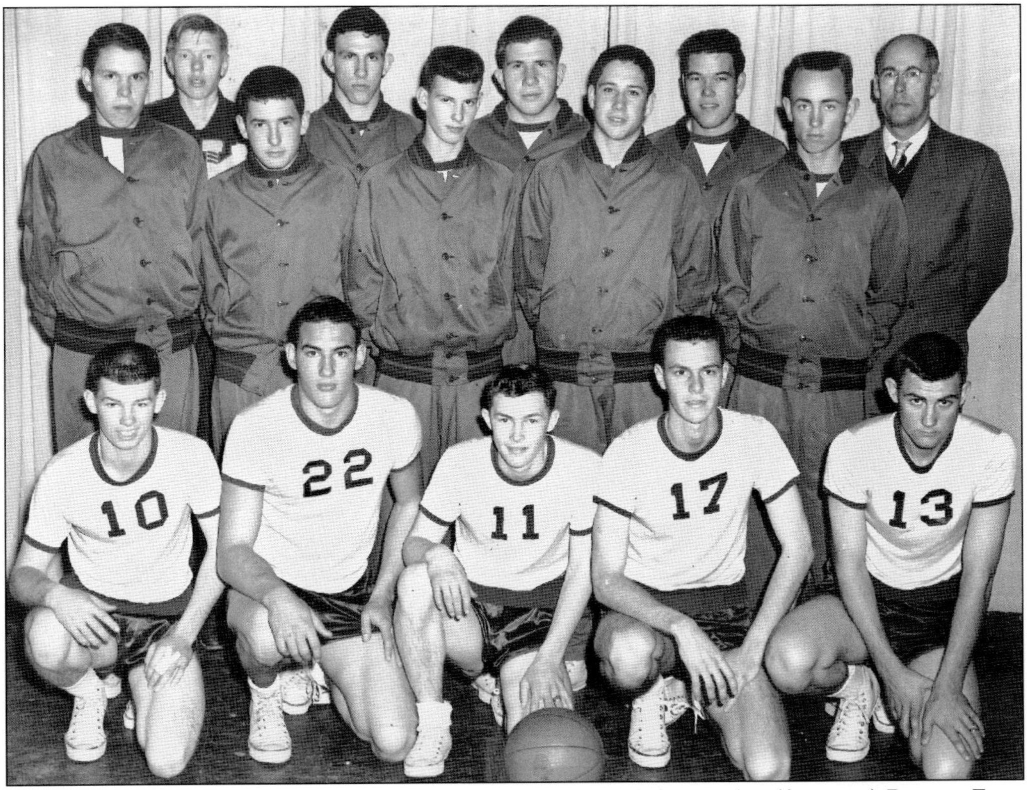
The District 33-B basketball champions of 1953 are, from left to right, (first row) Bennie Enis, Kenneth Hartin, Don Odneal, Loman Park, and Robert Wayne Wilburn; (second row) Dale Schulter, Red Maples, Gerald Copp, Terry Masten, Larry Enis, Glen Ray Adams, Bobby Boaz, Fletcher McBee, Wendell Bartlett, and coach W. W. Davis.

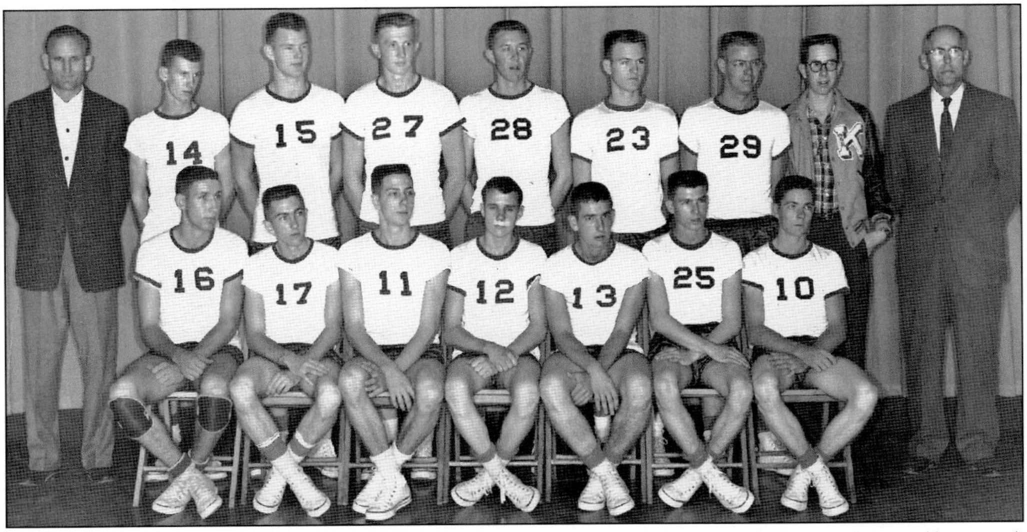
Krum's 1955 basketball team was guided by two coaches. Pictured from left to right are (first row) Billy Masten, Butch Murdock, Bobby Parkey, Jack Cofer, Gerald Copp, Wayne Riley, and Windy Fowler; (second row) coach Ed McReynolds, Larry Enis, Bubba Marshall, Ballard Hopkins, Garland Holley, Milton Finley, Billy McCarty, Bill Cole, and coach W. W. Davis.

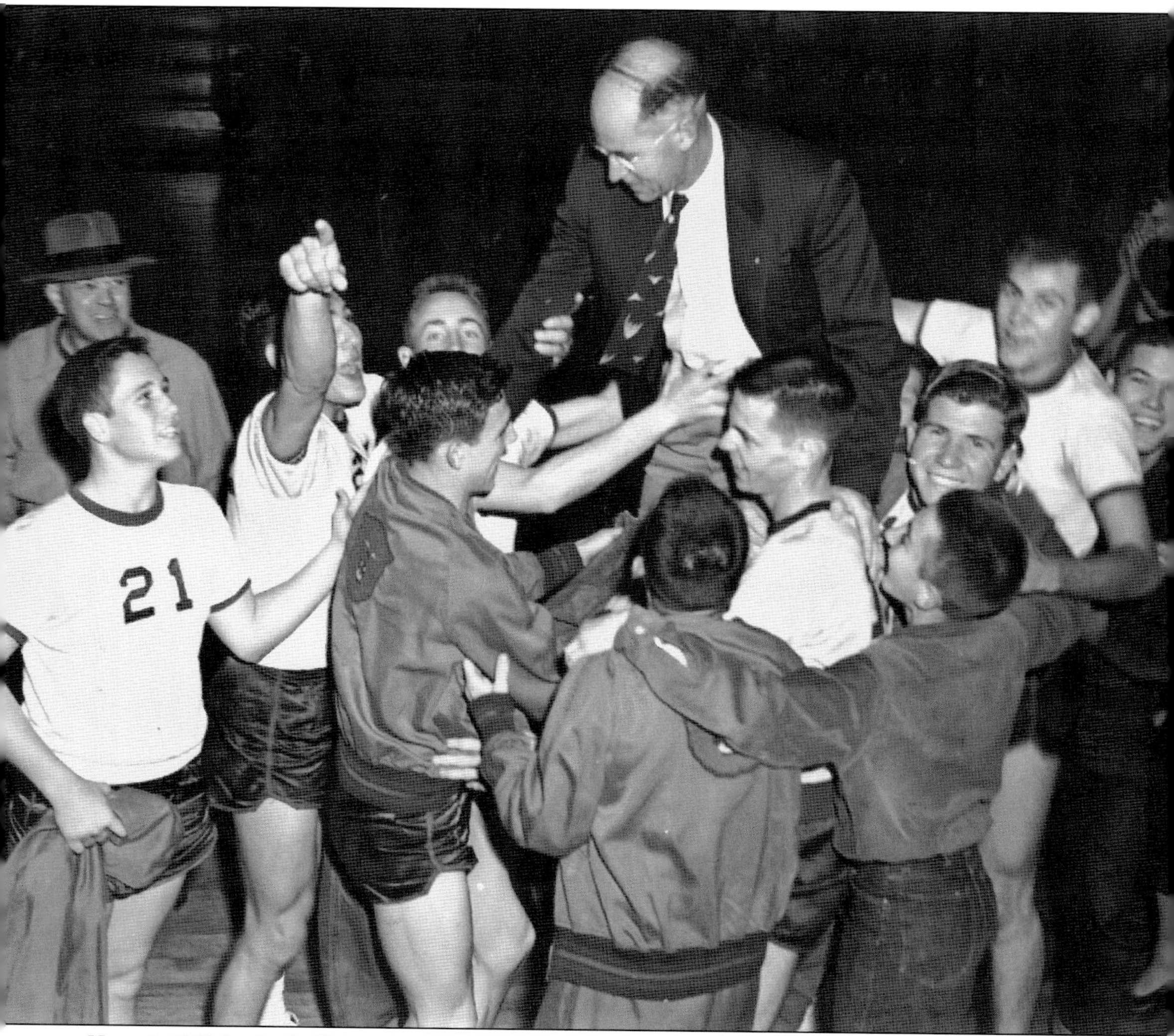

Krum's 1953 basketball team members lift coach W. W. Davis to their shoulders in celebration of winning the District 33-B championship that year. Coach Davis, who was also superintendent of schools and a math teacher, can be credited with beginning the winning tradition that Krum basketball teams have enjoyed over the years.

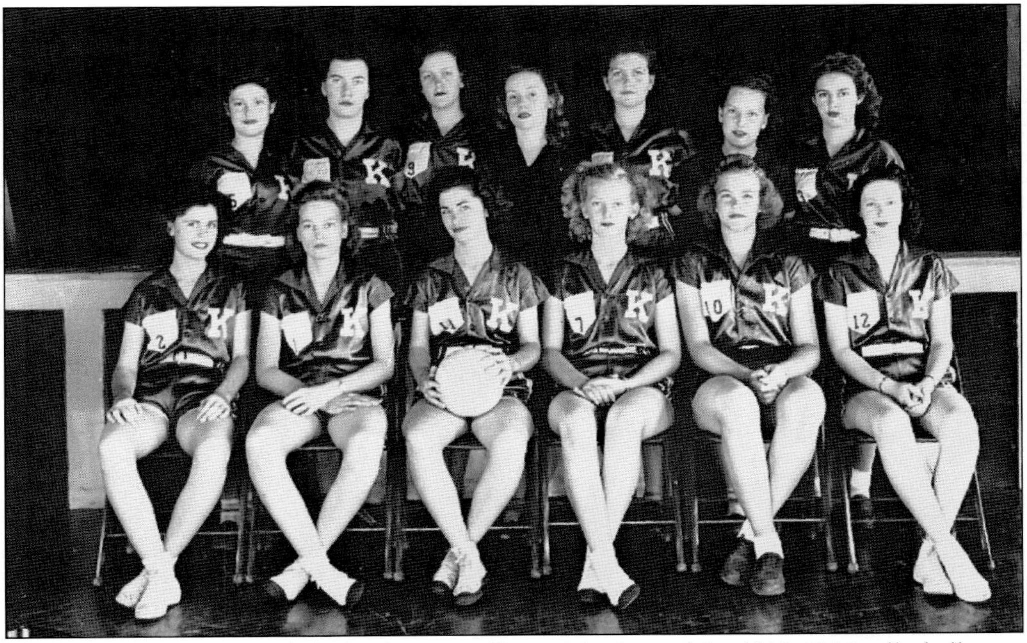

Volleyball is another popular school sport in Krum. Members of the 1945–1946 volleyball team are, left to right, (first row) Billie Cheatham, Melba Smith Willie, Pearl Cheatham, Gloria Ross, Rosa Hopkins, and Mary Ruth Miller; (second row) Gloria Cheatham, Omalie Mellin, Merle Phillips, coach Anna Sue Morgan, Dorothy Hicks, Wilma Dee Martin, and Imogene Harris.

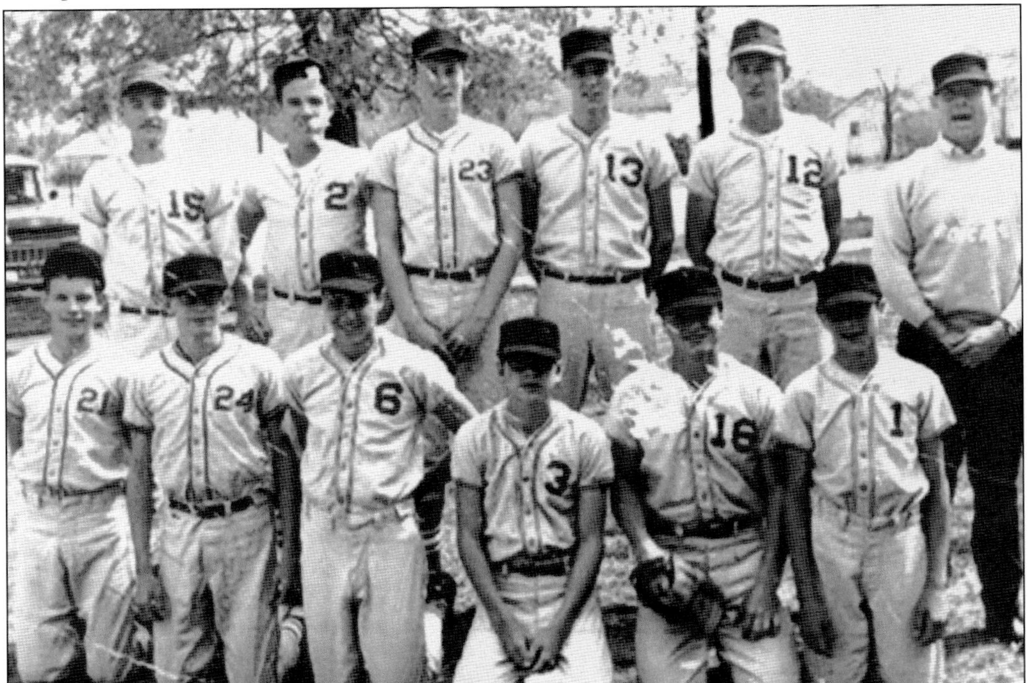

Krum's 1964 baseball team consisted of, from left to right, (first row) unidentified, Jack Hall, Eddie Sallee, unidentified, Tony Shurbet, and unidentified; (second row) Billy Koiner, Tommy Hartin, Donnie Merriefield, Rick Knight, Jack Standifer, and coach Tip Hall.

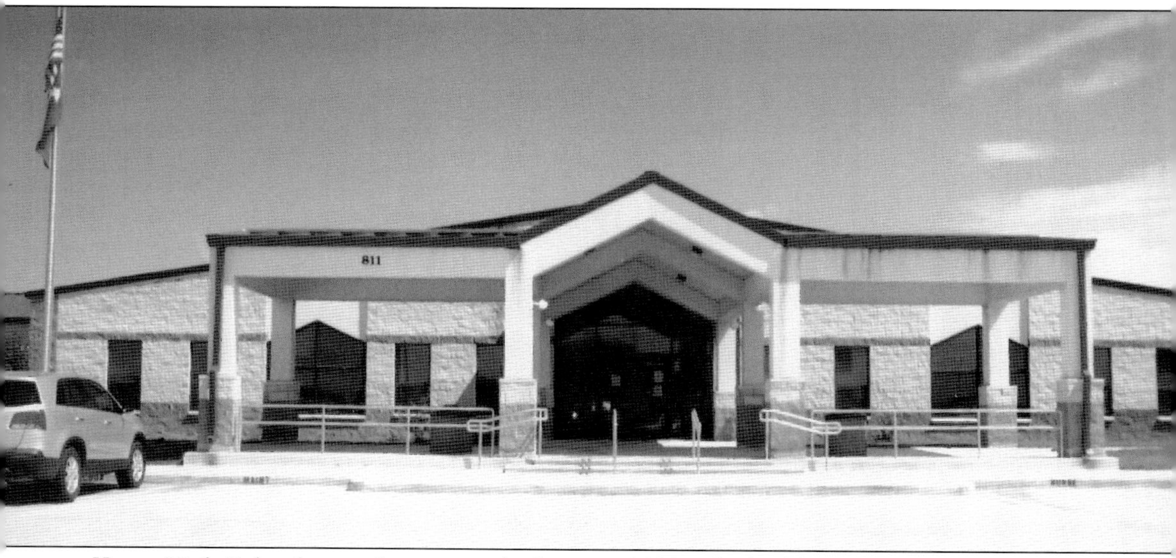

Krum High School moved into new facilities in 2003. The building sits on the back portion of the school property on the north side of East McCart Street. To the left (not shown) is the Bennie Enis Gymnasium, named for one of Krum's basketball legends, both as a player and as a very successful coach. To the right (also not shown) is a first-class auditorium and fine arts center completed in 2008. The old high school building is now Krum Middle School.

Four

The Churches

Religious worship has been a fundamental aspect in the lives of Krum's citizens, and four Christian denominations currently serve the town and its residents.

In 1876, members of the Jackson community established the First United Methodist Church, which met in the one-room schoolhouse, where the current Jackson Cemetery is located. In 1891, the schoolhouse was moved, along with the rest of the Jackson community, to the new settlement of Krum, 2 miles to the north, and the Methodists continued meeting in the building until they could build their own, which they did in 1901. They remained in this building until 1924, when they began construction of a new building at the intersection of McCart and Second Streets. Meeting for 10 years in their new basement, they completed a brick sanctuary in 1924. In 2010, they moved to a new sanctuary in the eastern part of Krum.

The First Baptist Church, organized in 1882 in the same Jackson Schoolhouse, was next on the scene. In 1886, the congregation moved to a new building located 3 miles down North Hickory Creek, where they remained for six years until moving into Krum in 1898. Dismantling their building on North Hickory Creek, they reassembled it on three lots in Krum located at the intersection of Lake and Second Streets. Then to make room for school expansion, they sold the lots to the school district and moved the building across the street. In 1961, the little white building was replaced by a brick sanctuary at the intersection of Lloyd and Second Streets. The Baptists remained there until 1992, when they moved to their current location on Gregg Road.

The Church of Christ, an offspring of the Church of Christ of Bolivar, had its official beginning in Krum in 1893. They met on Sunday afternoons in the one-room schoolhouse that accommodated the Methodist services in the mornings. In 1899, they built their own meetinghouse on North Third Street, which they used until it burned in 1929. They are still meeting in its replacement.

Krum's Christian Center Assembly of God was organized in January 1992 with 11 people present. The first pastor, Carl Lambert Jr., held the first few church services in the two-car garage of his home on Gregg Road until February 1992, when they moved into the brick building vacated by the Baptists. They remained there until 1994, when their current building at the intersection of Jackson and Britton Streets was erected. The Assembly of God's current attendance averages 170 people.

A fifth denomination, the Presbyterians, also had a presence in Krum. Organized in 1901 with 18 or more charter members, they grew to about 150 in 1916. Then a decline in membership set in. With only a few faithful members still attending, the church disbanded in 1942.

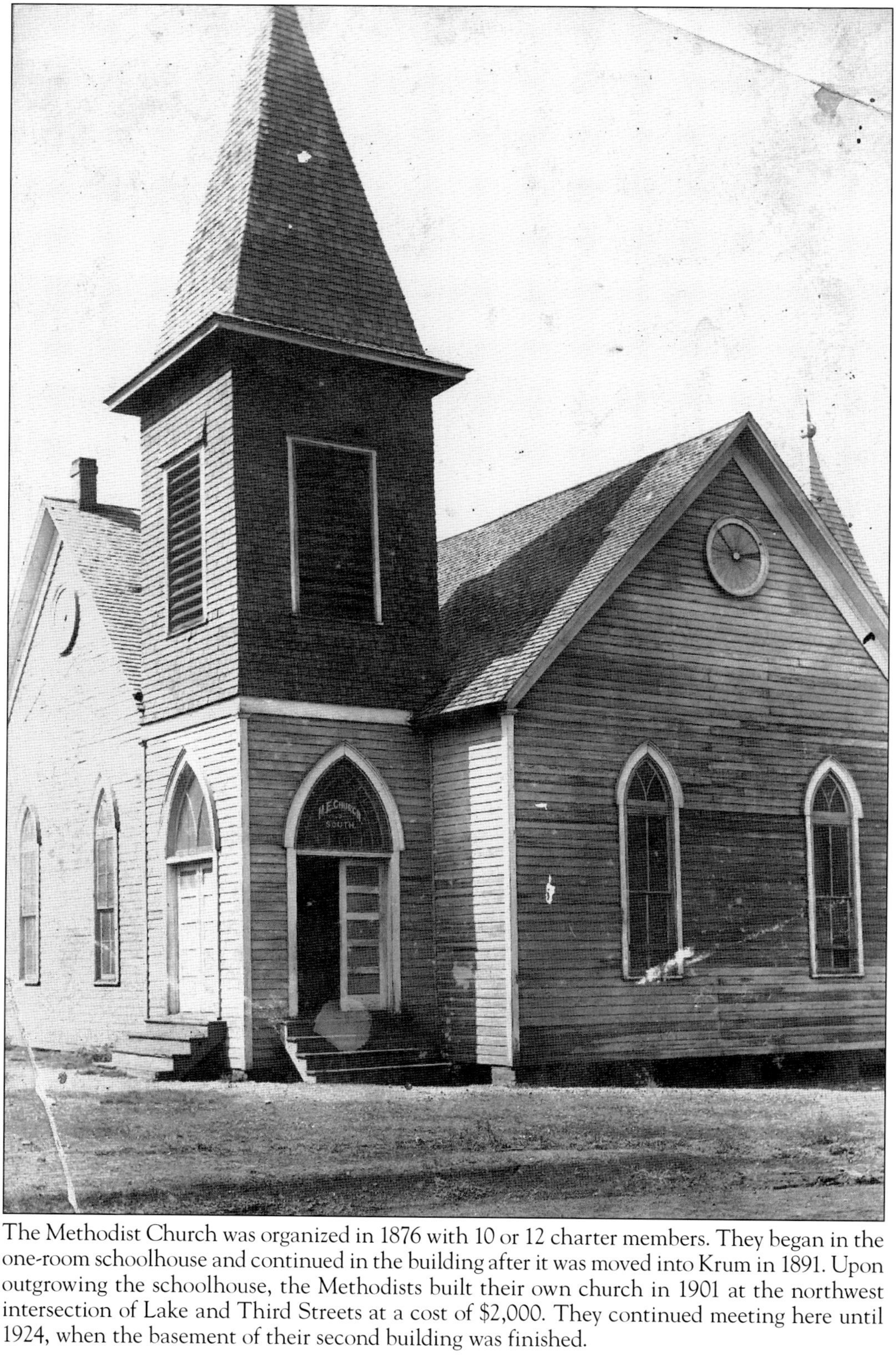

The Methodist Church was organized in 1876 with 10 or 12 charter members. They began in the one-room schoolhouse and continued in the building after it was moved into Krum in 1891. Upon outgrowing the schoolhouse, the Methodists built their own church in 1901 at the northwest intersection of Lake and Third Streets at a cost of $2,000. They continued meeting here until 1924, when the basement of their second building was finished.

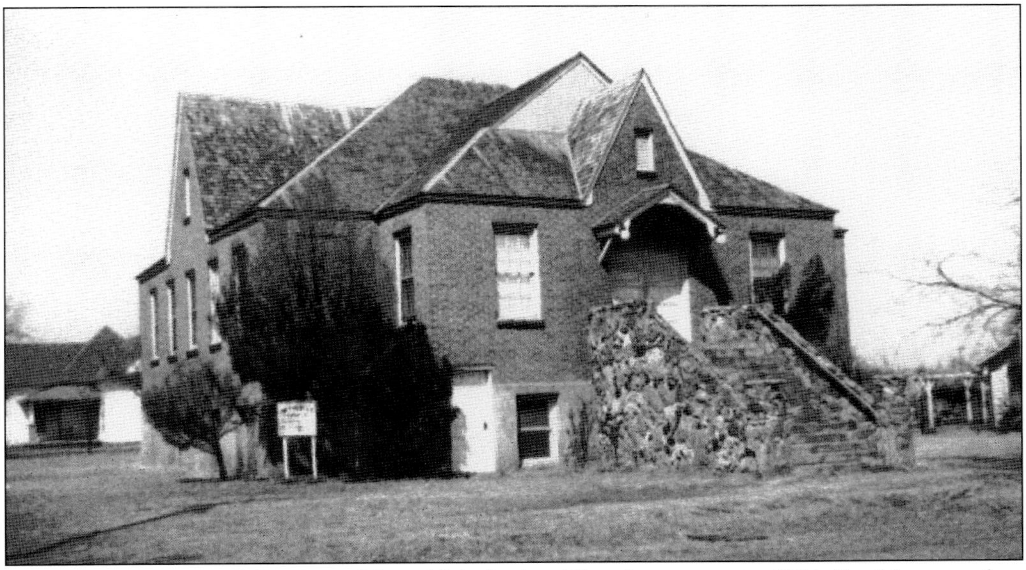

This was the home of the Krum United Methodist Church starting in 1924. For 10 years, they met in the basement until finishing the brick sanctuary in 1934. The rock work on the front steps was later replaced with brick. In 1975, the Martha Fowler Educational Building was added to the north side of the church.

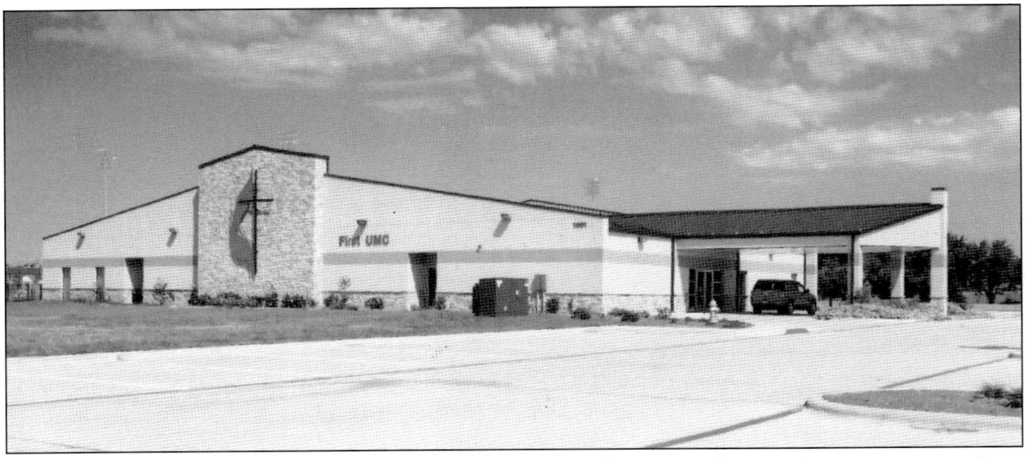

It was a happy day for the Methodists when, in 2010, they moved into a larger, more modern sanctuary in the eastern portion of Krum.

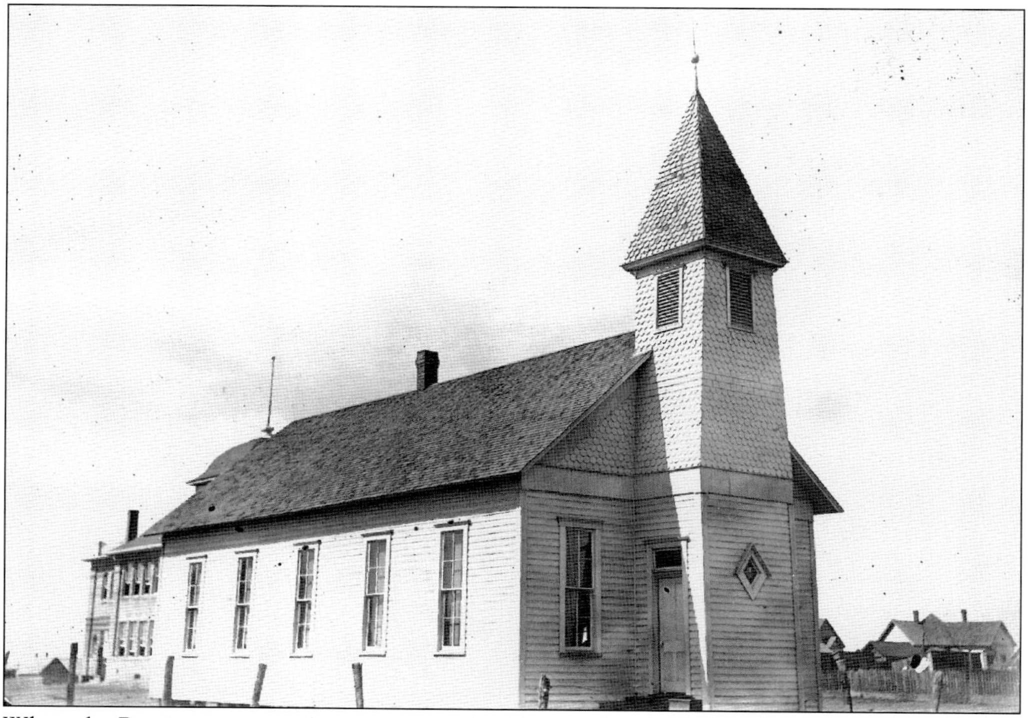

When the Baptists outgrew the one-room schoolhouse, they built this church on North Hickory Creek in 1886, and it became known as the North Hickory Creek Baptist Church. It remained there until 1898, when it was dismantled and moved into Krum to the northwest corner of Lake and Second Streets. Because of the expanding needs of the high school (in the same block), the church moved its building across the street in 1934 and continued using it until 1961, when the congregation constructed the brick building that now houses the Masonic Lodge.

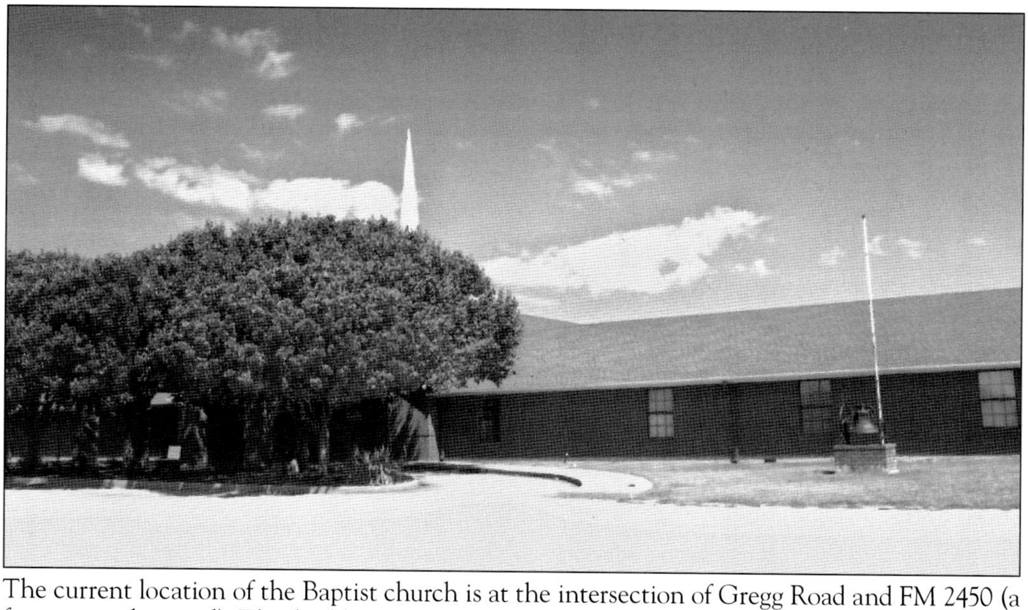

The current location of the Baptist church is at the intersection of Gregg Road and FM 2450 (a farm-to-market road). This building was constructed in 1994.

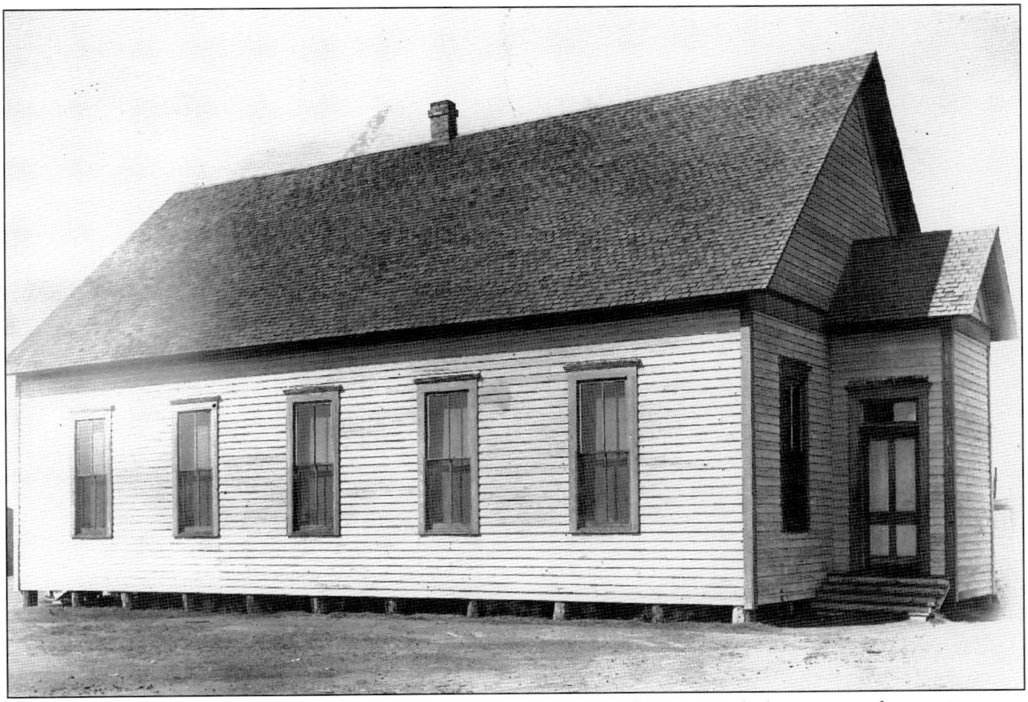

The Church of Christ also began in the one-room schoolhouse and then moved into its own building, erected in 1899 at the intersection of Third and Hancock Street.

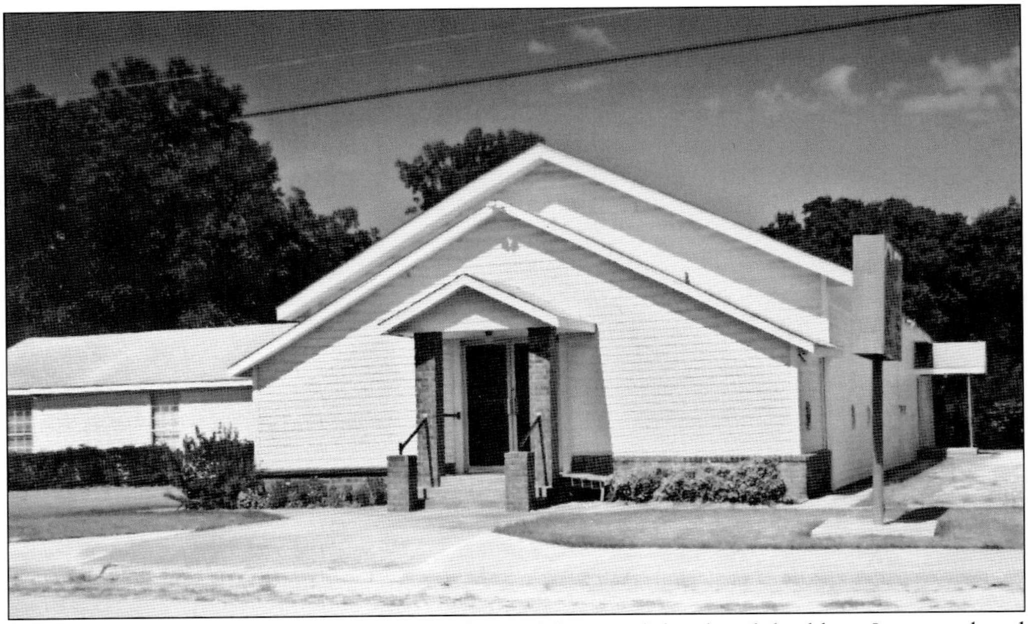

In 1929, a grass fire got away from the caretaker and destroyed the church building. It was replaced at the same location by the present Church of Christ building.

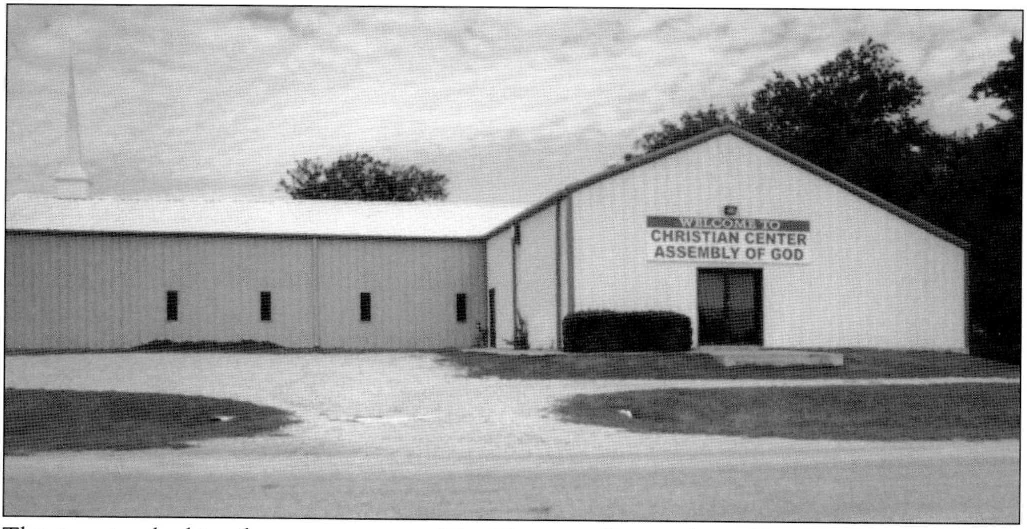

This is a view looking from east to west of the Christian Center Assembly of God building. Built in 1994, it is located in the central district of Krum, one block east of First Street and one block south of McCart Street.

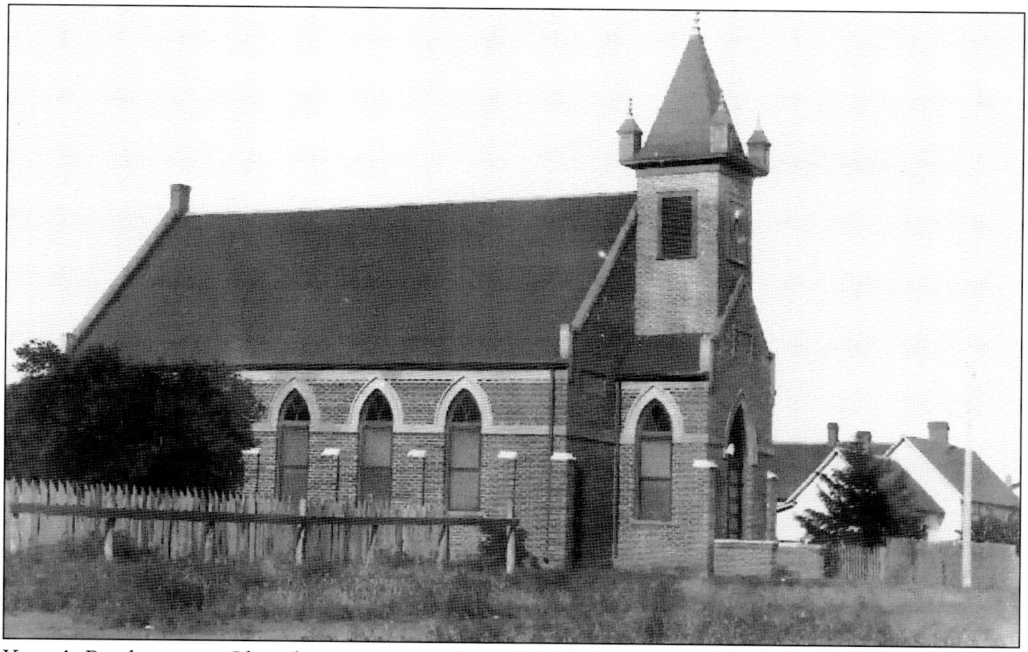

Krum's Presbyterian Church was organized in 1901. In 1903, a pastor was assigned to conduct services once a month, and the congregation began meeting in the Methodist building, where the Methodists were holding meetings only twice a month. In 1911, the Presbyterians moved into their own building located near the Kimbrough home on Britton Street.

Five

The Families

Krum has been blessed with families of ability, assertiveness, and high moral and cultural standards. They are well read, and they have good business acumen. They have worked well together in making a prosperous, family-oriented community. An indication of the desirability of the Krum environment is that descendents of many of the pioneer families are still here. Many have seen much of the world as a result of military and business travel, along with just being tourists and visitors to other places, yet Krum remains their home base. The old families are still represented here, and new families are now arriving in large numbers to live in the Krum environment while working in Denton or elsewhere in the Dallas–Fort Worth Metroplex.

The focus of this chapter is on the early families who have molded and shaped Krum into what it is today. In a close-knit community like Krum, interfamily marriages are to be expected, and many families are simply cousins of other families. In addition, the bond of community has always been present, with socials and other types of gatherings bringing different families together. Therefore, the first pictures in this chapter were selected to emphasize the close family relationships and the community spirit of Krum's early residents. The focus will then shift to presenting a selection of Krum's earlier individual families.

It is not possible, however, to give complete family histories in this volume, nor is it possible to include photographs of all members of families who are presented. It is hoped that a representative survey of Krum's leading early families will provide interest, inspiration, and motivation for Krum's current population to carry on the traditions and accomplishments that have already been established.

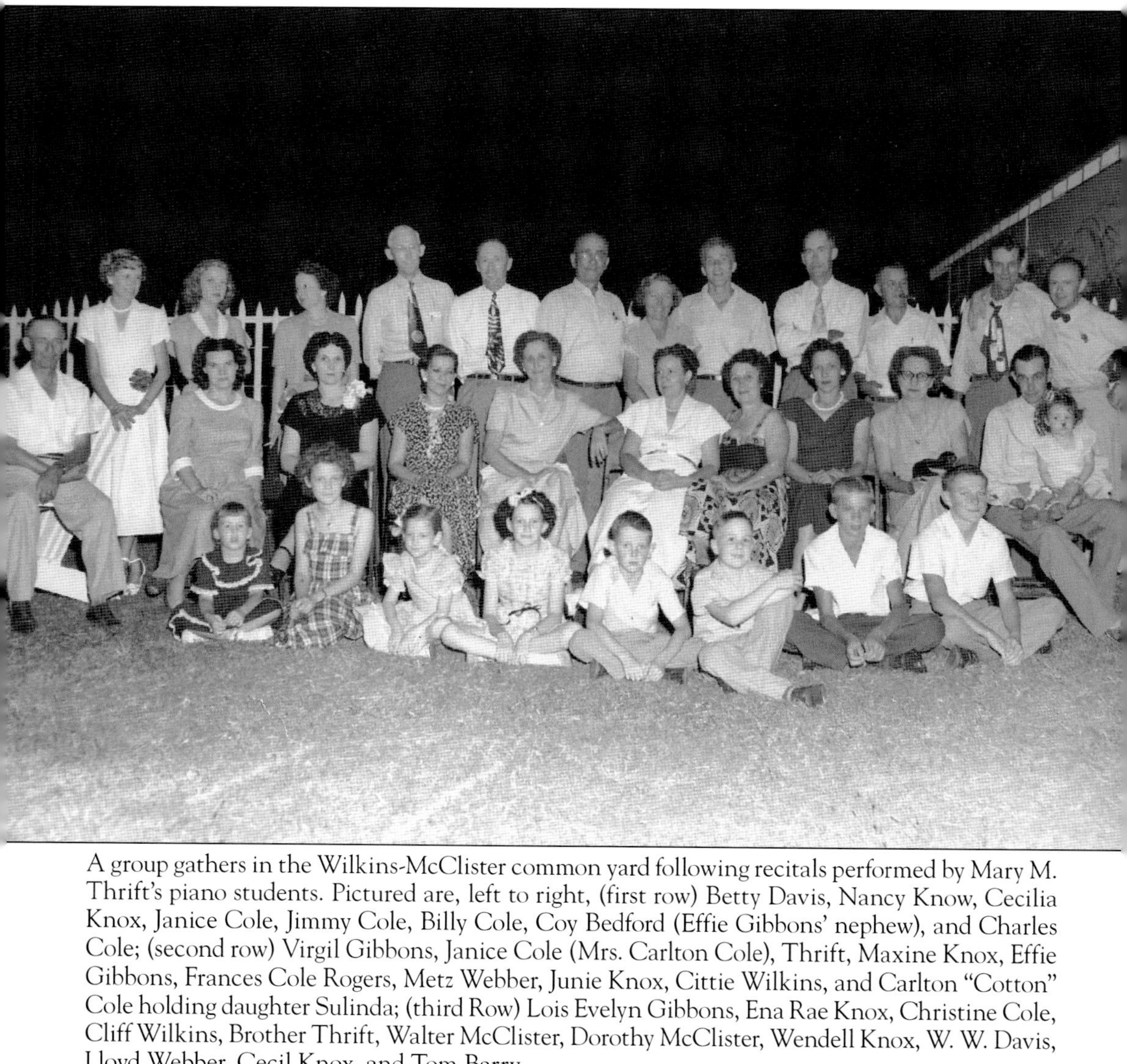

A group gathers in the Wilkins-McClister common yard following recitals performed by Mary M. Thrift's piano students. Pictured are, left to right, (first row) Betty Davis, Nancy Know, Cecilia Knox, Janice Cole, Jimmy Cole, Billy Cole, Coy Bedford (Effie Gibbons' nephew), and Charles Cole; (second row) Virgil Gibbons, Janice Cole (Mrs. Carlton Cole), Thrift, Maxine Knox, Effie Gibbons, Frances Cole Rogers, Metz Webber, Junie Knox, Cittie Wilkins, and Carlton "Cotton" Cole holding daughter Sulinda; (third Row) Lois Evelyn Gibbons, Ena Rae Knox, Christine Cole, Cliff Wilkins, Brother Thrift, Walter McClister, Dorothy McClister, Wendell Knox, W. W. Davis, Lloyd Webber, Cecil Knox, and Tom Barry.

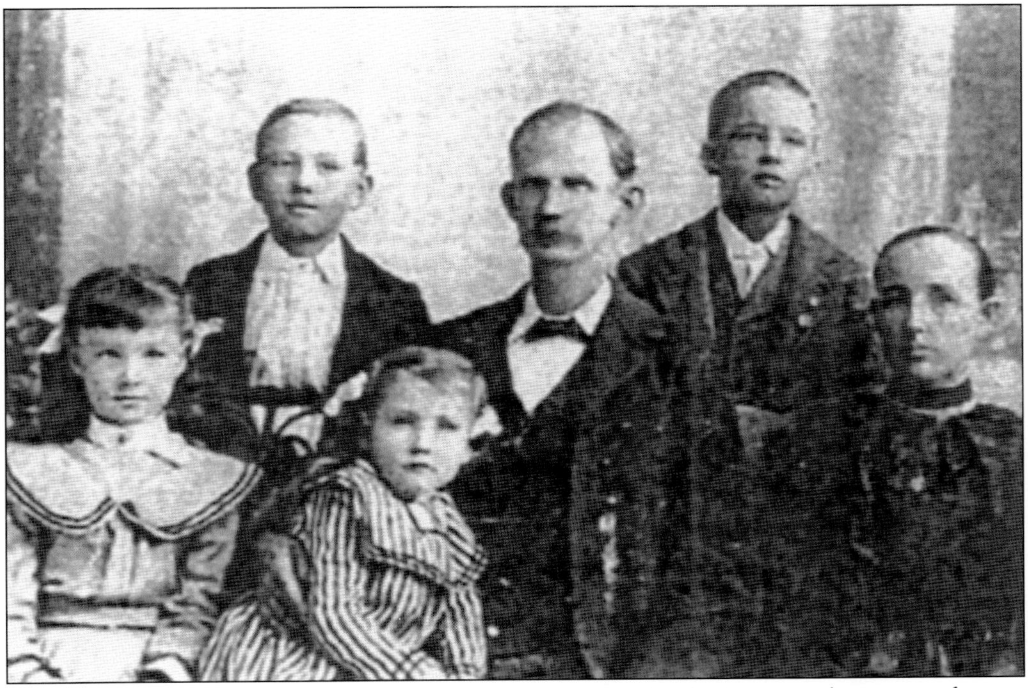

W. Y. "Wy" Barnett moved to Krum before 1882 and bought the Barnett place west of town. He was a charter member of the Hickory Creek Baptist Church, and he helped organize the Continental Bank and Trust Company in Krum. Pictured from left to right are Ava, Joe, Parolee, Wy, Fred, and Bessie Barnett.

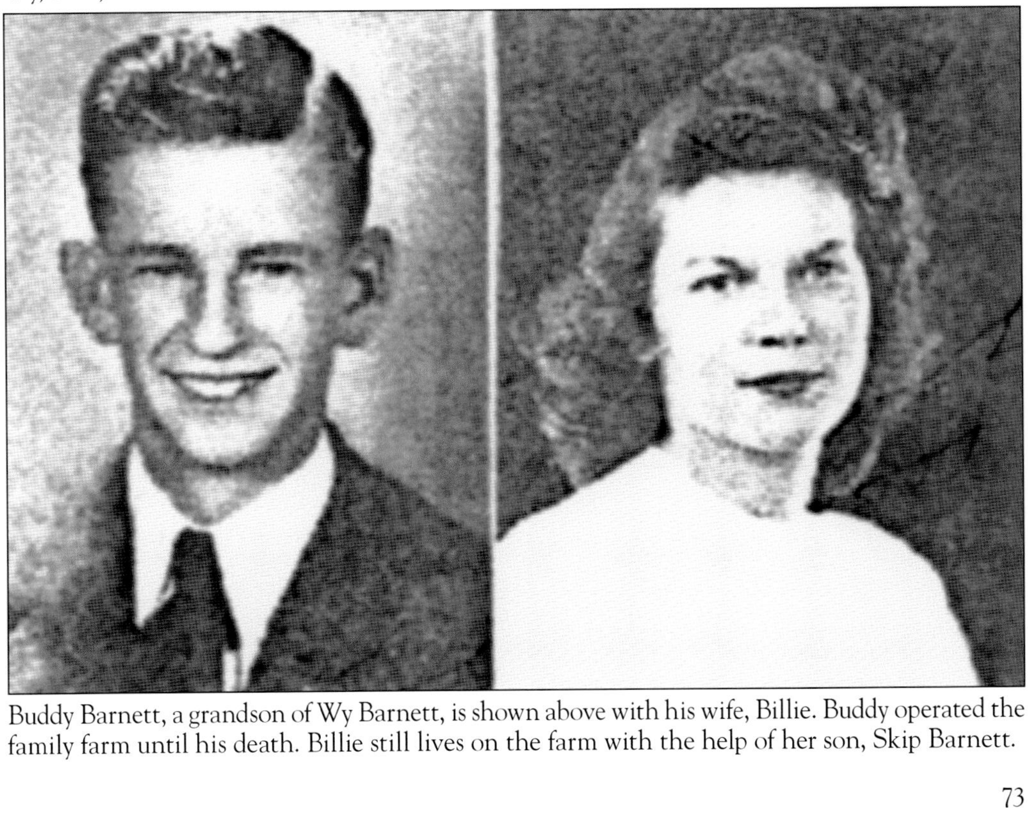

Buddy Barnett, a grandson of Wy Barnett, is shown above with his wife, Billie. Buddy operated the family farm until his death. Billie still lives on the farm with the help of her son, Skip Barnett.

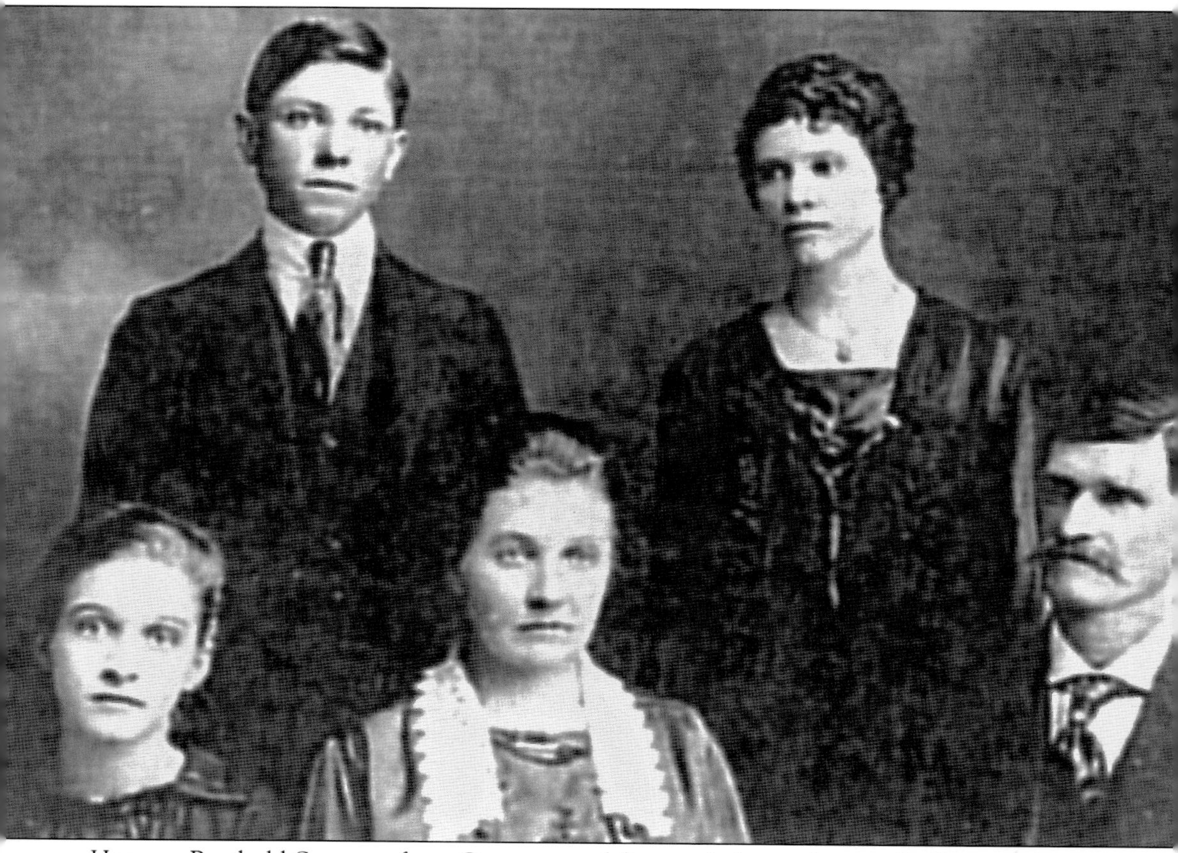

Herman Barthold Sr. came from Germany and first settled on a farm in Dallas and then in the Blue Mound area north of Krum. Herman and his wife, Mary, had eight children, five of whom—Augusta, Herman Jr., August, Fred, and Ida—settled on farms in the Krum area. These lands are still occupied by descendents of these five families. Herman Jr. is pictured here with his family. They are, from left to right, (first row) Lilly, Lena, and Herman Jr.; (second row) Herbert and Rosa.

Herbert Barthold stands beside his wife, Marjorie Knox Barthold. The couple had three children and farmed acres northeast of town. Marjorie was pianist at Krum Methodist Church for many years, and Herbert sang in the church choir in addition to being superintendent of the Sunday school.

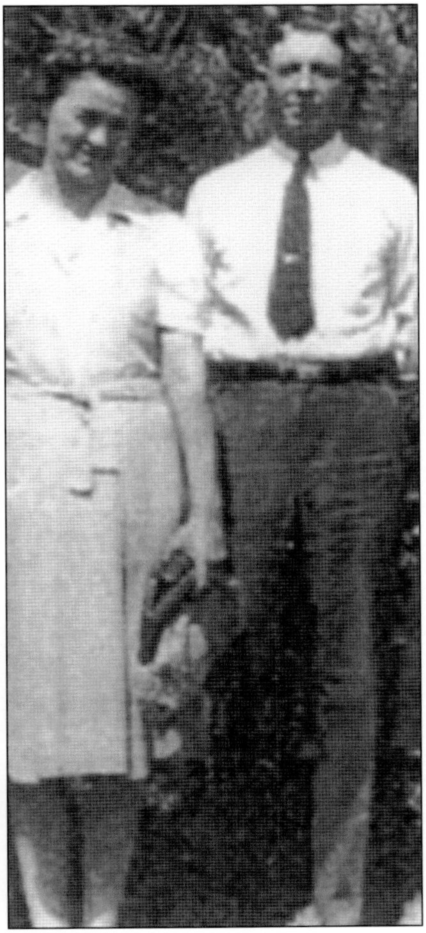

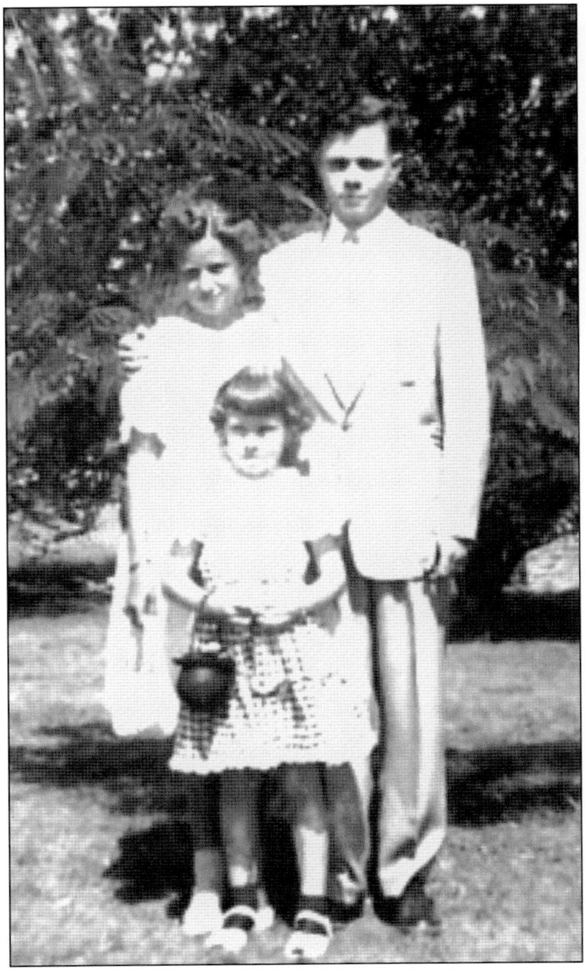

Children of Herbert and Marjorie Barthold are, from left to right, Susan, Jane, and Rodney. As adults, they have been quite active in local affairs.

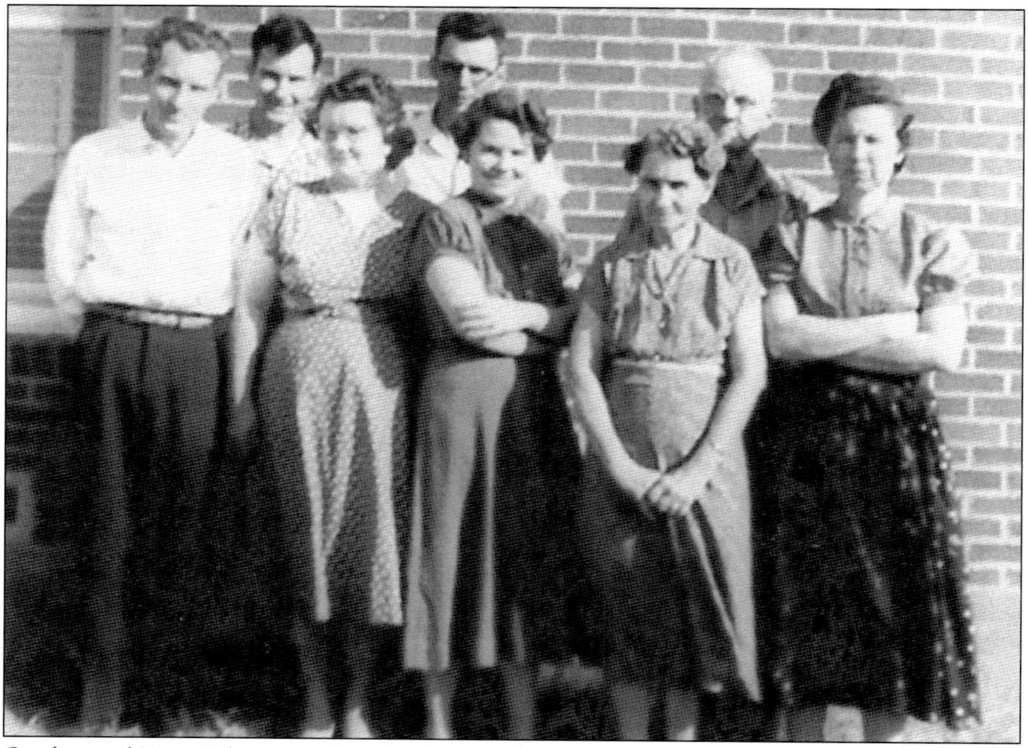

Gordon and Mary Bilyeu pose for a family picture with their grown children. Pictured are, from left to right, (first row) Dorotha, Theopal, Mary (mother), and Launa; (second row) J. C., Russell, Granville, and Gordon (father). Russell became a professor of mathematics at the University of North Texas. Granville, a 1951 valedictorian at Krum High School, moved to Hopewell, Virginia, where he received many honors including Citizen of the Year in 2003.

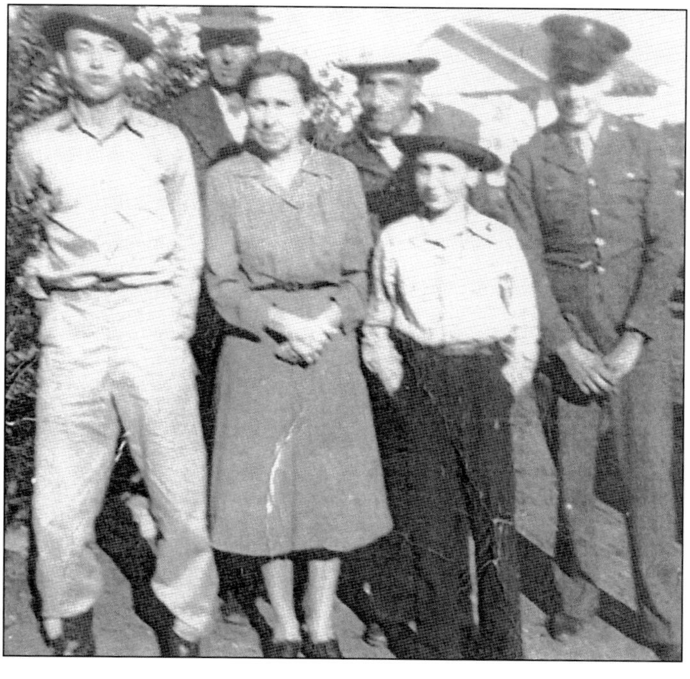

Borth family members include, from left to right, (first row) Myron, Annie K., and Jerome; (second row) Aaron, Herman, and Nickie. Myron has been associated with the Barry Insurance Agency since 1973.

Although the Bridges family has moved from Krum, they still return every year to renew friendships and memories at the homecoming festival held on the first weekend of May. At right are newly weds George Ezra Bridges and his bride, Minnie Ola Bridges.

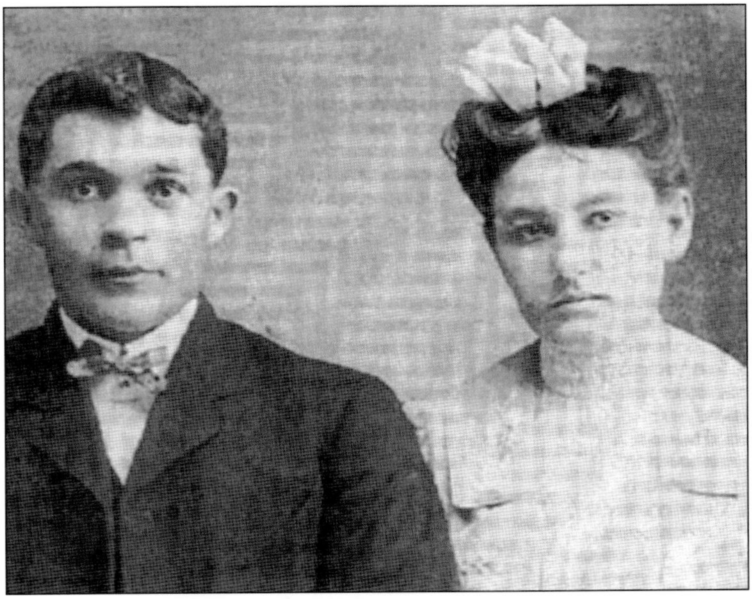

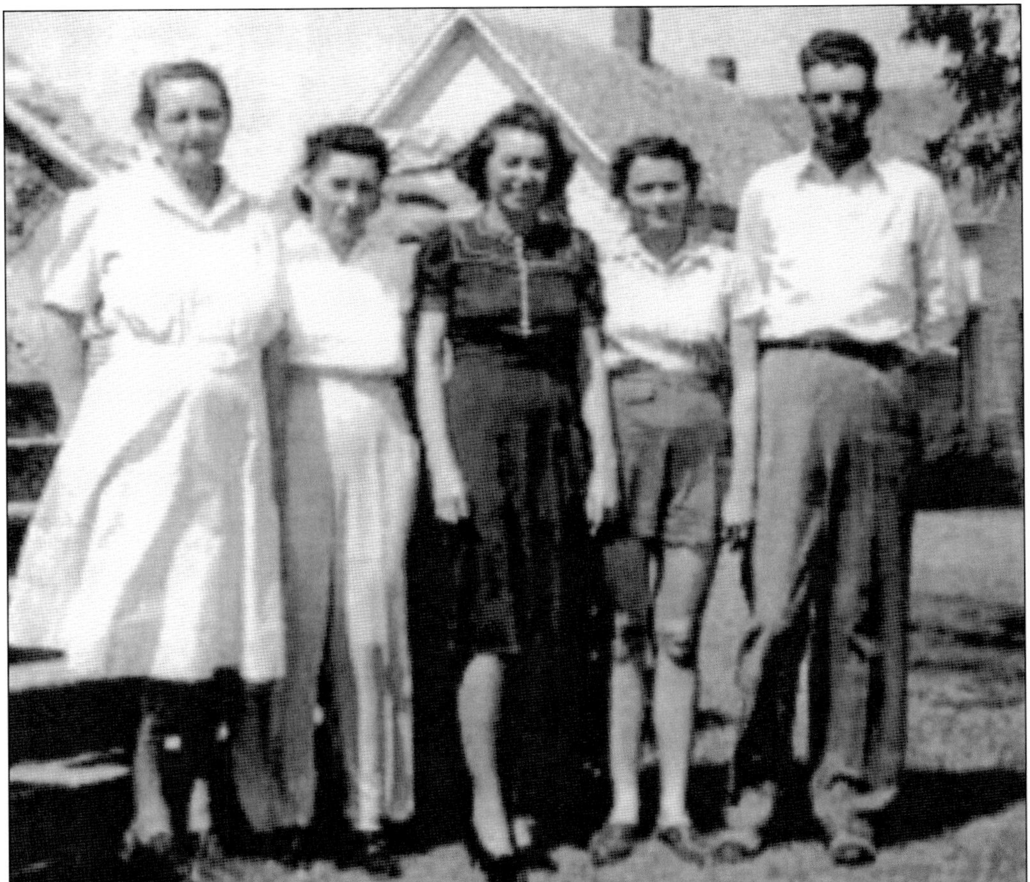

Members of the Bridges family include, from left to right, Minnie (mother), Ruby, Roberta, and Inez, with her husband, Curtis Oliver.

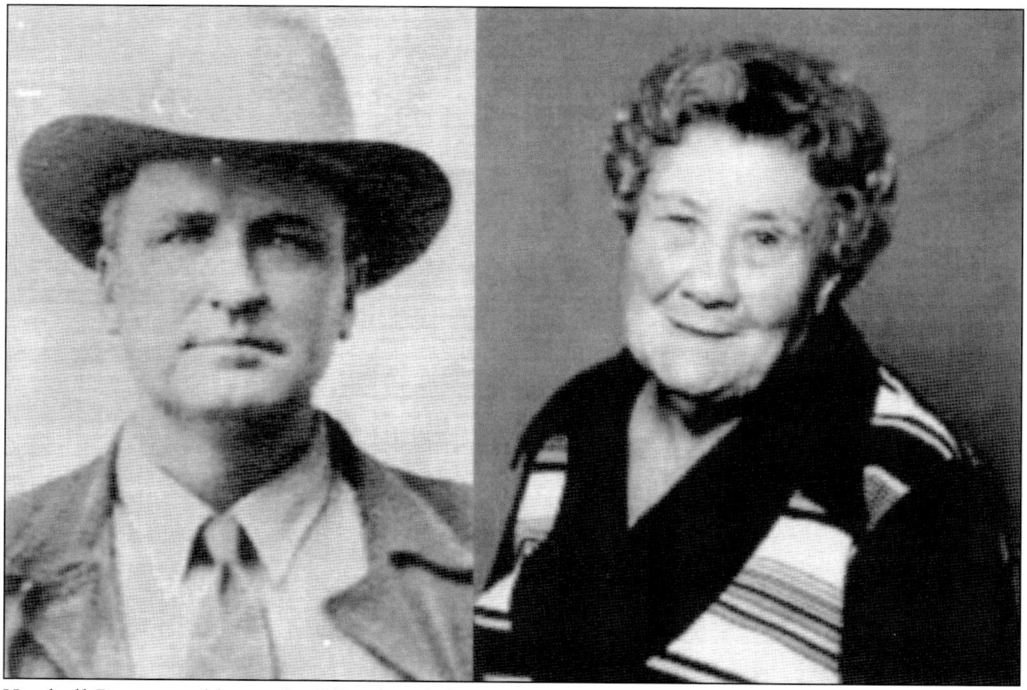

Kimball Brisco and his wife, Ollie, headed another of Krum's prominent early families.

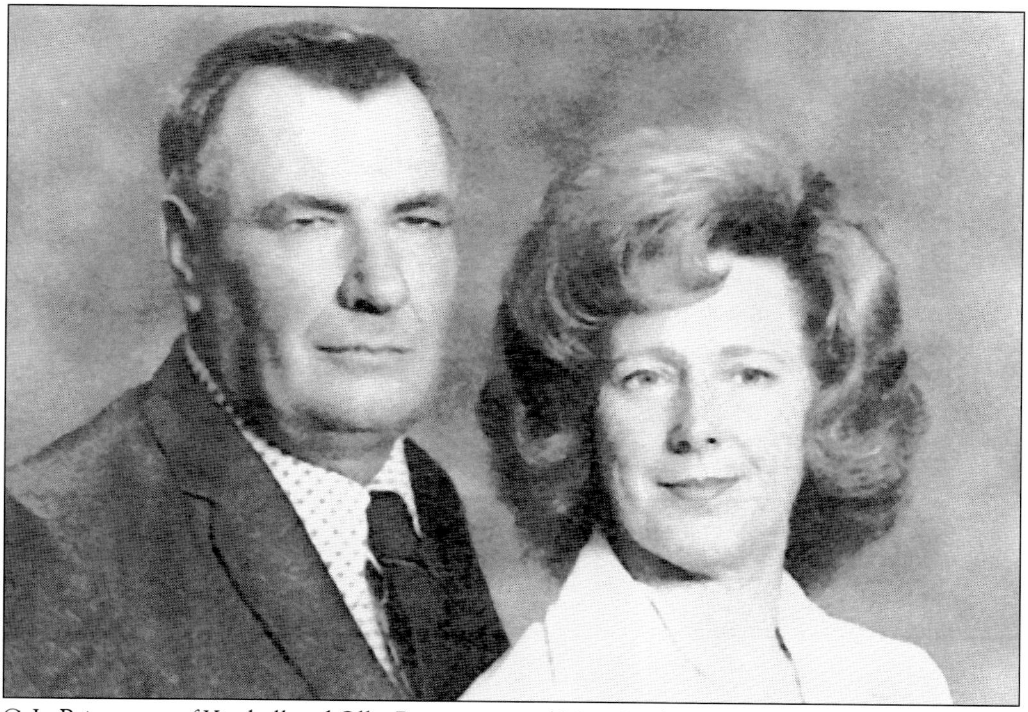

C. L. Brisco, son of Kimball and Ollie Brisco, married Mary Ruth Miller, daughter of Ava and John H. Miller. Mary Ruth was born on December 16, 1928. She was the secretary of the Krum schools for many years. C. L. and Mary Ruth had three children—Linda, Donna, and Charlene.

Members of the Cofer family are, from left to right, Johnny, C. C. (father), Lum, Fanny, and Jack.

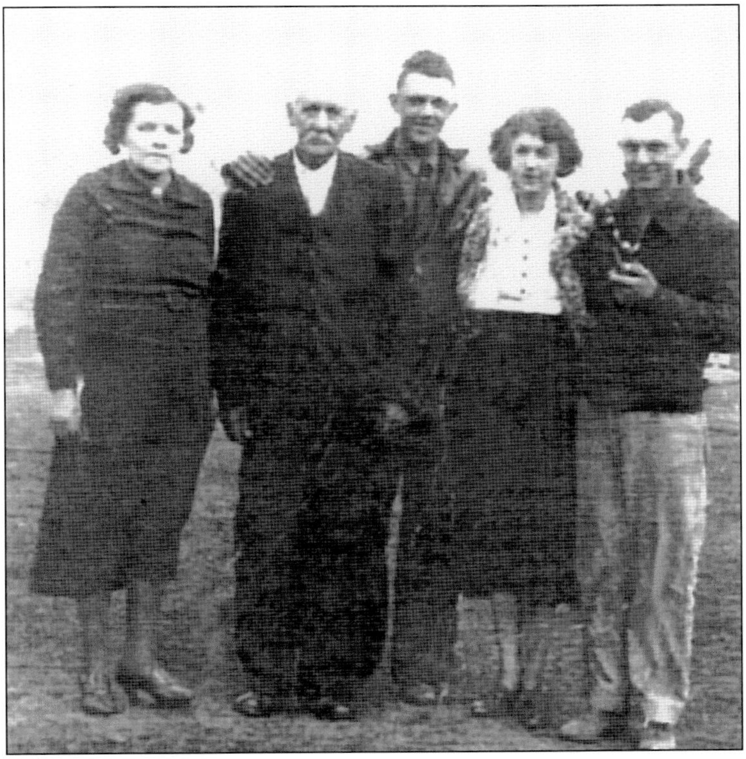

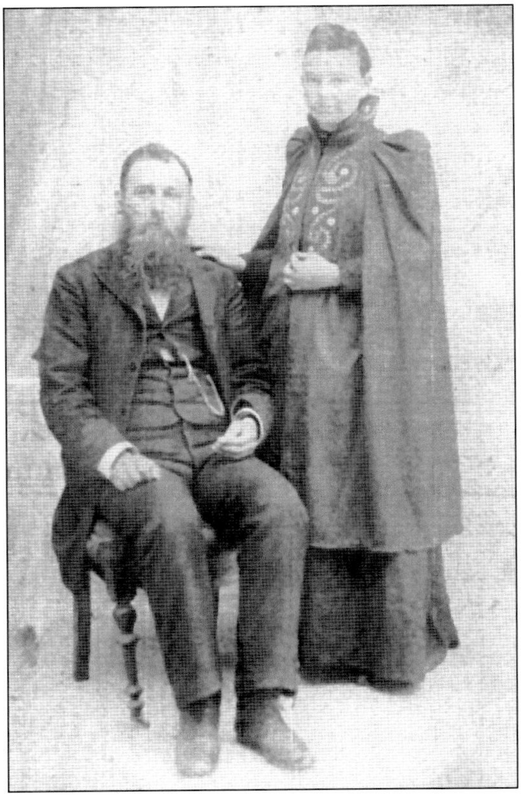

C. C. Cofer, who moved to Krum in 1893, has been referred to as the smartest person ever to live in Krum. As an ordained minister, he helped organize Krum's Church of Christ and became its first pastor. He preached there for 25 years. Cofer organized a correspondence college in Krum that granted bachelor degrees in Bible study. He also served as postmaster from 1899 to 1904. He is shown at the left with his wife, Sylvestus.

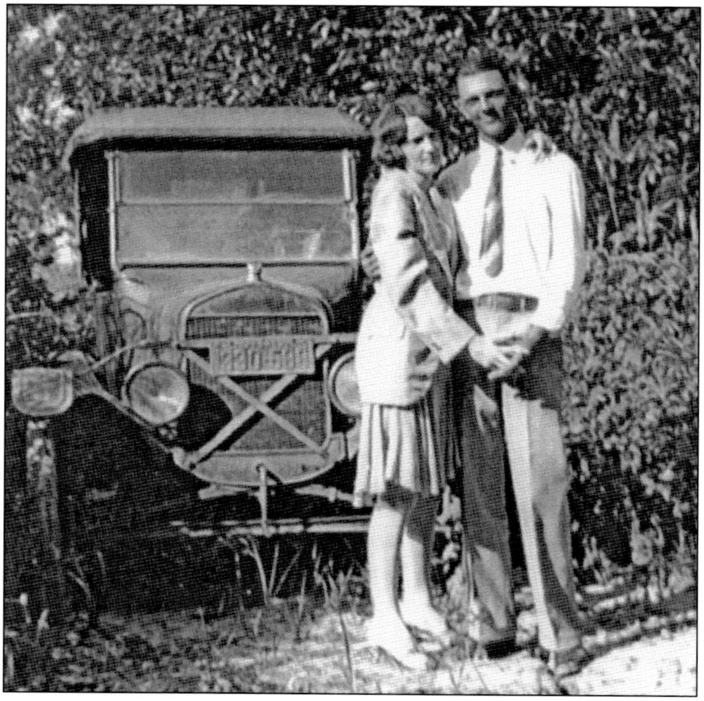

Lum Cofer stands proudly with his wife, Ruth, and his Model T Ford.

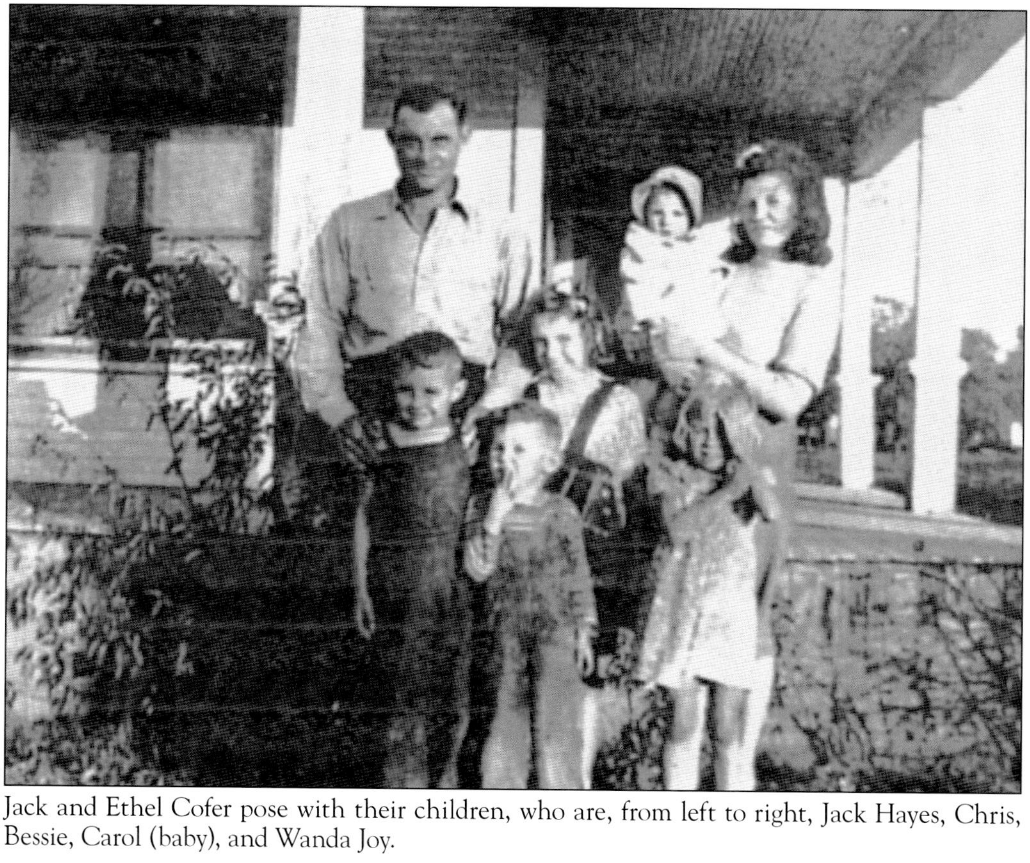

Jack and Ethel Cofer pose with their children, who are, from left to right, Jack Hayes, Chris, Bessie, Carol (baby), and Wanda Joy.

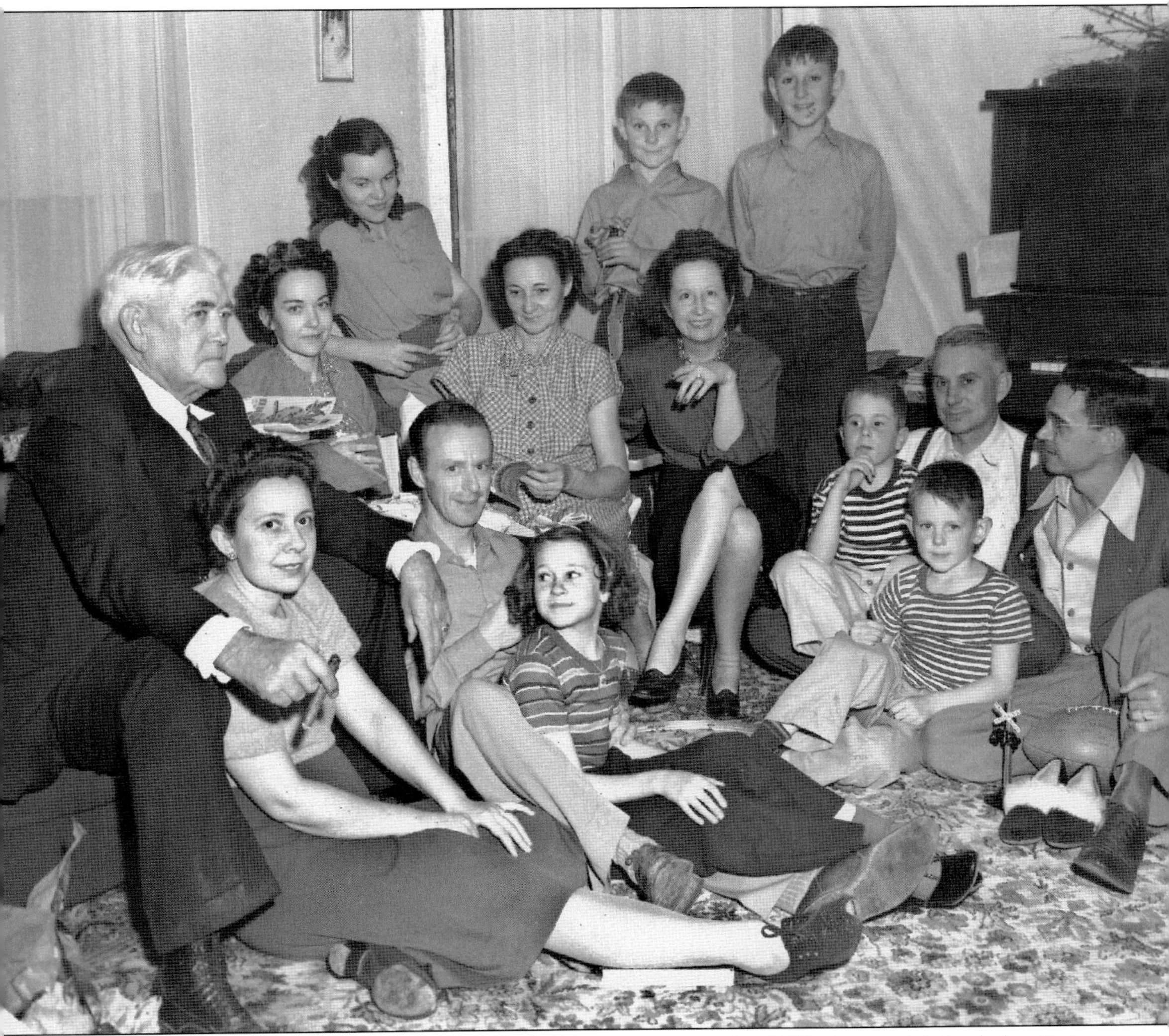

Ralph L. Cole Sr. was one of Krum's leading businessmen. In 1905, he established the R. L. Cole Grain and Elevator Company, and by 1912, he was the leading grain and cotton dealer in Denton County. Over the next four years, he added a feed mill, a coal yard, and a flour mill to his businesses. In addition, Cole served as president of the Commercial Club (forerunner of the Krum Lion's Club), and he was president of the Farmers and Merchants State Bank from 1947 until his death in 1948. Here Ralph L. Cole Sr. and his wife, Corine, are enjoying their children and grandchildren in the living room of their home during Christmas 1946. Shown are, from left to right, (first row) Frances, Tom Barry, Janice, Billy (striped shirt left), Weldon, Jimmy (striped shirt right), and Carlton; (second row) R. L. Sr., Mary L., Corine, and Christine; (third row) Janice (wife of Carlton), Charles, and R. L. "Buddy" Jr.

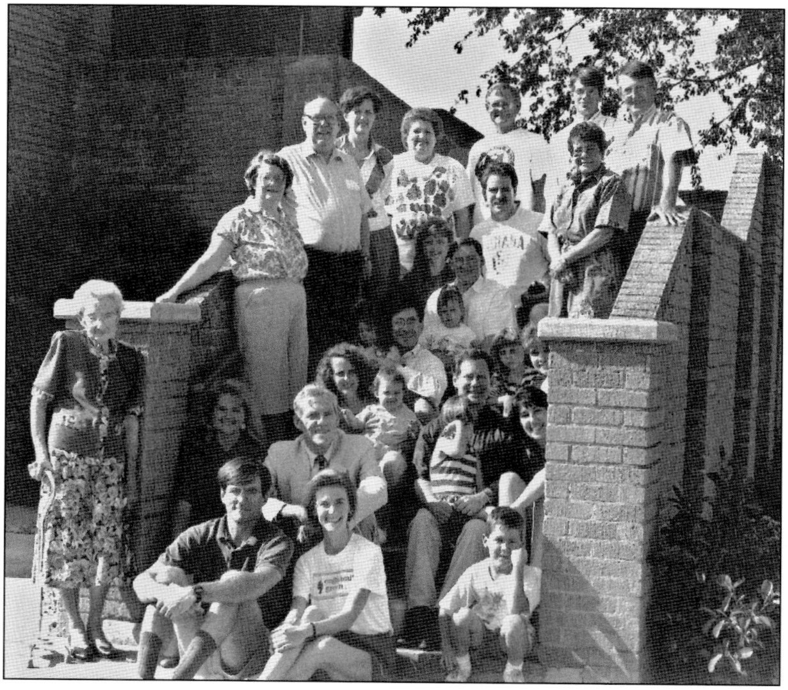

Gathered on the steps of the First United Methodist Church, which was across the street from the Cole home, are members of the Cole's extended family celebrating Corine Cole's 90th birthday.

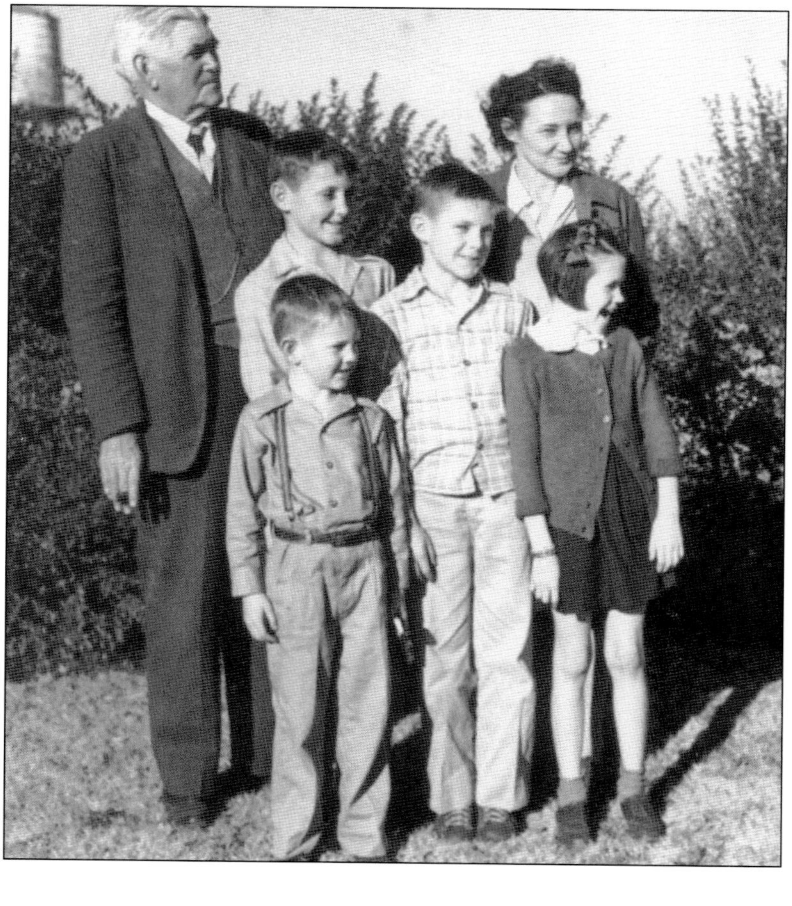

R. L. Cole and his wife, Corine, stand with their four children—from left to right, Buddy, Charles (front), Jimmy, and Janice.

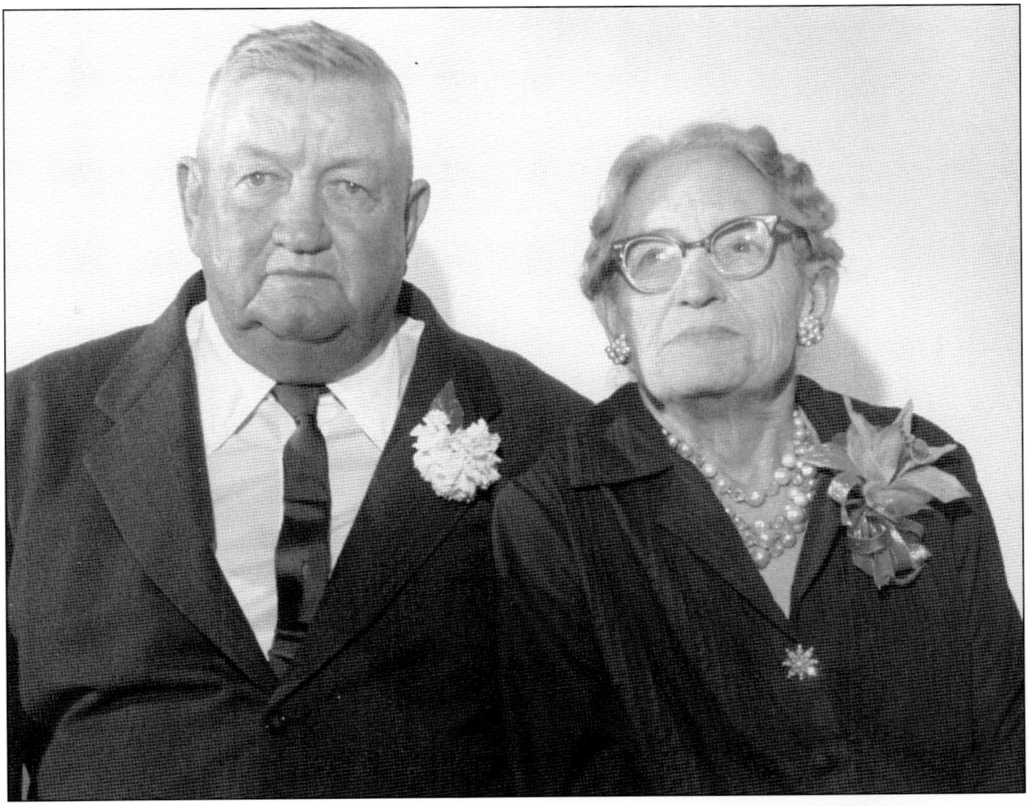

Earl Cox partnered with Will Koiner and Lee Koiner in establishing the Koiner Gin Company. Cox managed the business. In these photographs, Earl and his wife, Lillian, are celebrating their 50th wedding anniversary. Standing behind Earl and Lillian in the right photograph are their children—from left to right, Jiggs, Irene, Wayne, and Eunice.

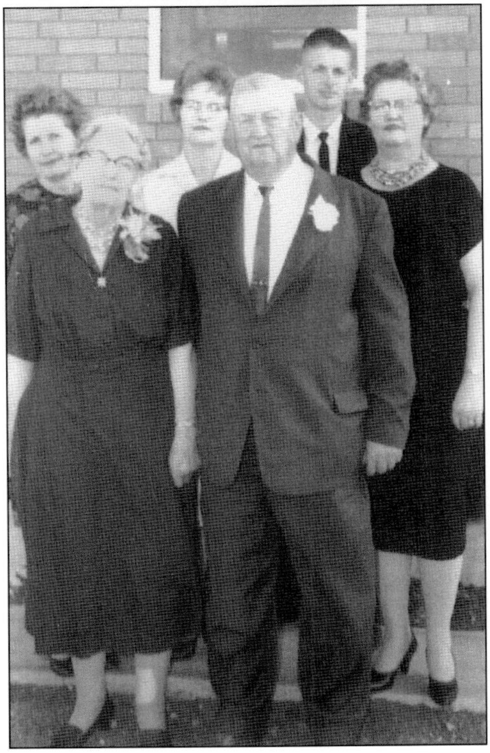

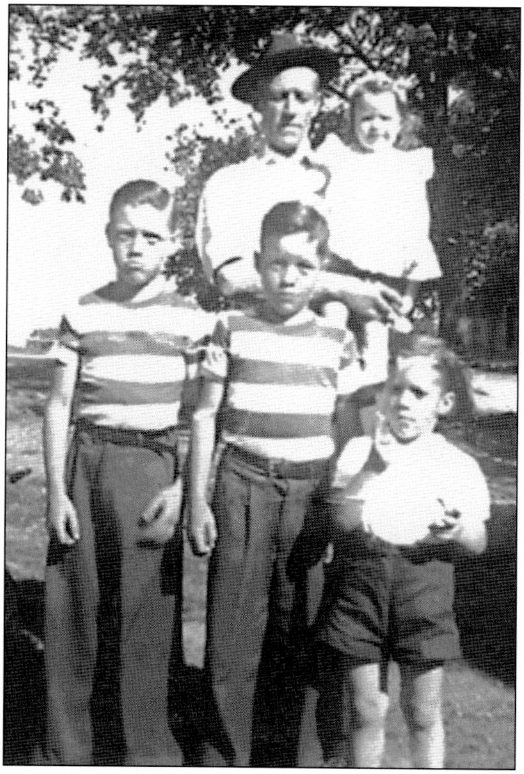

C. D. "Bud" and Blanche Dodd came to Krum in 1941 and quickly earned places for themselves in business and social life. Bud worked in the Lamm Grocery Store until 1945. He then opened his own grocery store next to the bank and operated it for 12 years. Blanche kept score for the Krum basketball teams for 25 years, worked at the Krum public library, and was the greeter at the Methodist church. She was such a respected person that the intermediate school was named in her honor. In the left photograph, Bud, holding young Kathryn, stands with his three sons—from left to right, Denney, Dan, and Don. The photograph below shows Blanche (center) celebrating her 90th birthday with her children, from left to right, Don, Dan, Denney, and Kathryn.

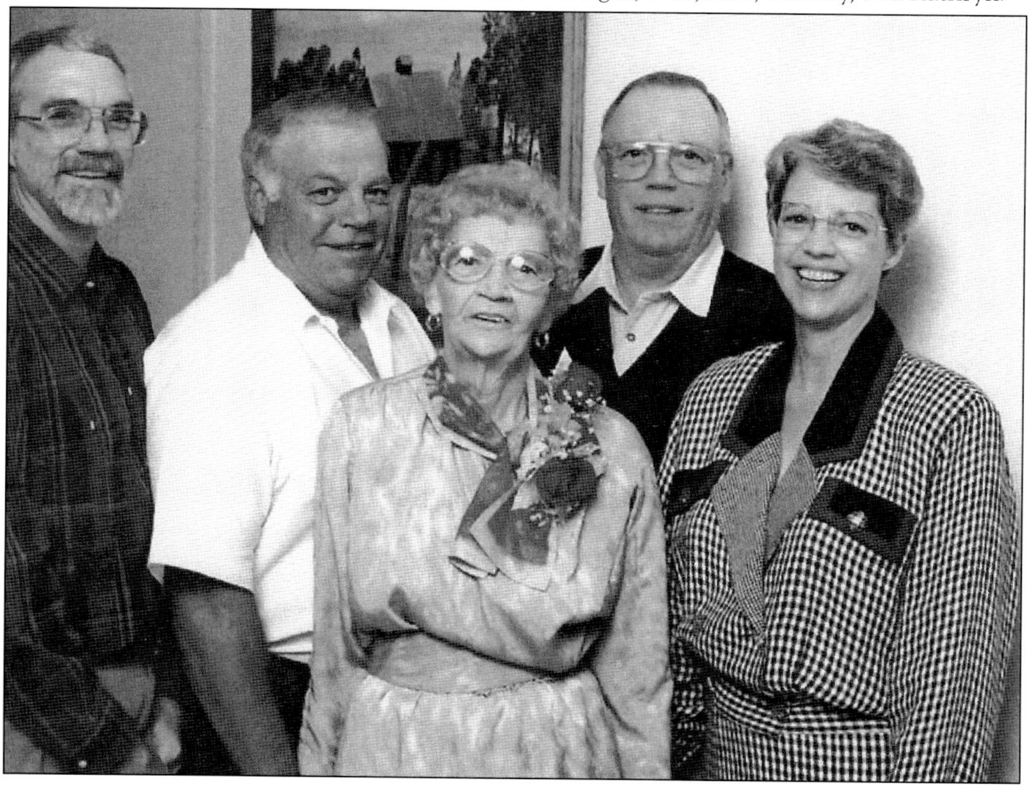

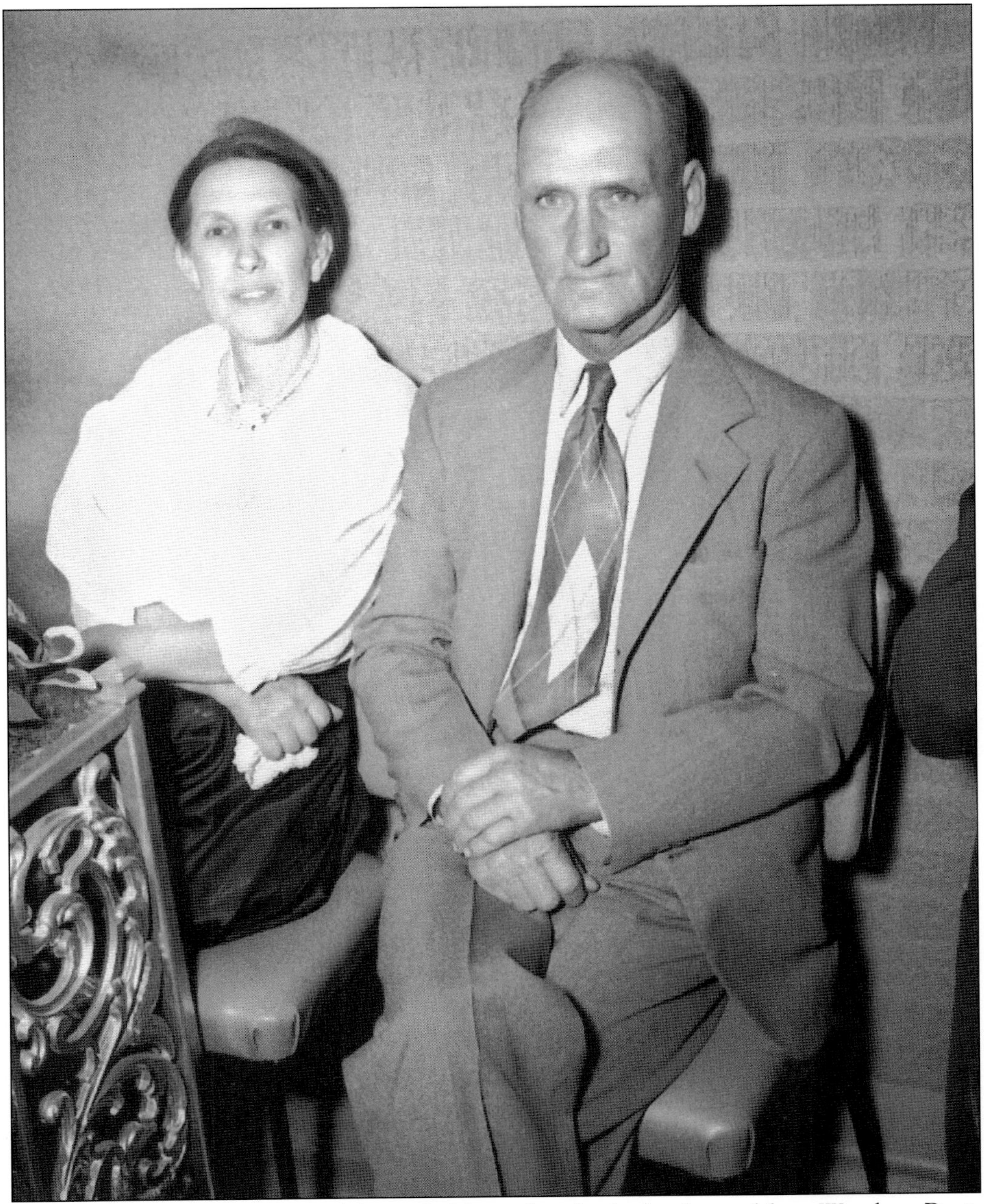

In 1950, Nelson Dyer, shown with his wife, Hattie, bought the lumberyard from Woodrow Davis and later leased it to the Ginnings brothers. Dyer owned an excavating business in Krum.

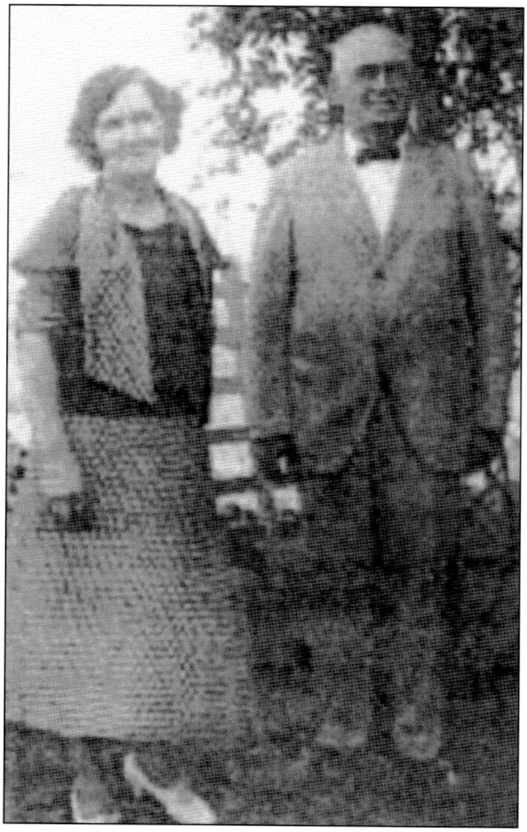

George Evans was a son of James A. Evans, who bought a farm just south of Krum in 1881. After James died, George and his wife, Maud, (left) bought the farm. Evans was progressive in all his endeavors. He sought to improve the strains of crops grown in the area, helped organize a livestock breeders association, taught two years at Jackson School, and was a charter member of the Literary and Debating Society.

Maud Evans (seated at right) visits with her children—from left to right, Emma, Bob, and Velma. Aunt Emma McGee stands behind Maud.

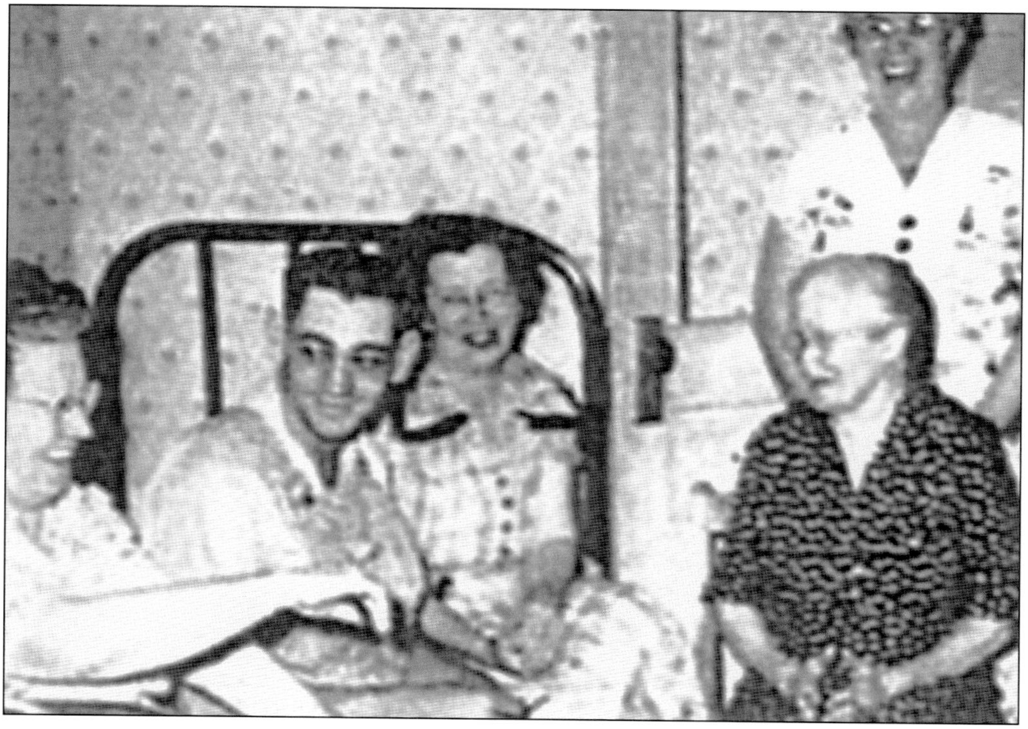

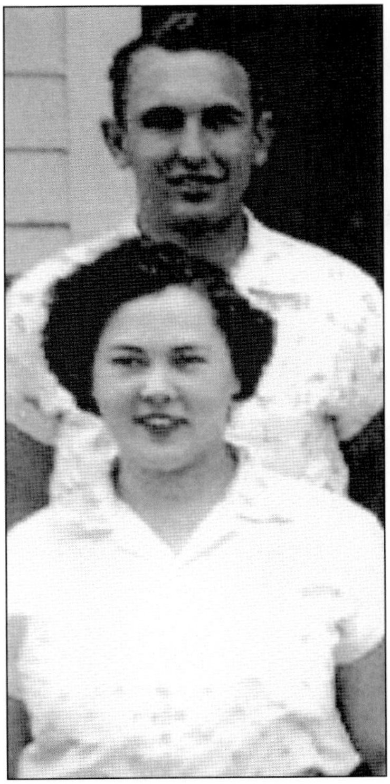

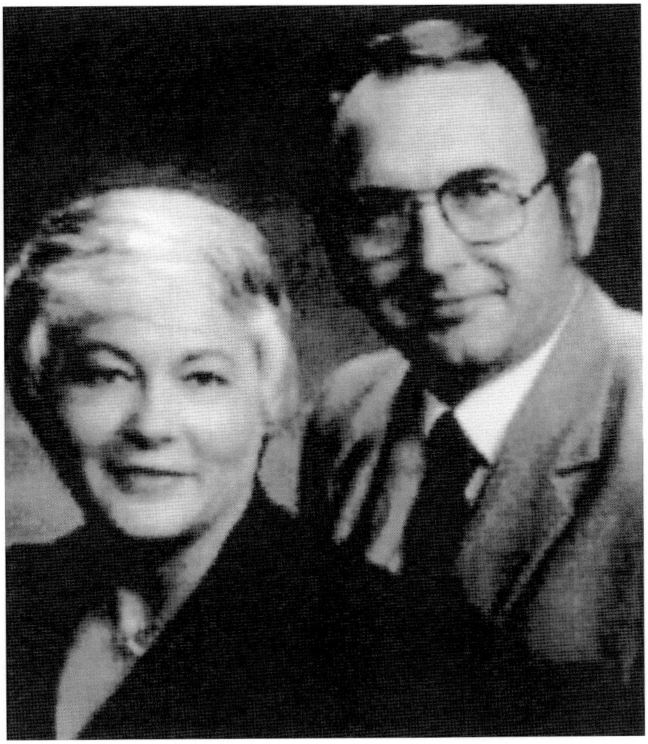

Jan and Dorothy Farris are seen in their younger years (left) and in their more mature years (right). Jan, a former mayor of Krum, is a son of Mary Wilkins by her first husband. Dorothy is a daughter of Lewis and Beulah Standifer.

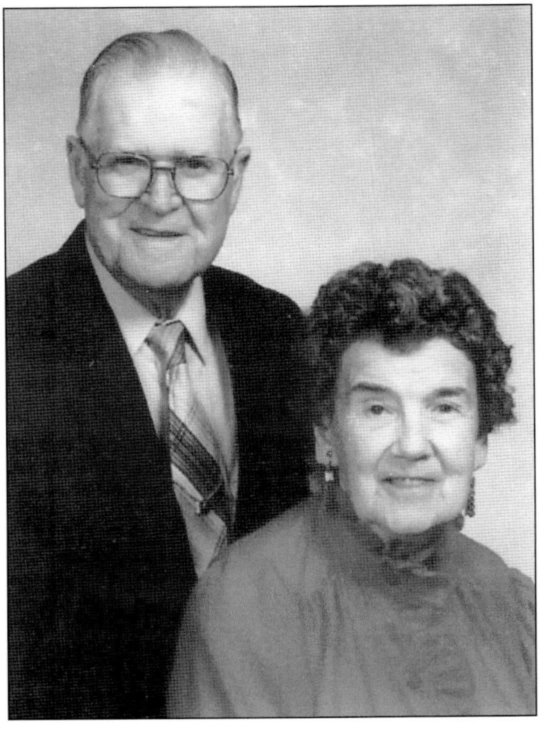

Morris Ferrell and his wife, Pauline, are pictured in the mid-1980s. Morris served as Krum's postmaster from 1934 until 1972. While Morris was in the navy for three years during World War II, Pauline, among others, filled in until his return.

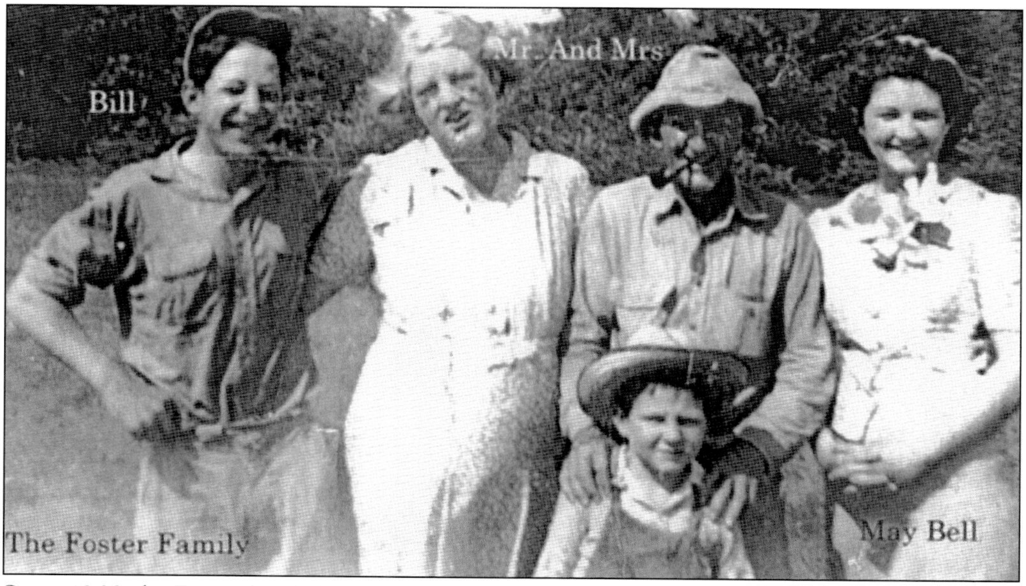

Since 1966, the Foster family has owned and operated the Foster's Saddle Shop on Interstate 35, 4 miles east of downtown Krum. Bill Foster and his wife, Billie Louise (not shown), started the business after learning leather and saddle work from Frank Leddy in Fort Worth while Bill was recuperating from a leg amputation. Bill is seen here with his family, from left to right, his mother, Edith; his father, Elliot; his brother, Gene (front); and his sister, May Bell.

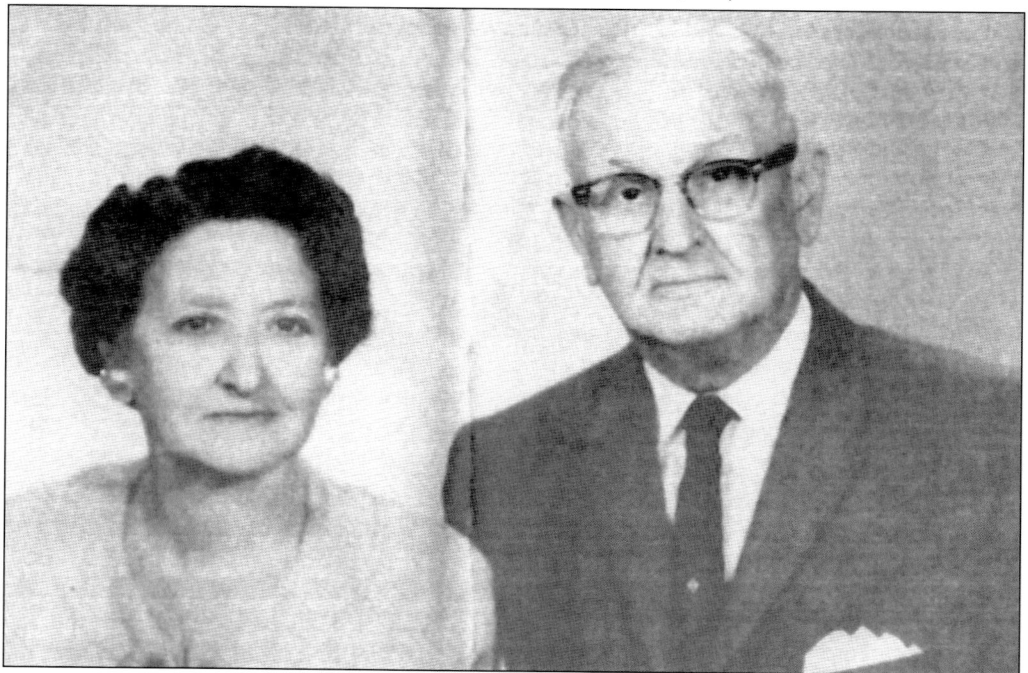

Pet and C. R. Fowler were longtime residents of Krum. C. R. Fowler moved to Krum from Denton in 1912, and in 1914, he married Pet Miller, daughter of John H. Miller. He established the C. R. Fowler Hardware Store, which he operated for 60 years, until his death in 1972. His son, "Pin," then operated the store. Pin (Francis) was elected as Krum's first mayor in 1954 and served for many years. He married Martha Dedmon Brooks, and their children were Jimmy and Pam.

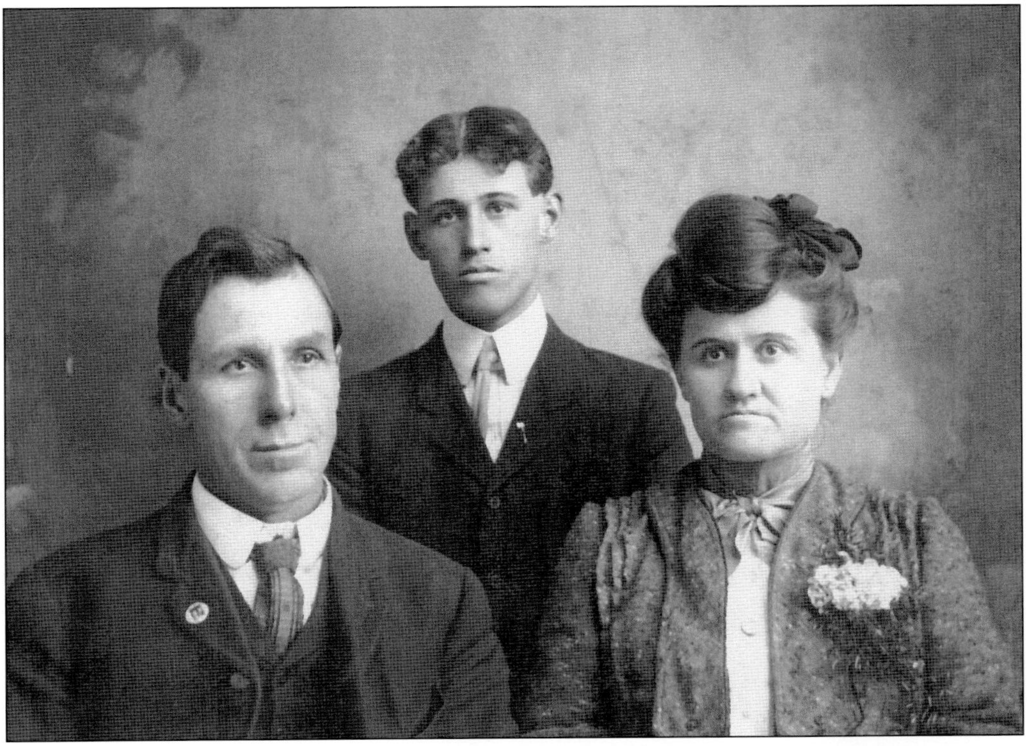

Dr. James Caughy Gose and his wife, Annie Lee (Chance), pose with their son, Sylvan Paul. James practiced medicine in Krum from 1898 until his death in 1945. He is remembered by many for his Christian faith. Each morning and evening, he would gather everyone in his home into the living room, where he would lead the family in prayer.

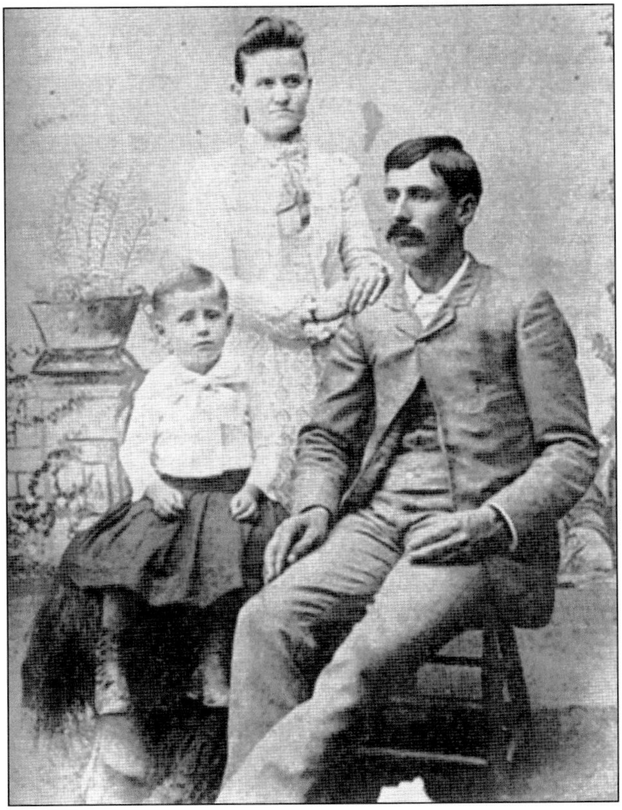

Shown here at an earlier age, James and Annie Lee pose with their young son, Sylvan Paul. James gave up his mustache in later years.

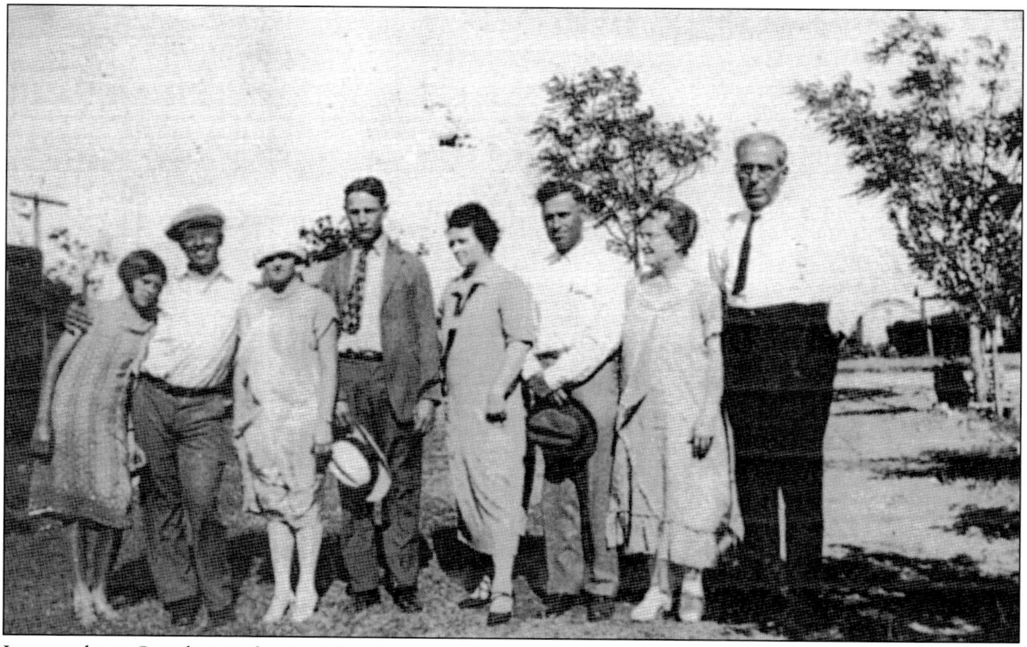

It must be a Sunday gathering for the Gose family. Pictured from left to right are Una, Paul, Ila Mae (Gose) Muncy, Herman Muncy, Vessie (Koiner), Sylvan Paul, Annie Lee (Chance), and James. Una, Paul, and Ila Mae are the children of Vessie and Sylvan Paul, Herman is Ila Mae's husband, and Annie Lee and James are the parents of Sylvan Paul.

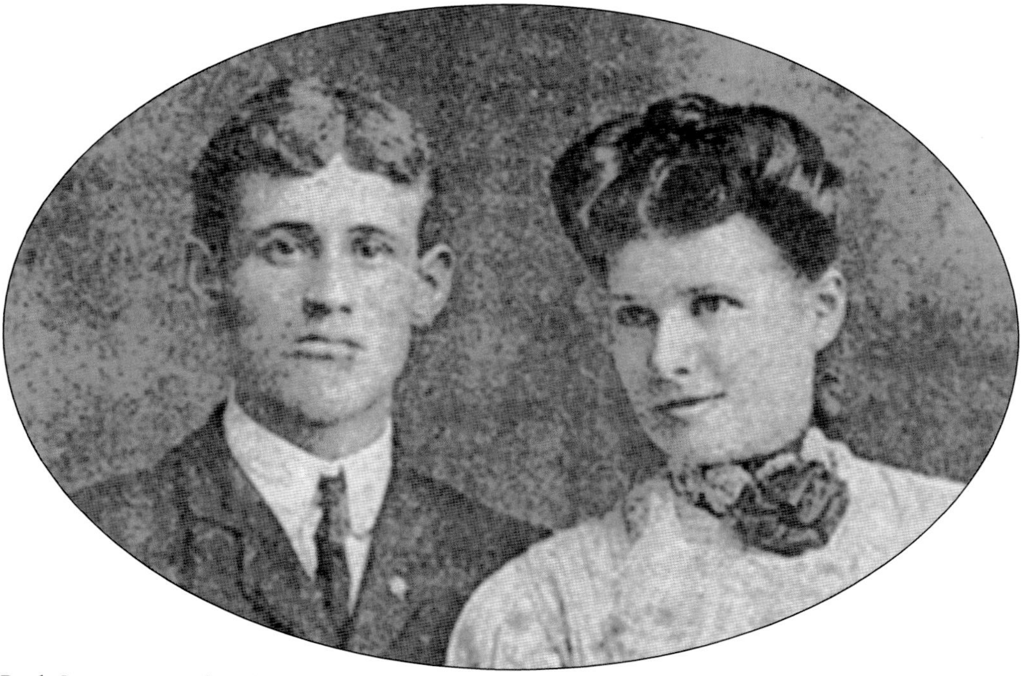

Paul Gose, pictured with his wife, Vessie, became a part owner in the Krum Water Works. He also built homes and was a beekeeper.

Russell and Gracie Helton stand in their front yard. Gracie was a daughter of Fletcher and Ethel McBee. The Heltons moved from Stony to Krum when the Stony School closed in 1946.

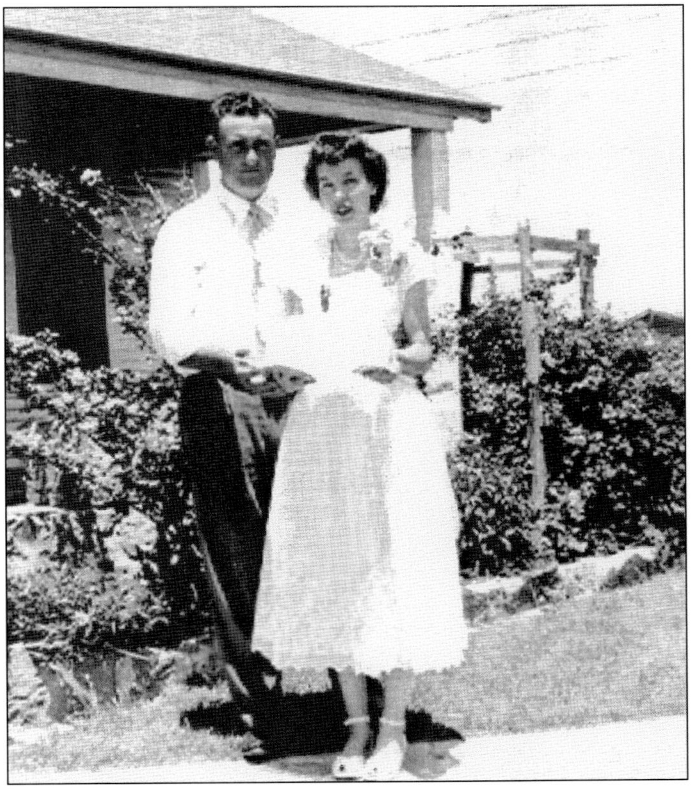

From left to right, Deanne Wilkins, Bonnie Bunnell, and Vickie Helton pose in this photograph. Deanne and Bonnie were cousins, and their mothers were part of the Helton family.

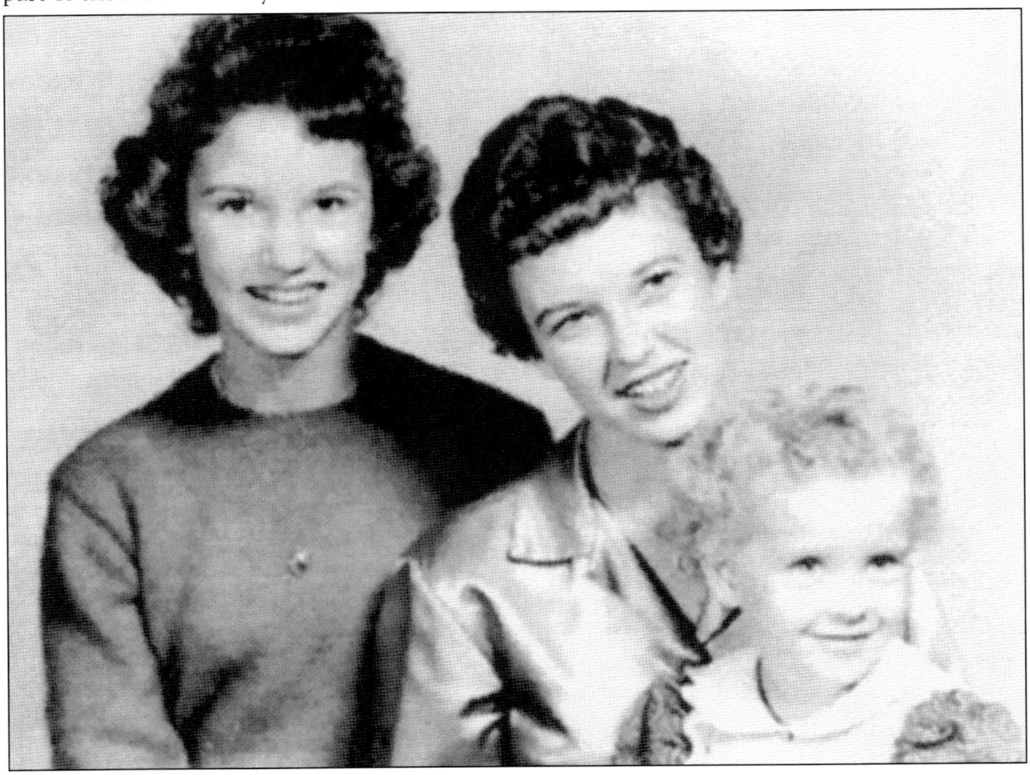

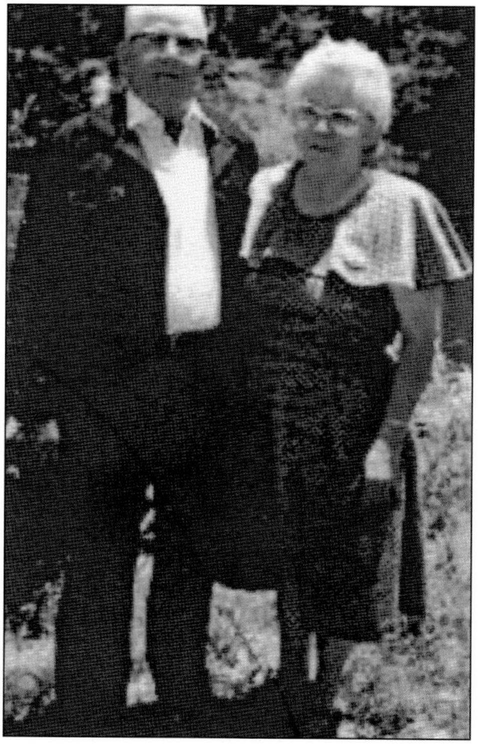

Melvin Johnson married Omie Riley, and T. E. Sauter married Omie's sister, Ollie Riley. Both families lived on portions of their old home place. Melvin and Omie are shown here.

This photograph shows, from left to right, Marjorie, Tom, Joyce, Wilma, Donald, Omie, Terry, Linda, and Raymond Johnson.

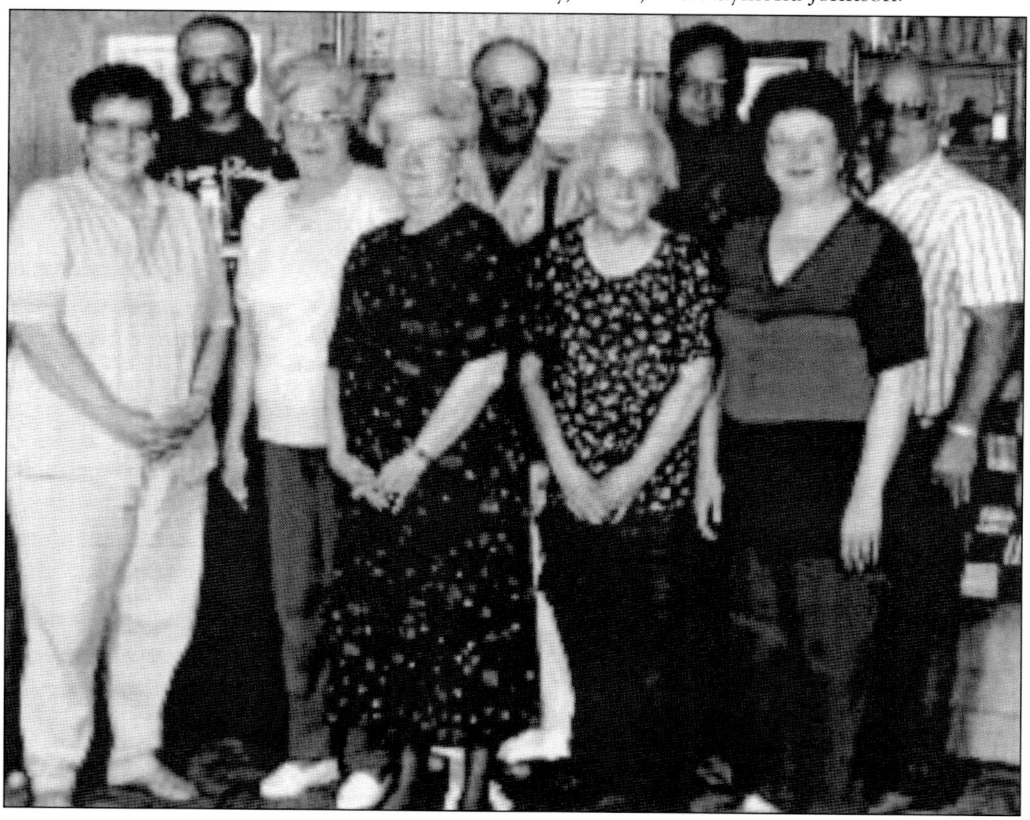

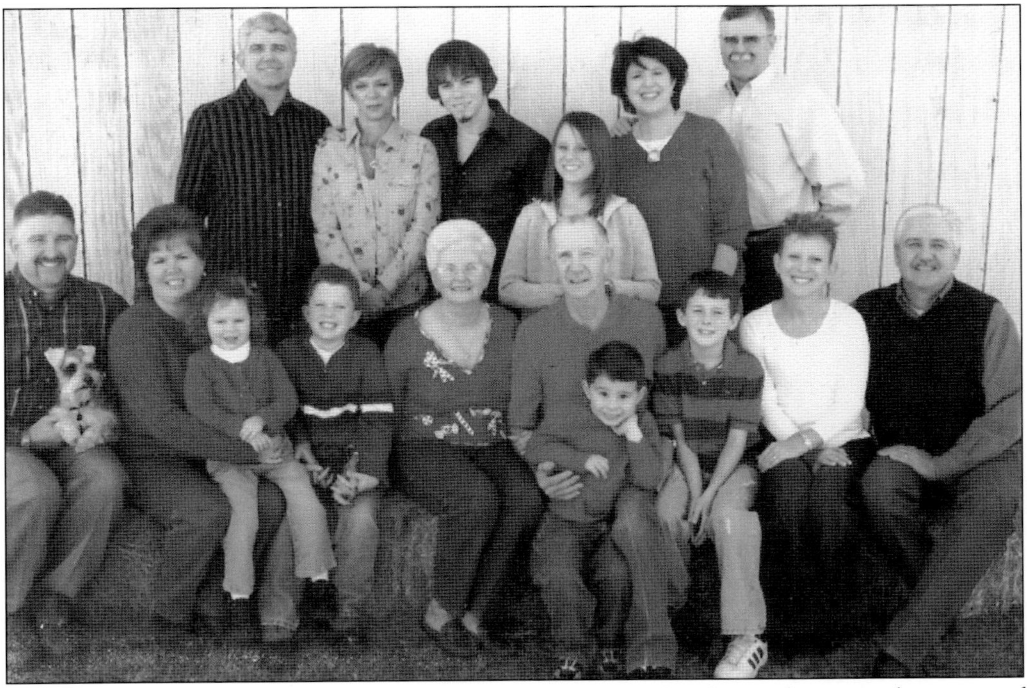

Clyde Knight and his wife, Evelyna, operated Krum's chicken hatchery. They were the source of baby chicks and eggs for Krum stores and residents for many years. Here their descendants are gathered together for Christmas 2005. They are, from left to right, (first row) Chipper, Sonya, Rachel, Tanner, Sue, Jack, Ben (front), Drew, Dixie, and Terry; (second row) Jimmy, Janet, Milyes, Lauren, Nina, and Randy.

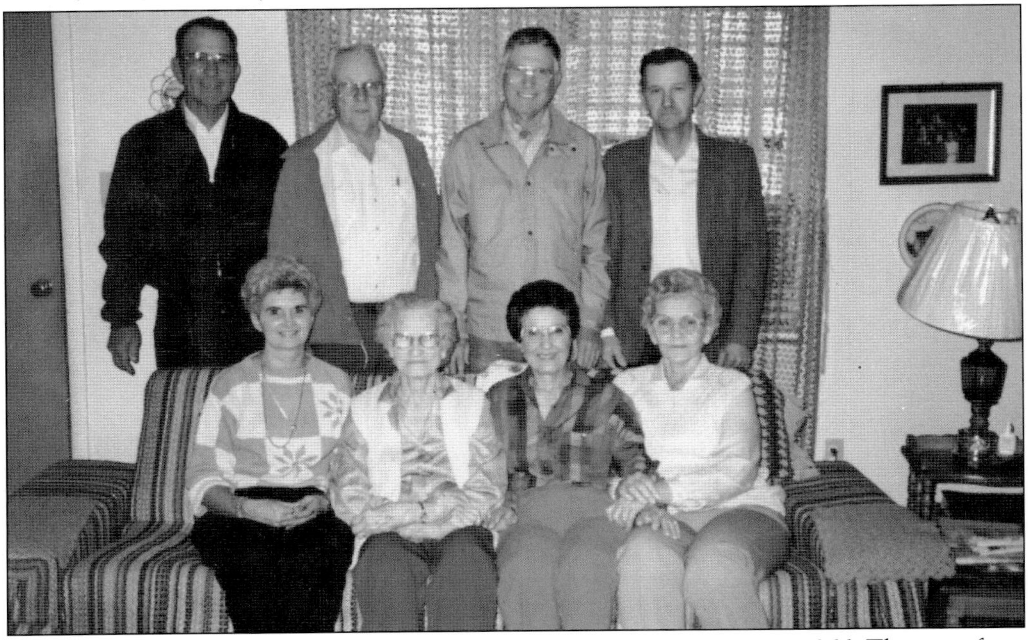

The Knight family is gathered together to celebrate Thanksgiving Day in 1966. They are, from left to right, (first row) Sue, Evalena (mother), Estie Jeter, and Dorothy; (second row) Dugan, James Jeter (son-in-law), Brantley "Preach," and Jack.

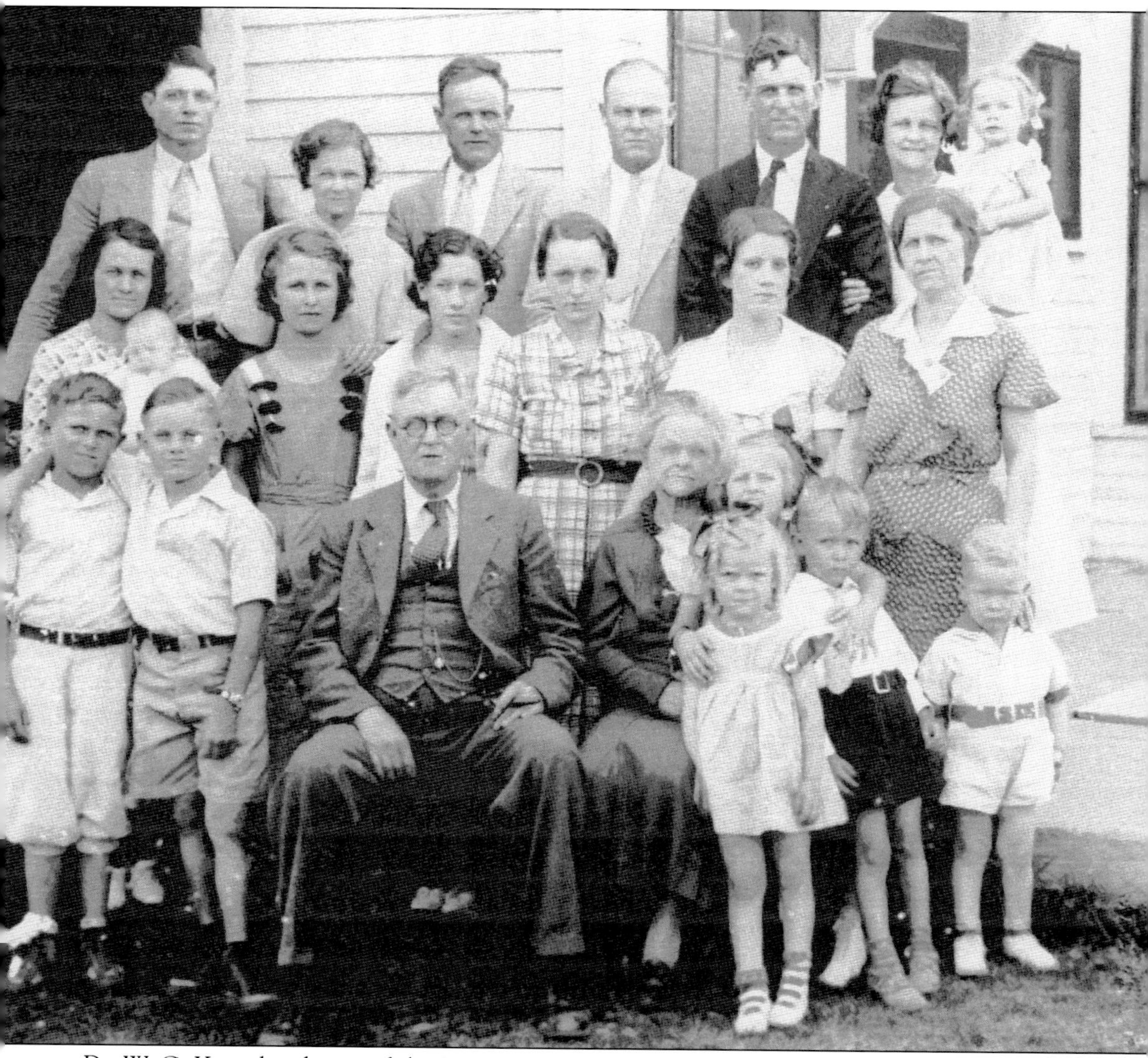

Dr. W. G. Knox lived west of the Joe Barnett farm on a ranch purchased with money some of his sons accumulated in the gold fields of Colorado and Alaska. One of those sons, Alvin Henry Knox, became a doctor and set up a practice in Pilot Grove, Grayson County, where he also had a small farm and cotton gin. Intrigued with the potential of Denton County, the younger Dr. Knox moved to Krum in 1909 and became a farmer and banker. He established the First State Bank, which became the Farmers and Merchants State Bank. He was also a charter member of the Texas Cotton Ginners Association. In this photograph Dr. A. H. and Bertha Knox celebrate their 50th anniversary. Pictured, from left to right, are (first row) Richard, Cecil Scott, Alvin Henry, Bertha, Sally, Ena (front), Dale, and Wendell; (second row) Marjorie, Rodney (baby), Patricia, Junie, Colene, Maxine, and Edith; (third row) Herbert, Helen, Howell, Douglas, Cecil, Ruth, and Ann.

David and Emma Koiner had three sons—Will, Jim, and John—who all bought farms in the Hawkeye area north of Krum. When Will gave up farming, he became caretaker of the Church of Christ in Krum. Two of Jim's sons—Will and Lee—established the Koiner Gin in Krum. John donated the land on which the Hawkeye School was built. Additional generations of Koiners have followed.

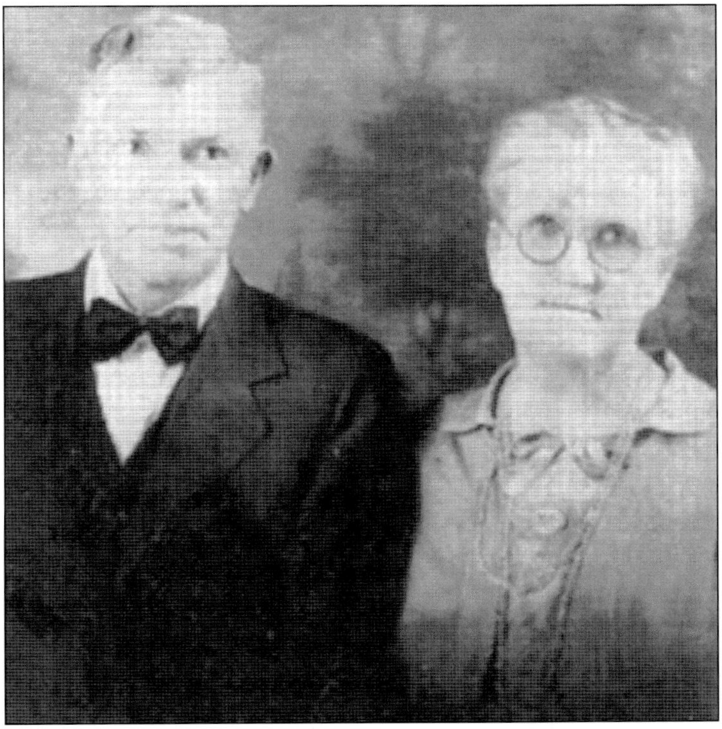

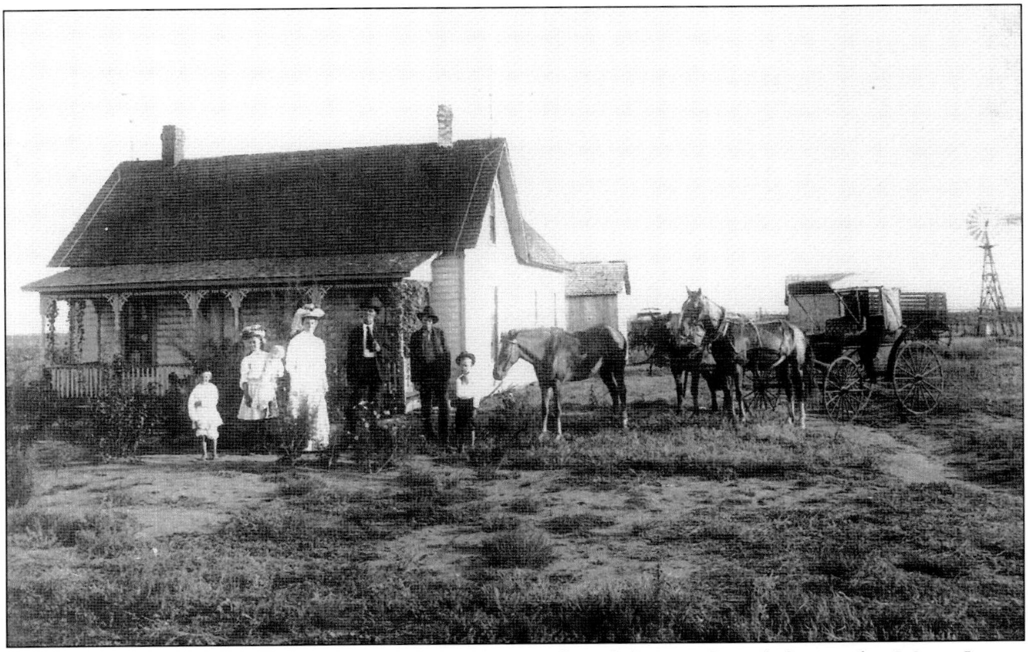

Members of the Jim Koiner family are shown here. The adults are, from left to right, Mary, Irene, Wayne, and Eunice.

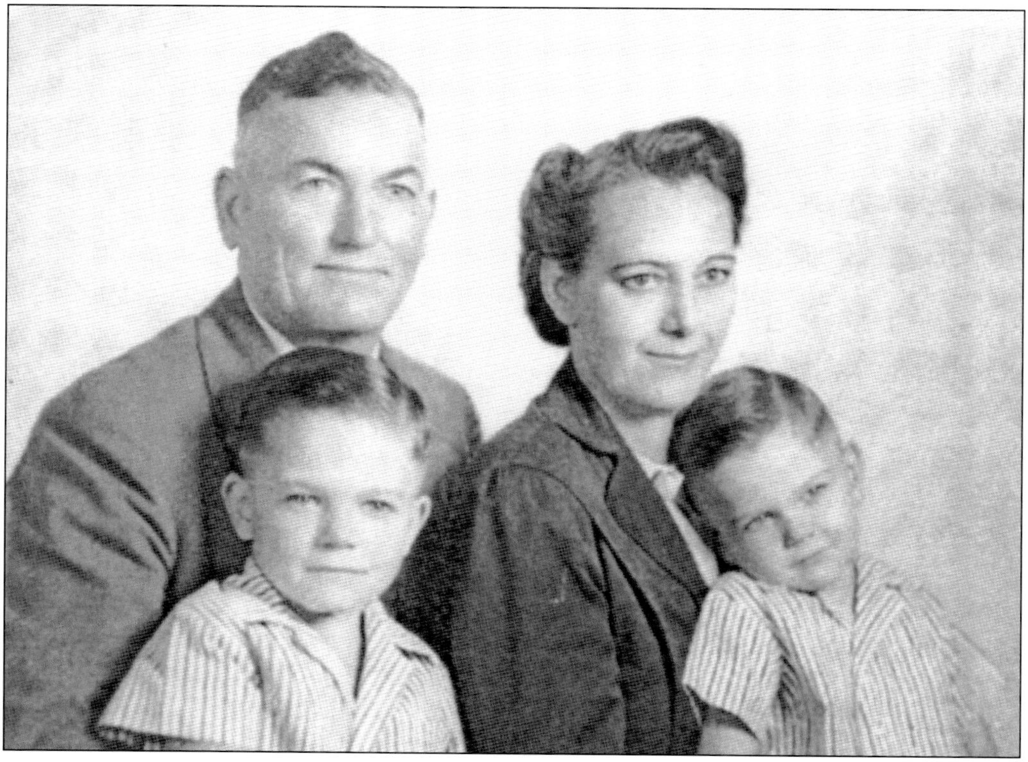

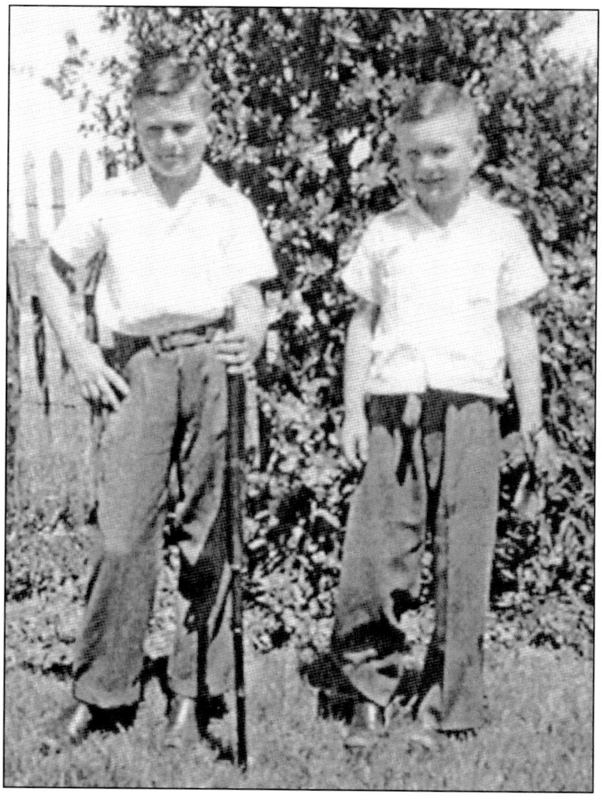

John and Verda Koiner pose with their sons, John and Wylie. The Koiners are descended from Silas Koiner, who traveled from Missouri with his wife. They settled in Denton in 1883.

When the two brothers, John and Wylie Koiner, grew up, they both became highly decorated officers in the nation's military services.

Members of the Lamm family pictured here are, from left to right, (first row) Harve holding his son Ed, Eurna, and Harve's wife; (second row) Homer and Velma. The picture below shows baby Ed as an adult. Harve Lamm moved with his immediate family to Krum in 1903. His brother, Ed, who was already there, was managing the Krum Mill and Elevator Company. Harve entered into a partnership with J. O. McClister in McClister's General Merchandise Store. After the store burned in 1906, Lamm bought the grocery end of the business and moved it down the street. The following year, with C. C. Gibbins as a partner, Lamm built a brick store on the south side of McCart Street. It continued in operation until being sold in 1969.

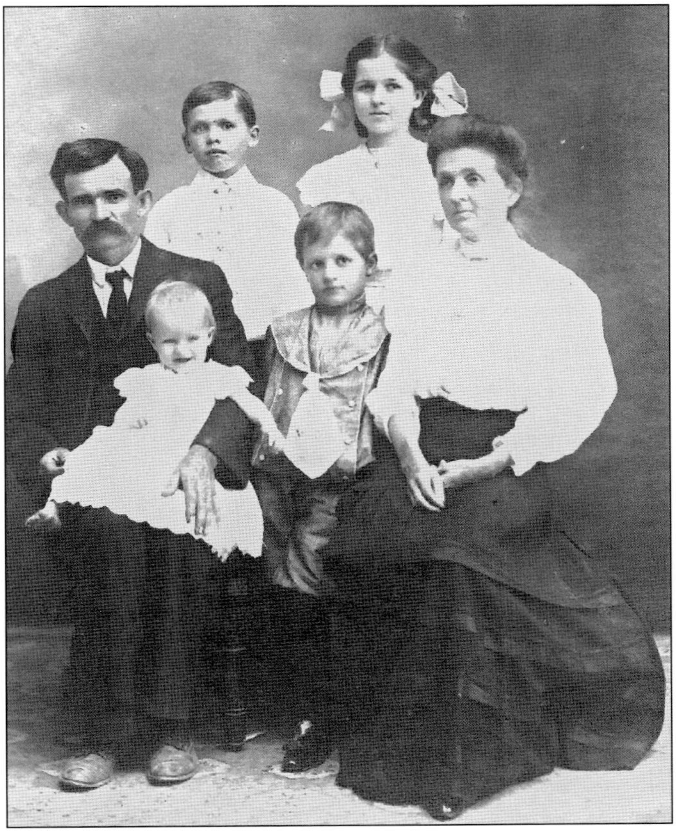

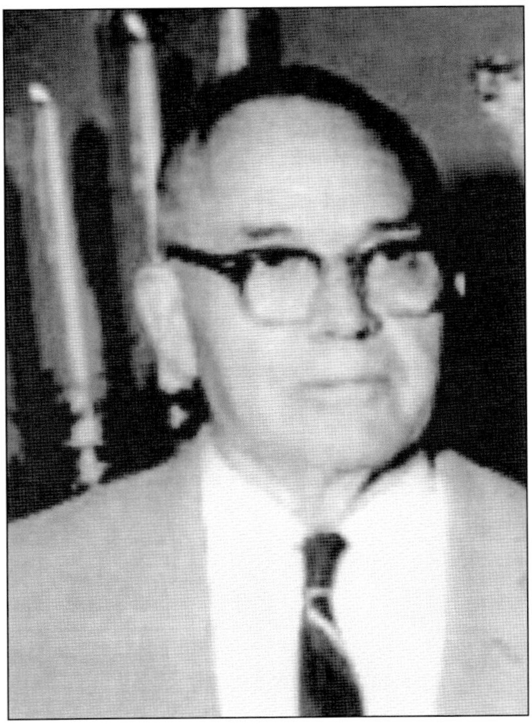

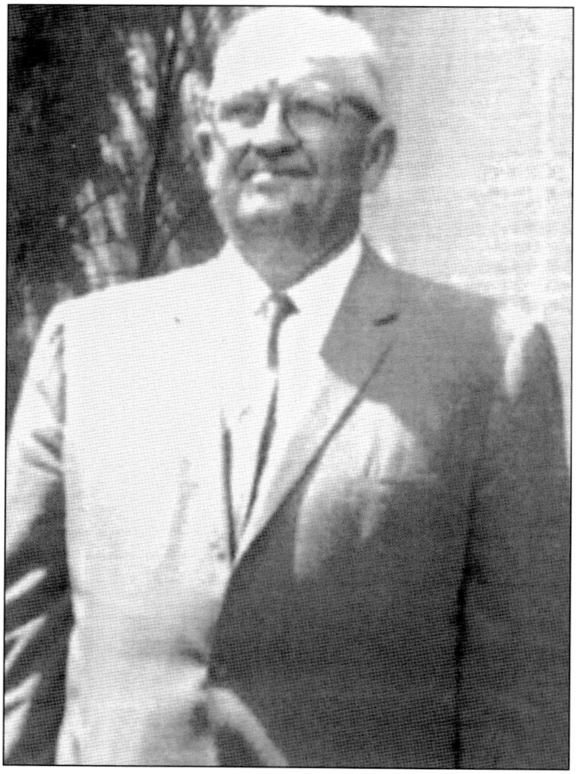

Homer Lamm married Frances Brumley. He, along with his brother Ed, continued operating the Lamm Grocery Store after their father's death. In his younger years, Homer hauled freight from the depot in a mule-drawn dray and delivered groceries house to house in a light wagon drawn by ponies.

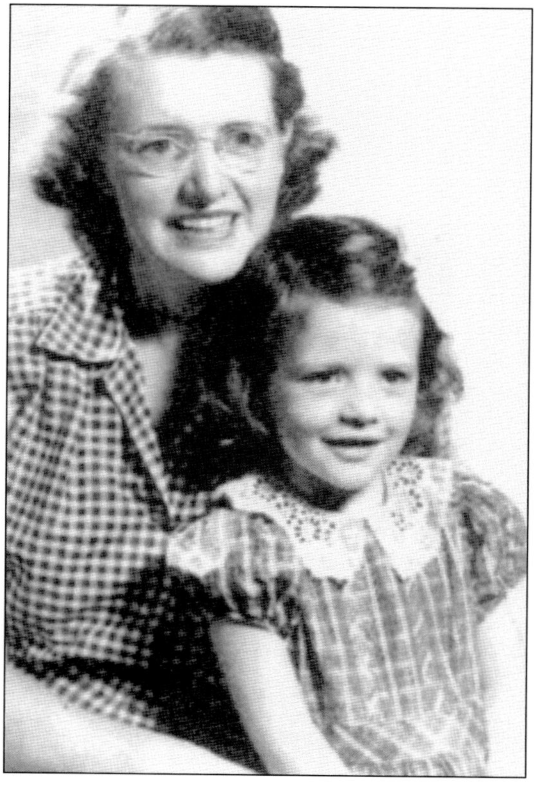

Following Homer's death, his wife, Frances, shown with their daughter Martha, remained in the family home, where she modernized the kitchen, bathrooms, and laundry room while retaining the overall ambience.

In 1912, Tom Lamonica and his bride, Jessie, moved to Krum, where he took over management of the lumberyard. At one time, Lamonica also managed the Rest Hour Theater.

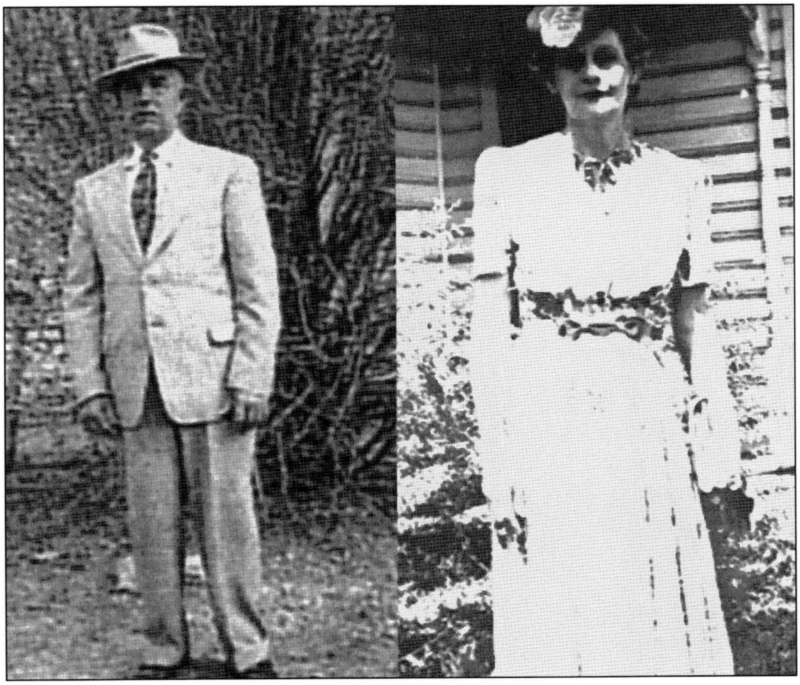

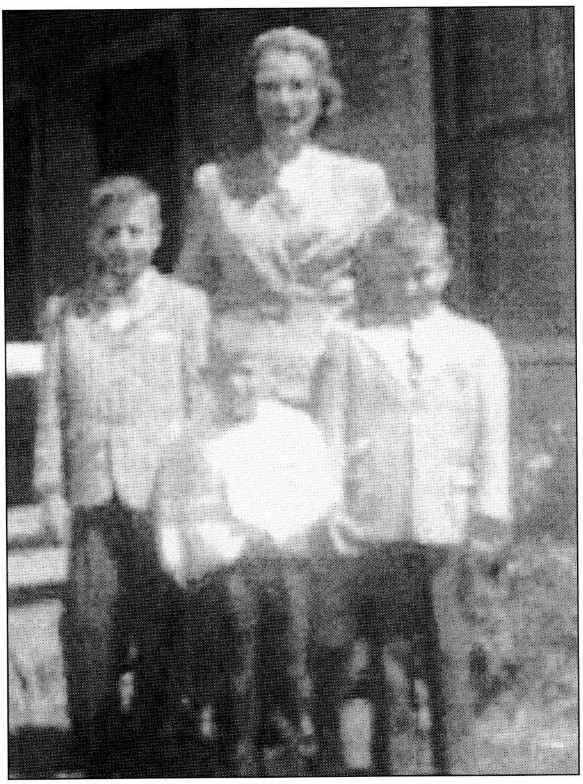

George Lamonica was a son of Tom and Jessie. George and his wife, Marie, had three sons—shown with their mother, from left to right, Larry, Gary, and David. Larry served two terms as Krum's mayor.

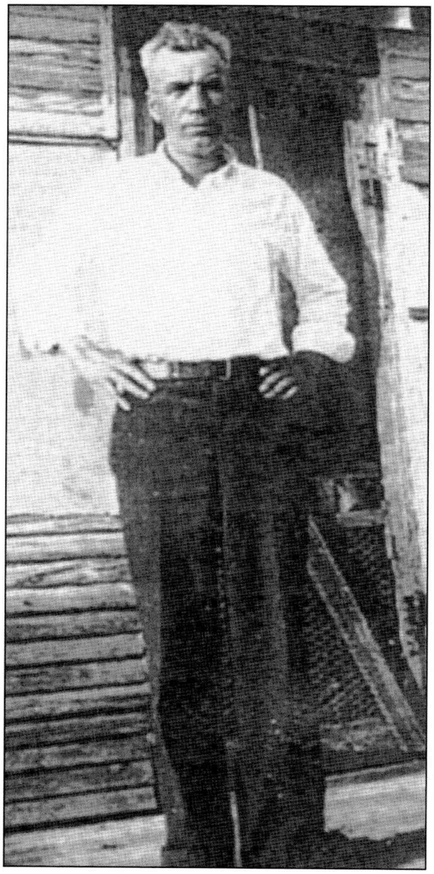

Fletcher McBee (left) worked for the Santa Fe Railroad as a section hand. He and his wife, Ethel, had three children. Pictured below, from left to right, they are Alvin, Gracie, and Fletcher Wayne. Gracie married Russell Helton.

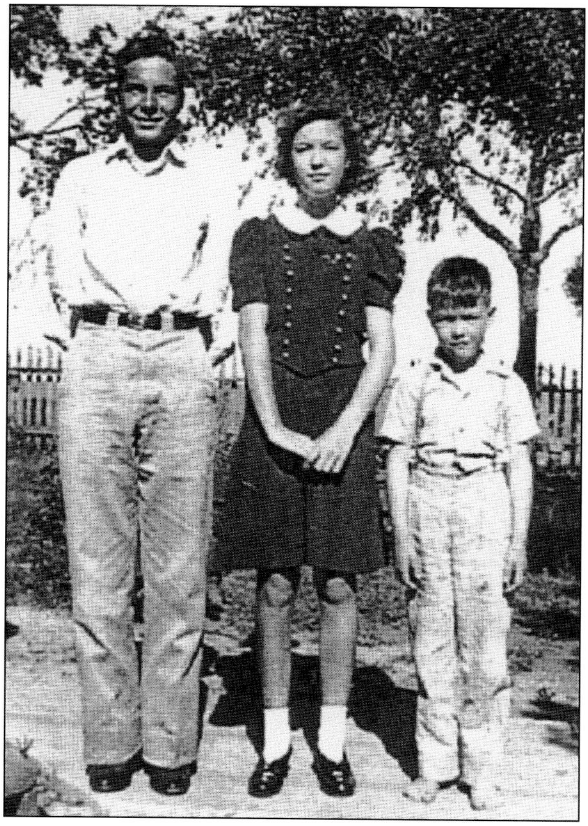

J. O. McClister was another of Krum's outstanding businessmen. Bringing his family to Krum in 1900, he joined his brother Andrew in establishing a general merchandise store. Sales were very good, and after constructing several additions as the business expanded, the building eventually covered the whole lot. Then on Christmas Eve 1906, a fire started in the next-door store, and the entire north side of McCart Street burned. McClister immediately erected a brick store and continued in the dry goods business, while selling his grocery business to Harve Lamm. In 1940, McClister's son, Walter, opened a garage and a successful Chrysler-Plymouth dealership in the Muncy Building. J. O. and Mattie McClister are shown at right, and below, from left to right, are Mattie McClister, Mary McGee, and Maude Crawford.

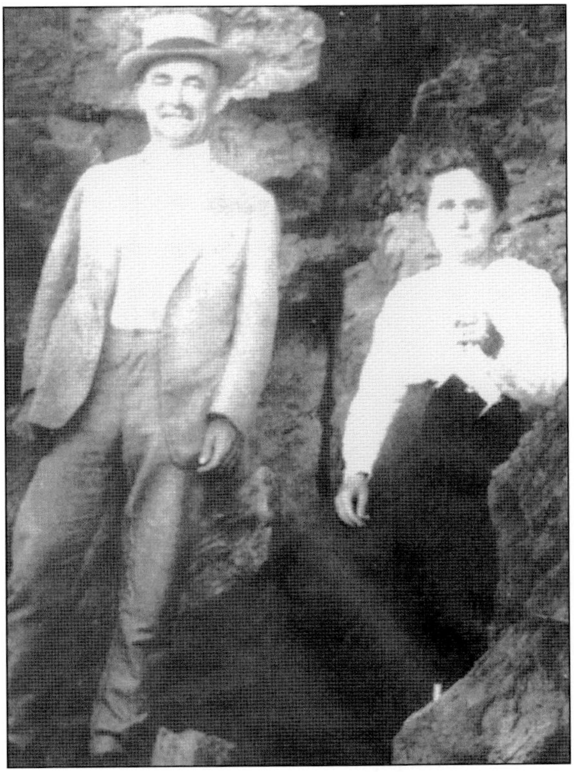

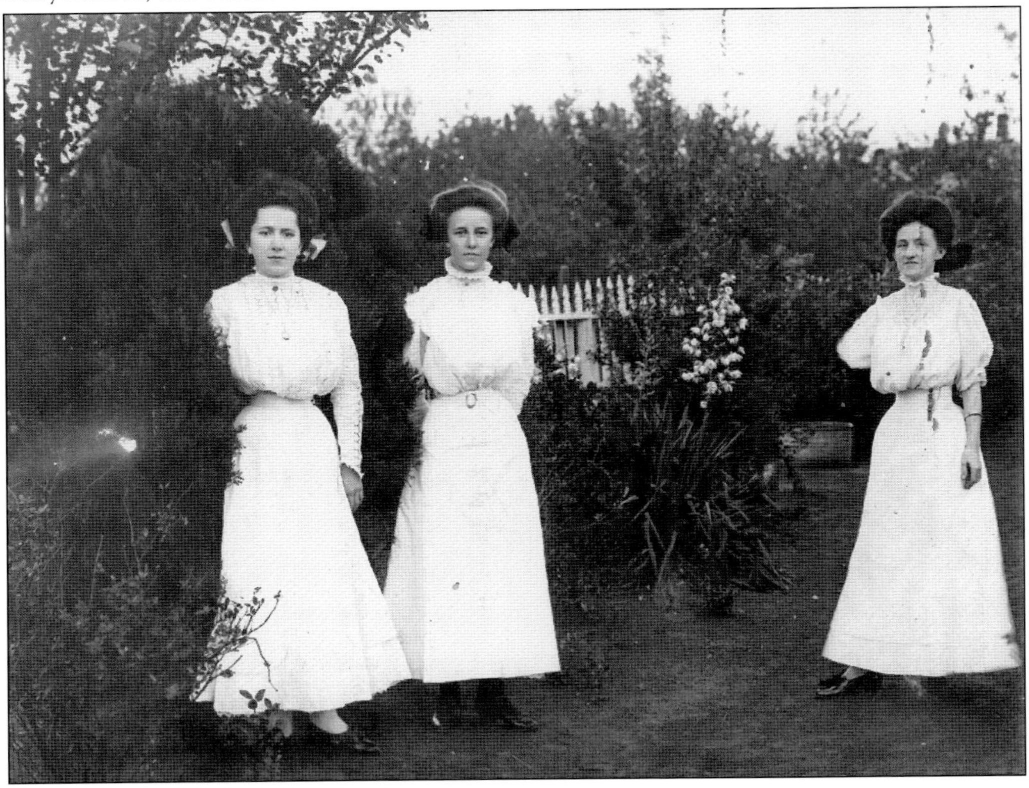

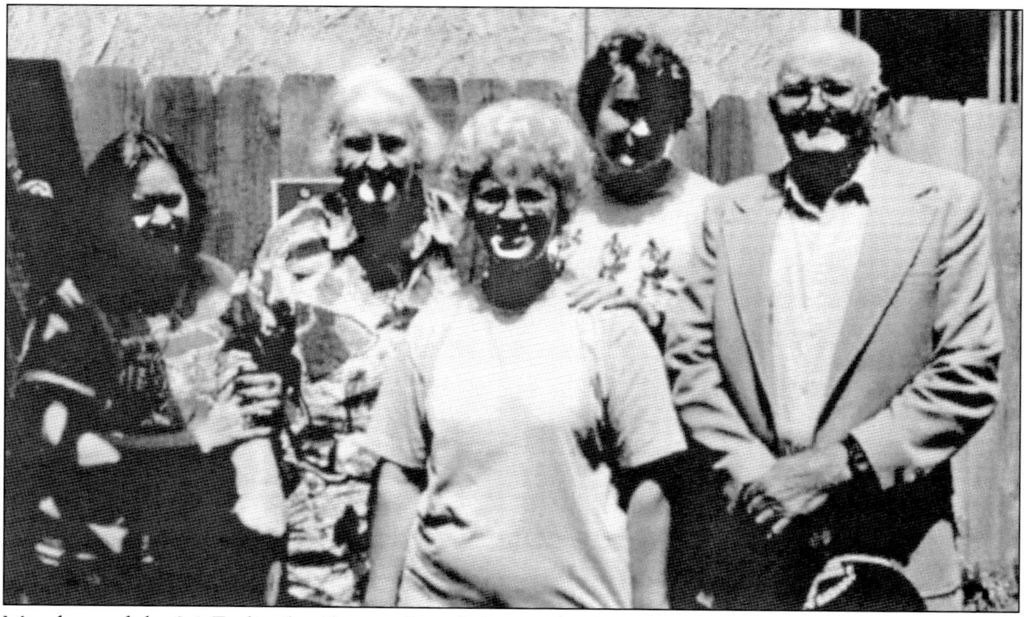

Members of the McFarlin family are, from left to right, Linnie, Bessie, Cecil Ann, Yvonne, and Russell. Cecil Ann married Wayne Cox, son of Earl and Lilian Cox.

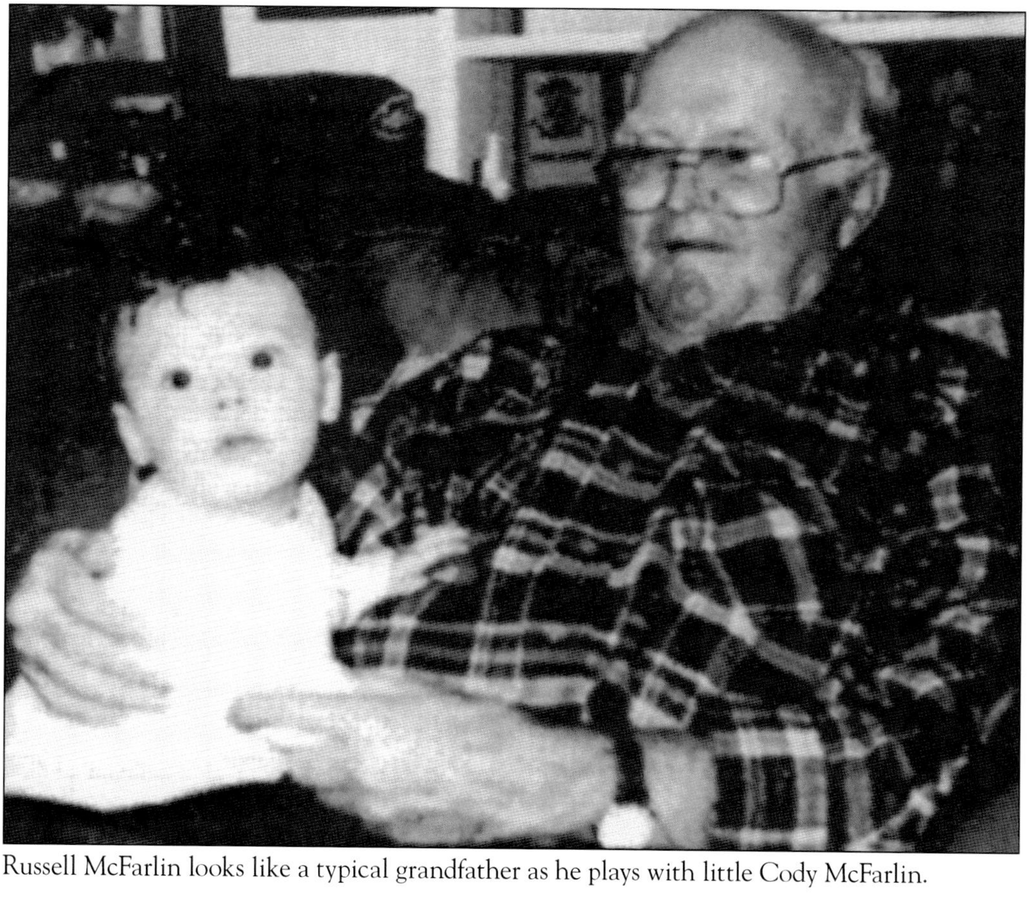

Russell McFarlin looks like a typical grandfather as he plays with little Cody McFarlin.

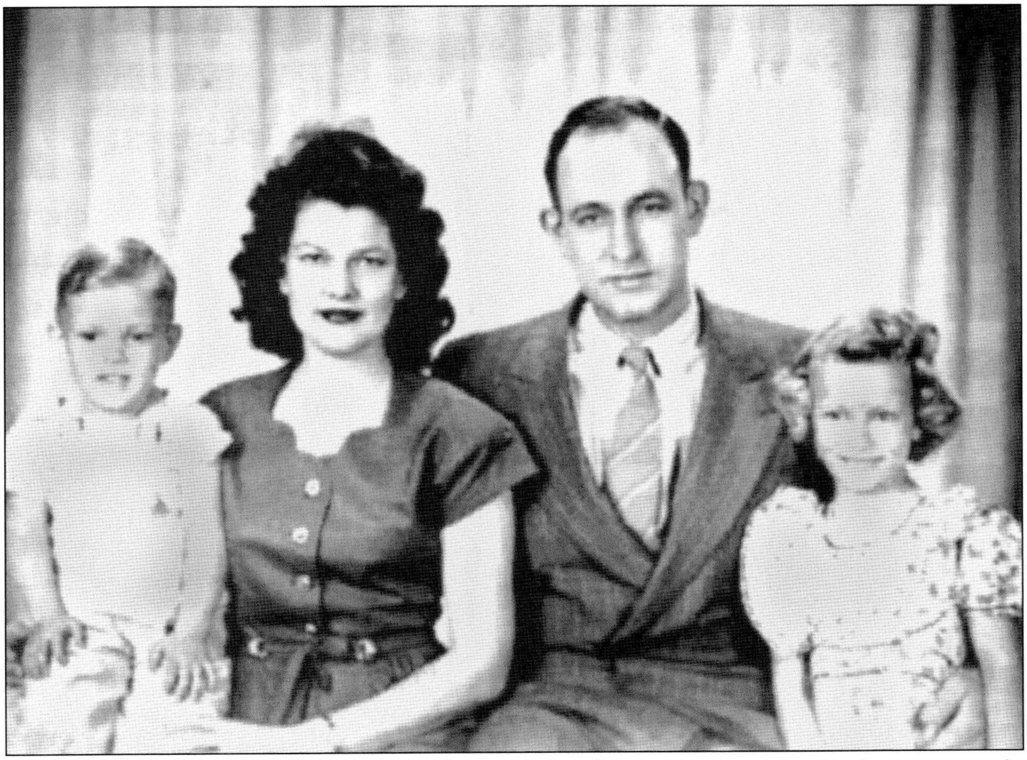

Staunch members of the Baptist Church, the McKinney family poses together for this photograph: (from left to right) Jerry, Burtis, Ned, and Glenda. As an adult, Jerry went into the ministry.

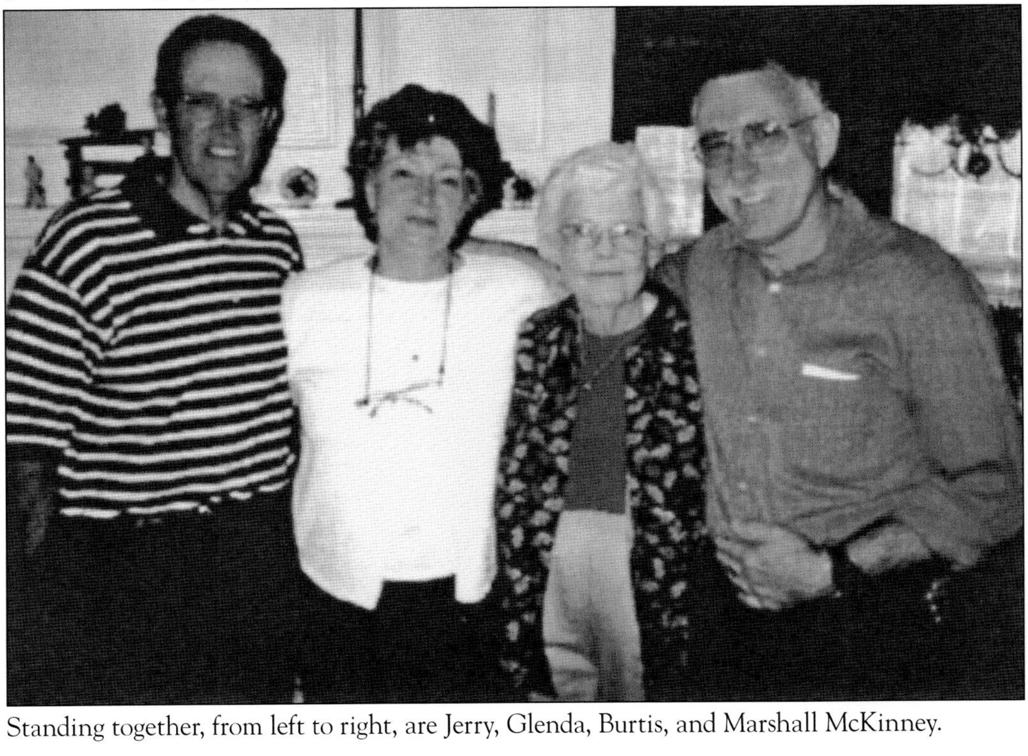

Standing together, from left to right, are Jerry, Glenda, Burtis, and Marshall McKinney.

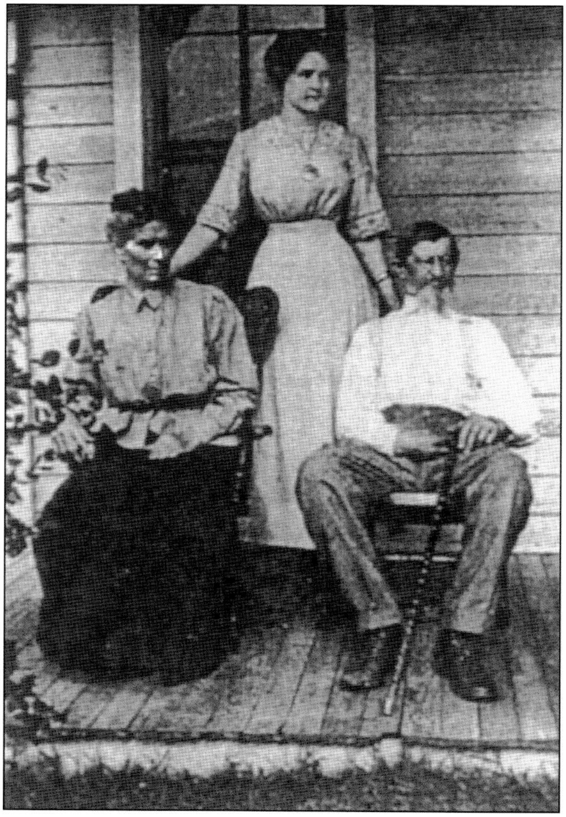

John Miller is believed to have been the first German American immigrant to the Krum area. In 1879, Miller married Augusta Barthold, daughter of another German family, and in 1886, they moved to a farm 1 mile east of Krum. One son, Joe, married Ava Barnett and became a pioneer family of the Plainview community. A daughter, Pet Miller, married Clarence R. Fowler, who established the C. R. Fowler Hardware Store. A son of the Fowlers, Francis W. "Pin" Fowler, became Krum's first mayor. At left, Augusta and John Miller sit while their daughter Pet stands behind. Below, the Miller men are, from left to right, John (father), Jack, Harry, John H., Barnett, Ralph, and Joe.

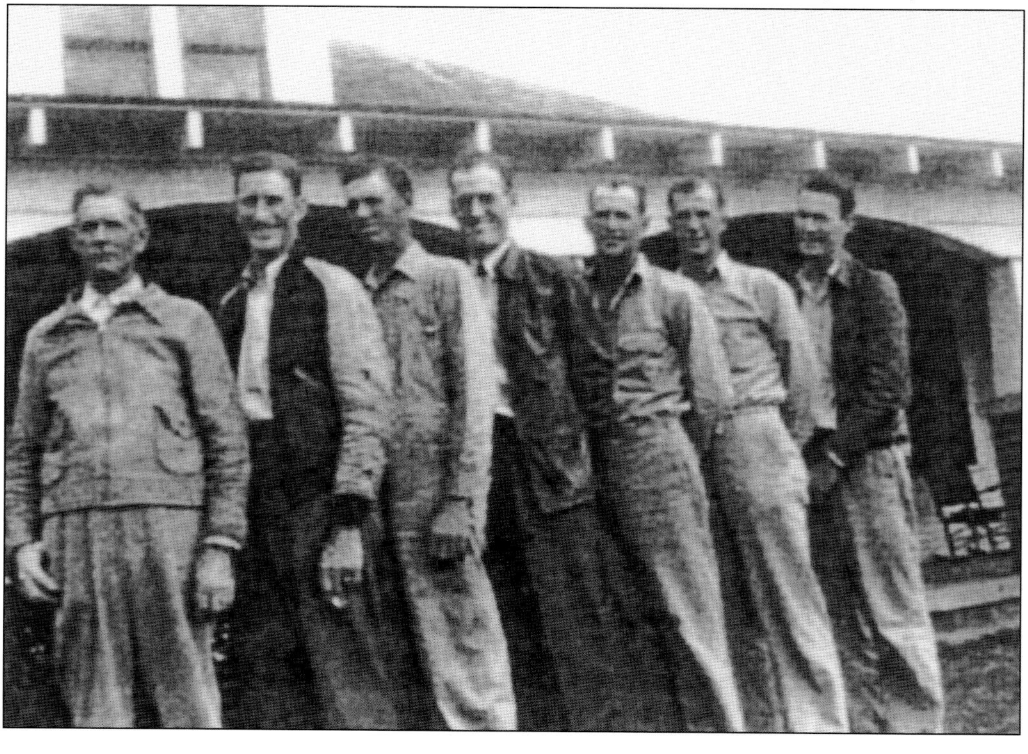

Newlyweds Alfred Saxton Monschke and Ruth Preston Monschke look forward to the future in this 1940 photograph. Albert was born on his parent's farm east of Krum where the Ryland Homes subdivision is now located. Ruth was born in Celina, Texas. The Monschkes were married on October 5, 1940.

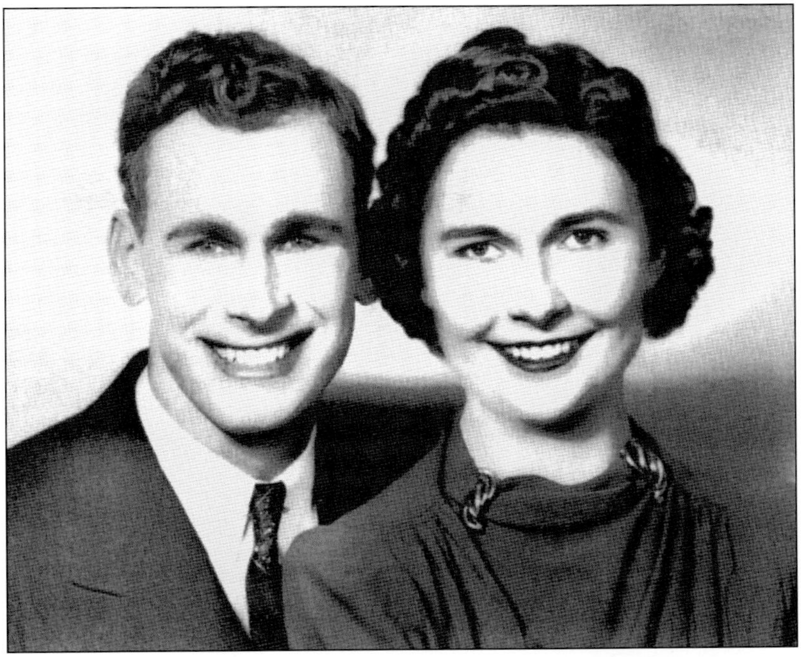

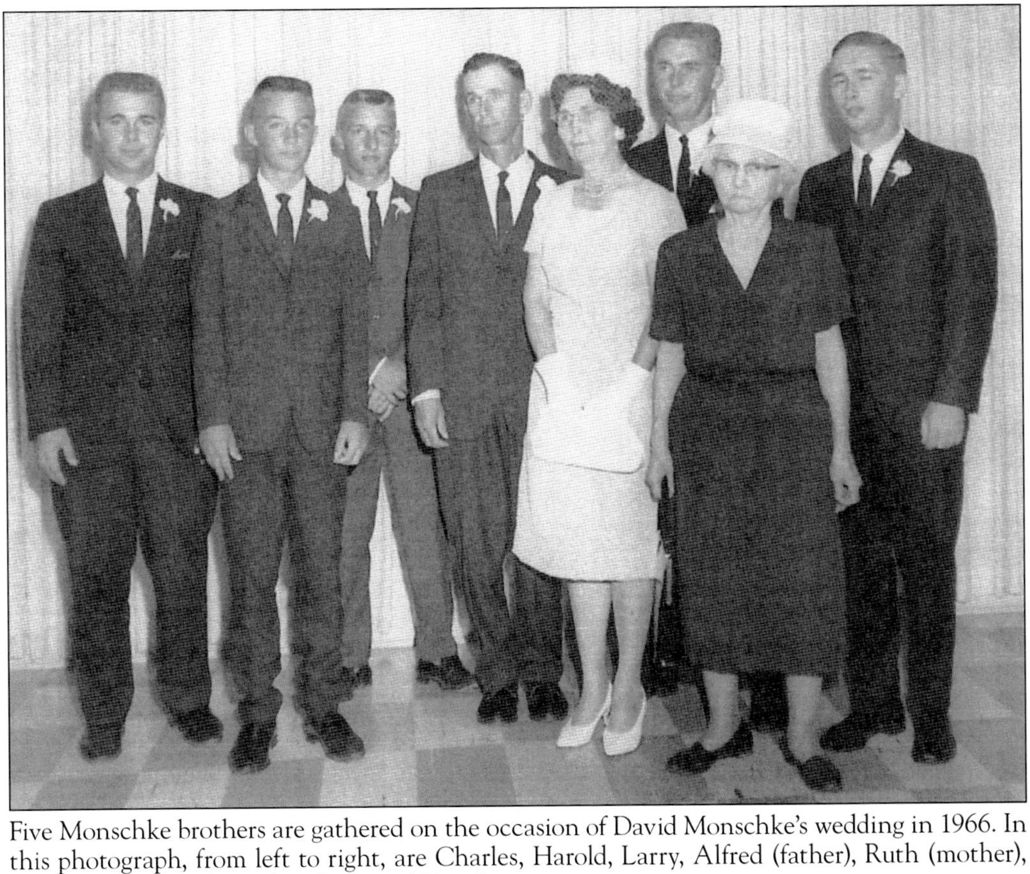

Five Monschke brothers are gathered on the occasion of David Monschke's wedding in 1966. In this photograph, from left to right, are Charles, Harold, Larry, Alfred (father), Ruth (mother), Paul, Annie Belle (grandmother), and David.

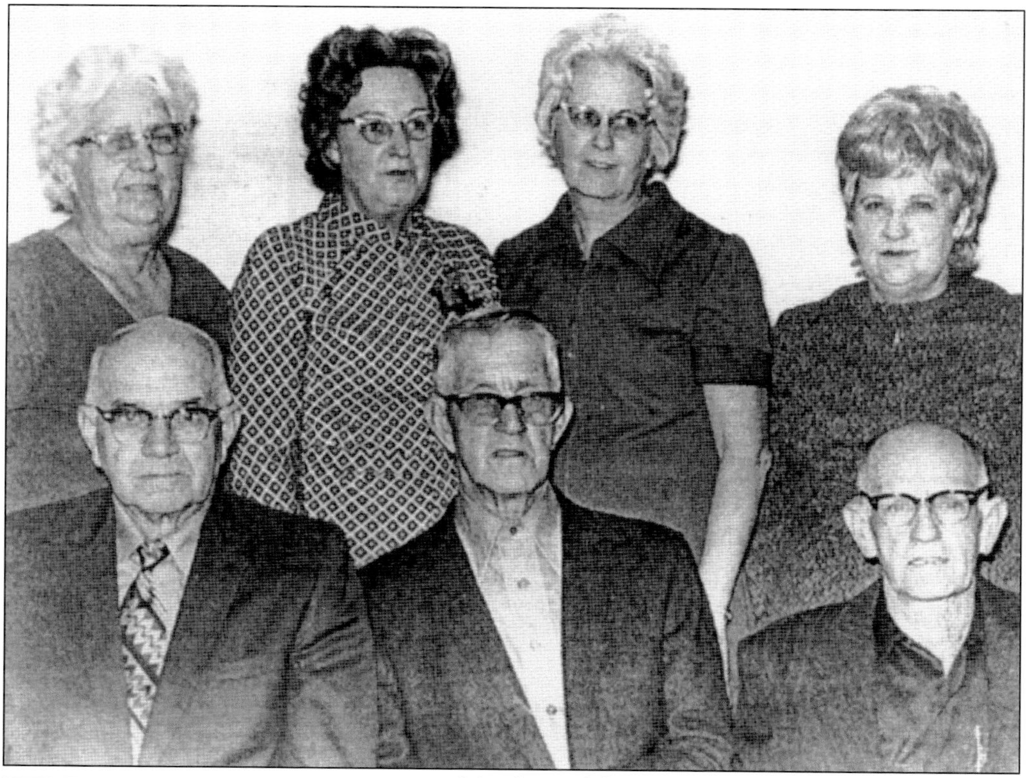

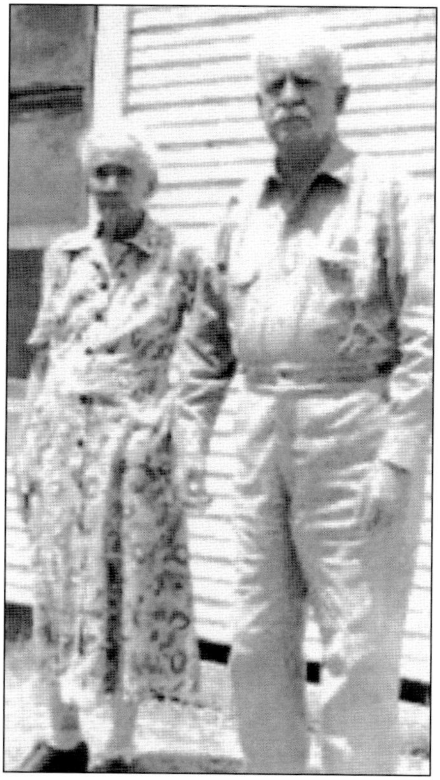

Members of the Park family pictured are, from left to right, (first row) Loren, Earl, and Mutt; (second row) Martha, Jean, Mable, and Joan.

The John E. Riley family came to Krum in 1910 and bought a farm west of Krum. Eight children grew up on the family farm—Jim, Henry, Annie, Iva, J. O., Ollie, Omie, and Ben. Pictured at left are John E. Riley and his wife, Isabel.

S. T. and Georgia Rankin lived on the old Egan place out on Egan Road. They were successful farmers.

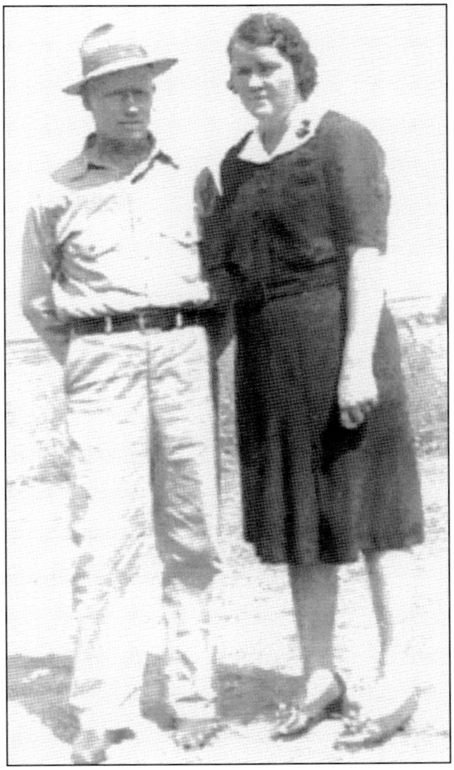

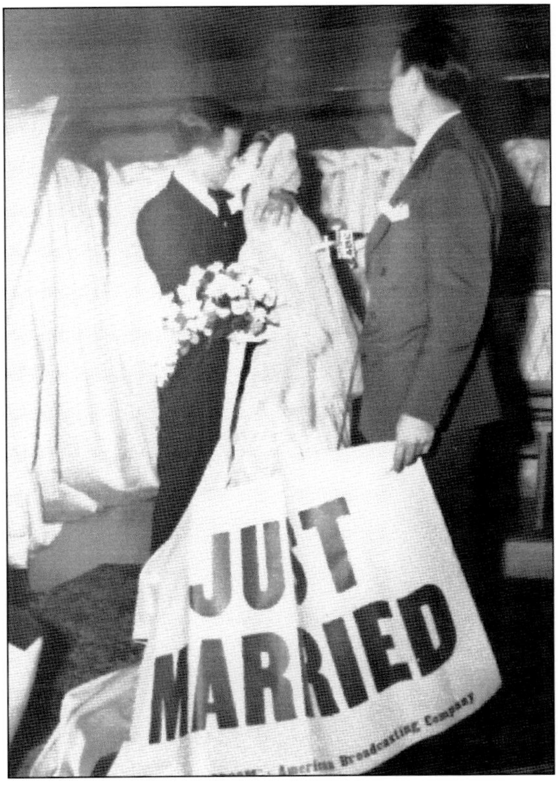

In June 1946, Dorothy Ruth Rankin, daughter of S. T. and Georgia Rankin, married W. H. McDaniel. The wedding took place on the *Bride and Groom* radio show aired nationwide from Hollywood by the American Broadcasting Company. The network paid for their honeymoon at Carlsbad by the Sea.

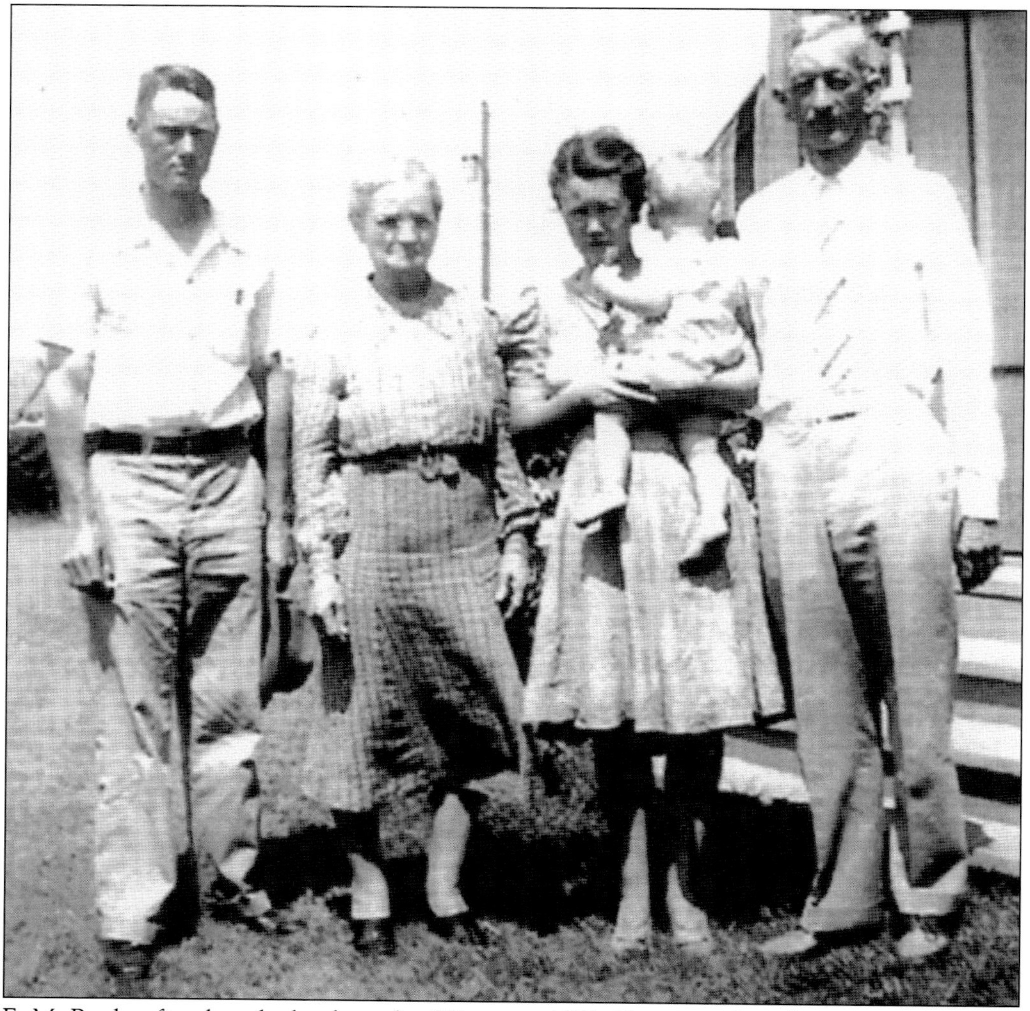

E. M. Rucker first bought land north of Krum in 1888. He married Mollie Batis, daughter of C. F. Batis, and they built a home just east of town. Rucker was instrumental in establishing the Continental Bank and Trust Company in Krum, and he remained on the board of the Farmers and Merchants State Bank when the two banks merged in 1910. Descendants of E. M. Rucker are shown here. They are, from left to right, George Wilkins, Molly Rucker, Frances Rucker, Frank Wilkins, and Reuban Rucker.

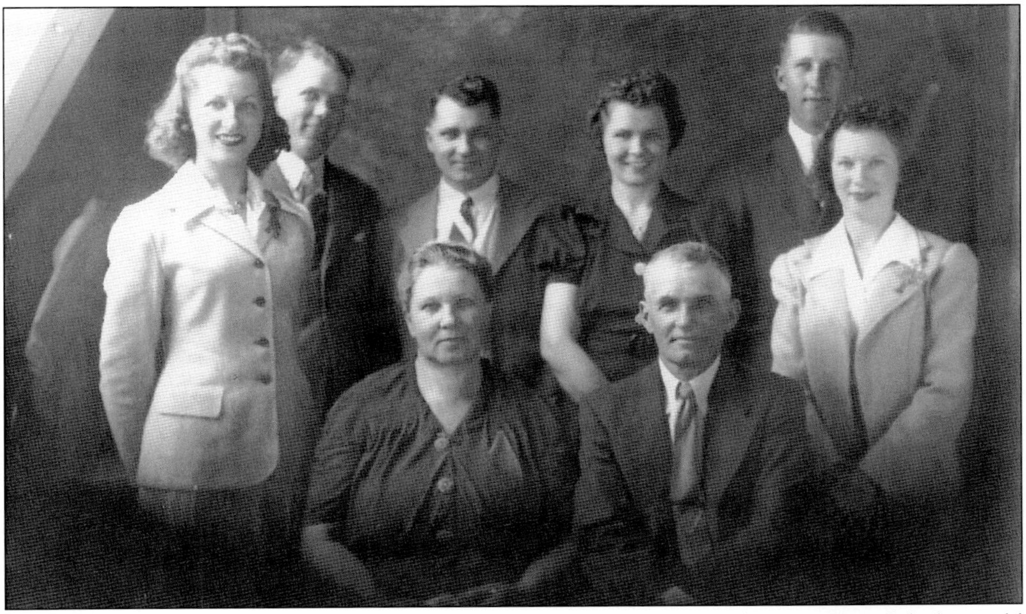

The Schultz family was another German family to settle in and around Krum. Frau Schultz could always be counted on to provide sauerkraut for anyone who was hungry. The Schultzes are, from left to right, (first row) Bertha and Ernest; (second row) Ella, Adolph, Erwin, Milda, Robert, and Hattie.

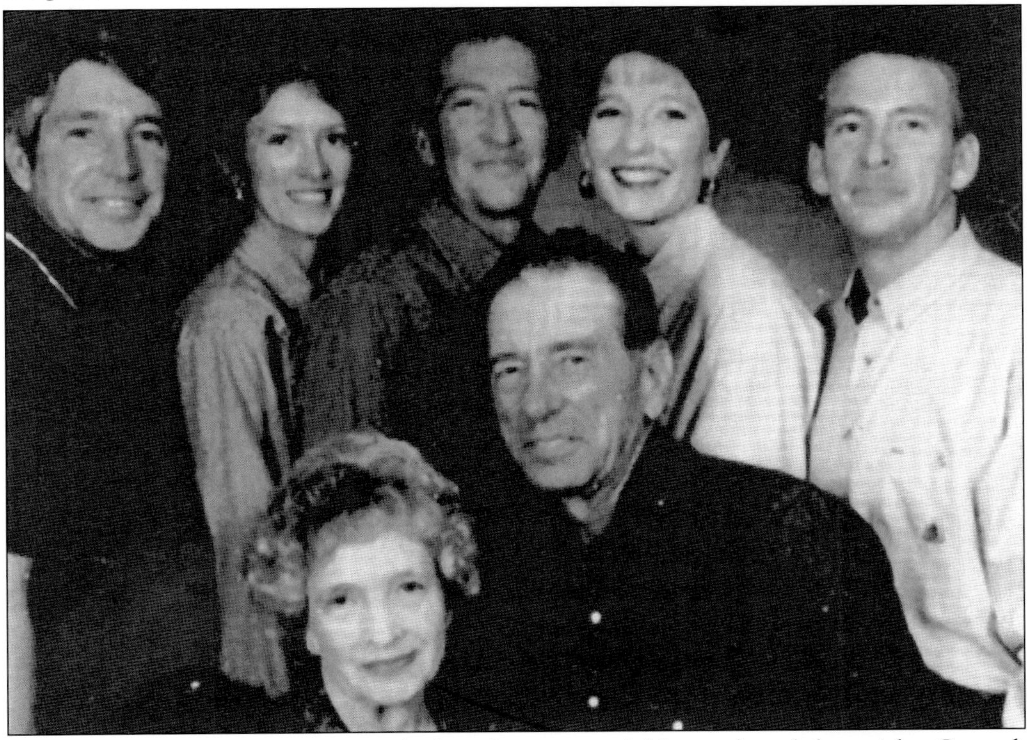

Anetta and Gary Shifflett pose with their five grown children—from left to right, Conrad, Beverly, Carl, Angela, and Travis. The Shiffletts are descended from S. J. Shifflett, who moved to Krum in 1898. For many years, Conrad was "Mr. Everything" in Krum: police chief, fire chief, and utilities manager.

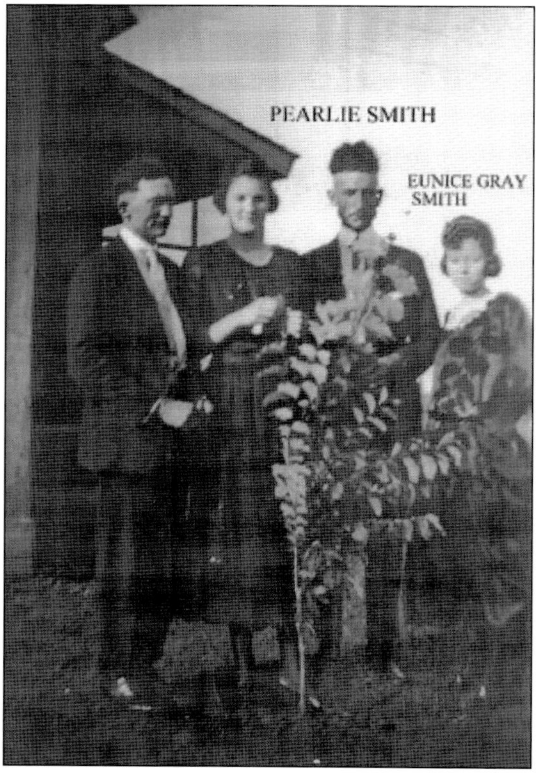

The Smith family, descendants of William M. and Missouri Smith, were prominent in north-central Texas, primarily in Grayson, Denton, and Montague Counties. With regard to the Krum branch of the family, Andrew Smith was a son of William M. and Missouri. Andrew married Nora Baxter, and two of their sons were William Pearlie Smith and John Henry Smith. Pearlie married Eunice Leola Gray, and they had two daughters. Eunice died at a relatively young age, and Pearlie then married Nettie Neeley. Pictured at left, Pearlie and Eunice are standing beside two unidentified friends.

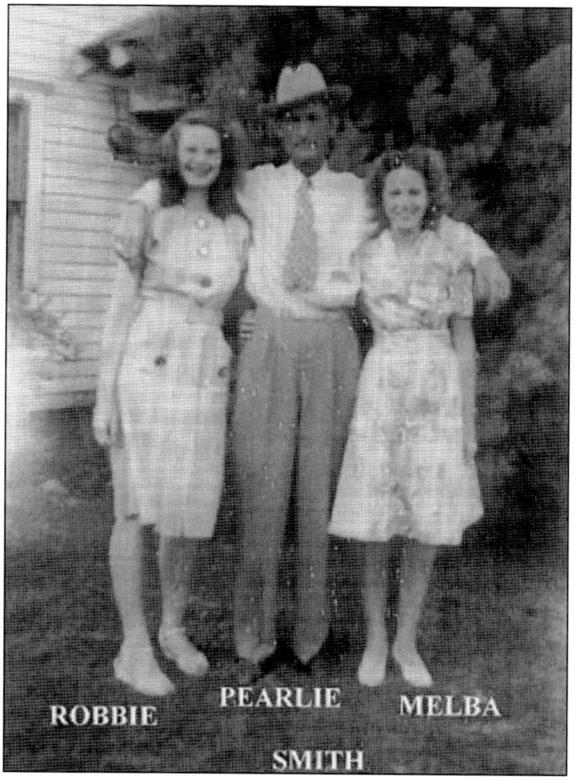

Pearlie Smith is pictured here with his two daughters—Robbie (left) and Melba (right).

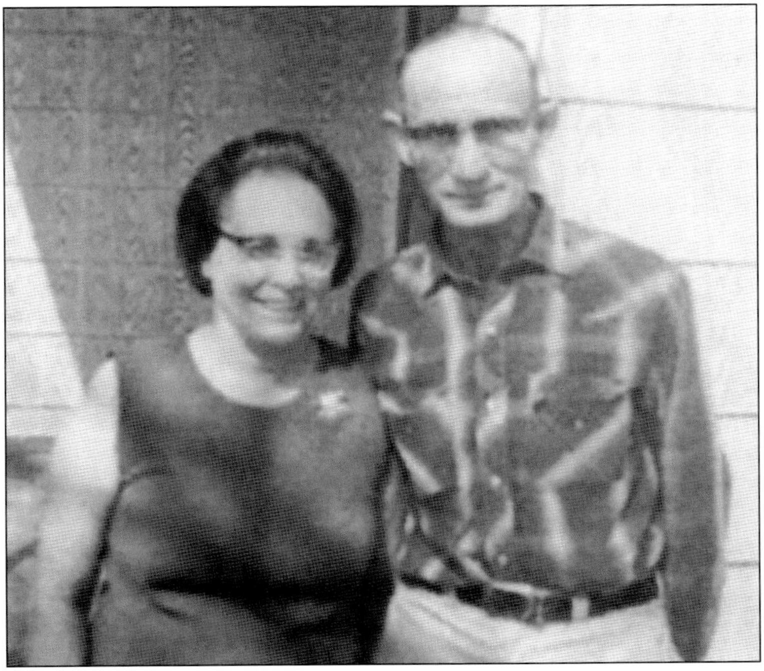

Lewis and Beulah Standifer stand together for this photograph. Lewis worked for the Santa Fe Railroad as a section hand. He also built Krum's Community Cellar, which served as a bomb shelter for many practice exercises.

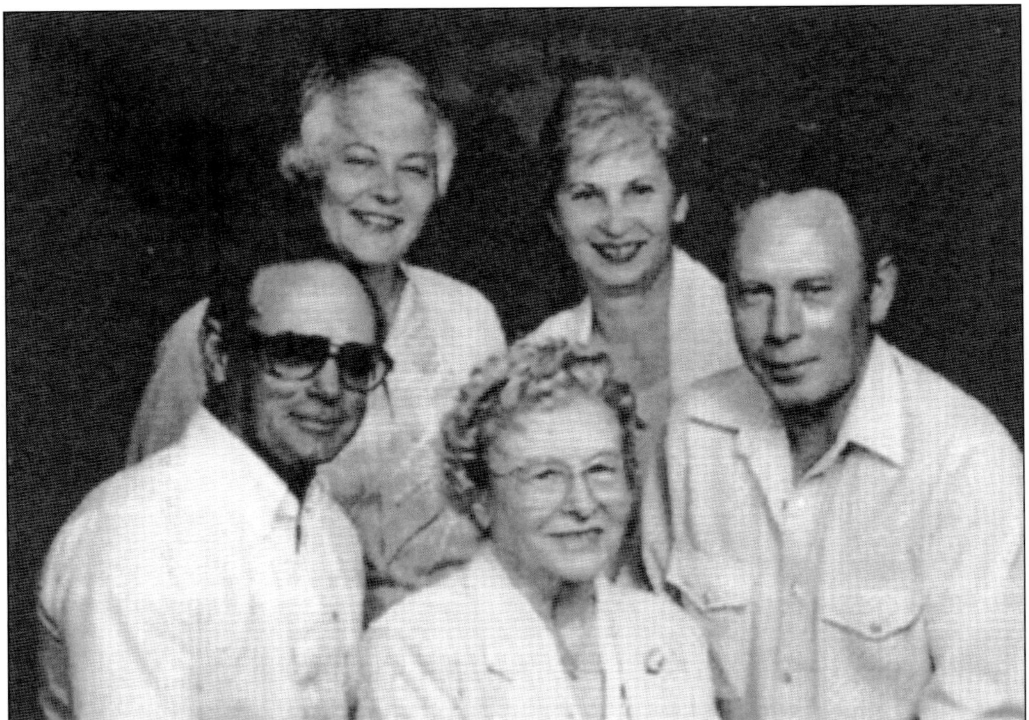

Beulah Standifer is surrounded by her children. They are, from left to right, Wendell, Dorothy, Jean, and Buddy.

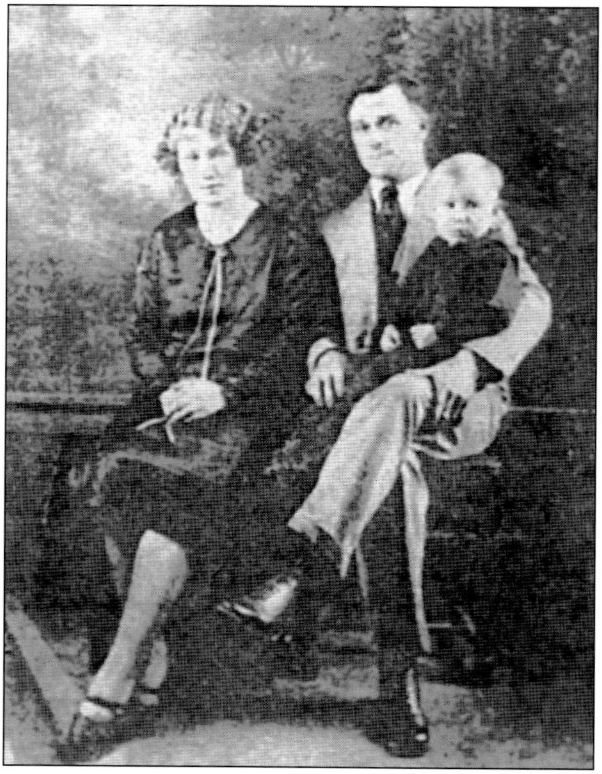

Velma and J. A. Stone sit with young William Edward on his father's lap. Velma was a daughter of George and Maud Evans, who "walked" to Krum from Arkansas. When George died in 1938, Maud moved into Krum proper from their farm. Velma and her husband, J. A. Stone, then operated her family farm until their deaths.

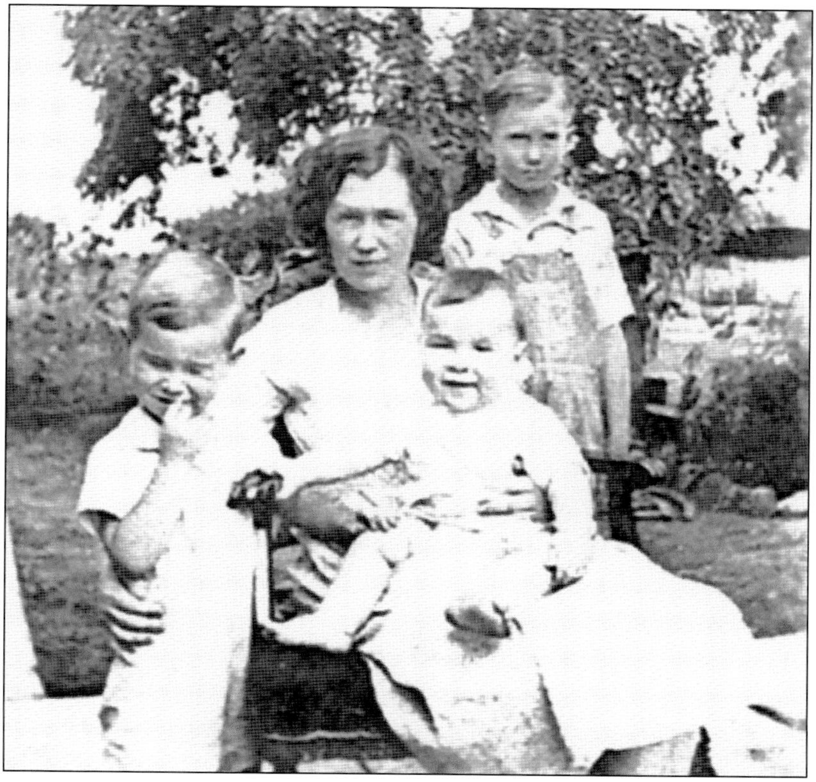

Velma Stone is surrounded by her three sons—from left to right, William Edward, Glen, and Dale.

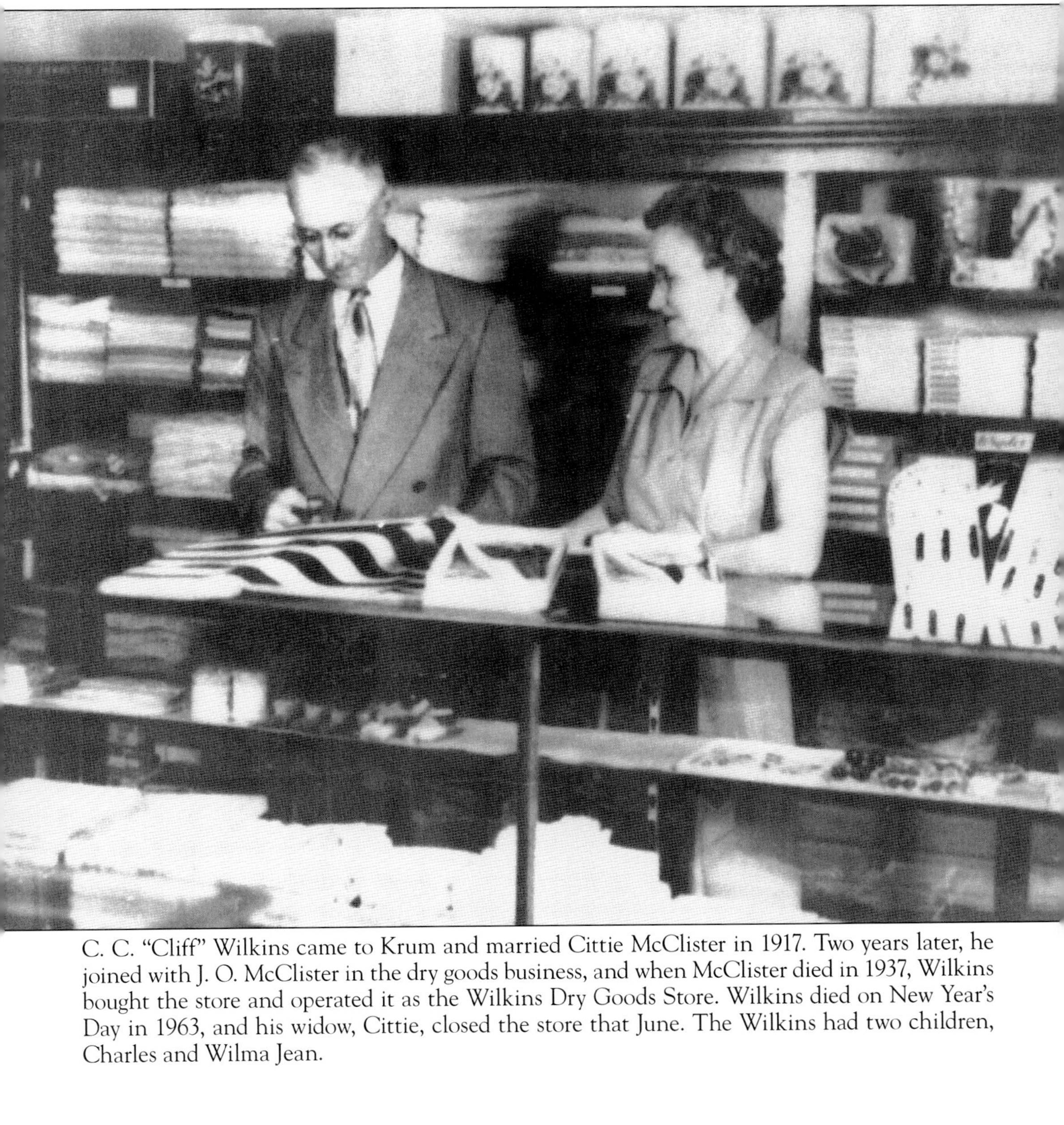

C. C. "Cliff" Wilkins came to Krum and married Cittie McClister in 1917. Two years later, he joined with J. O. McClister in the dry goods business, and when McClister died in 1937, Wilkins bought the store and operated it as the Wilkins Dry Goods Store. Wilkins died on New Year's Day in 1963, and his widow, Cittie, closed the store that June. The Wilkins had two children, Charles and Wilma Jean.

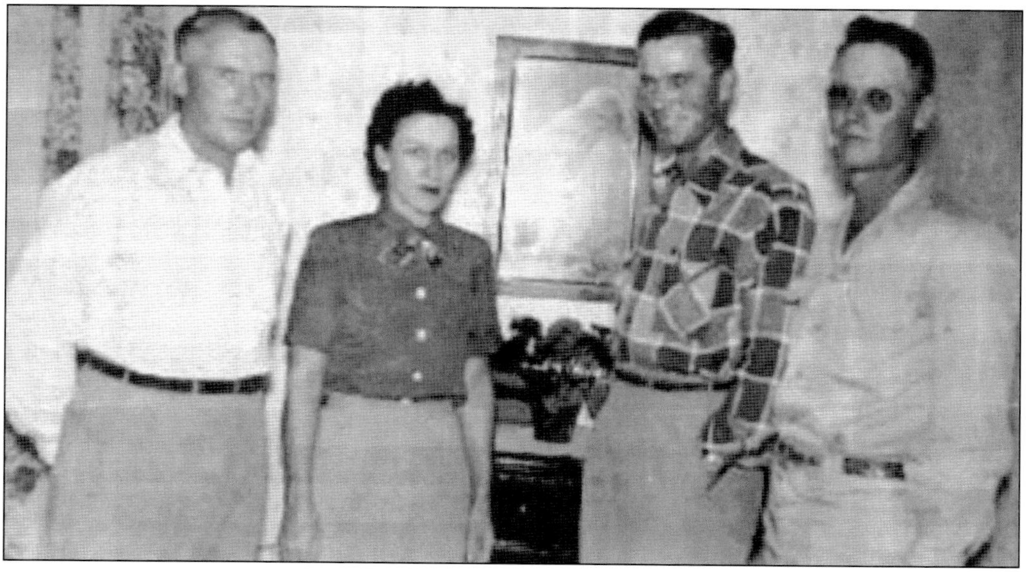

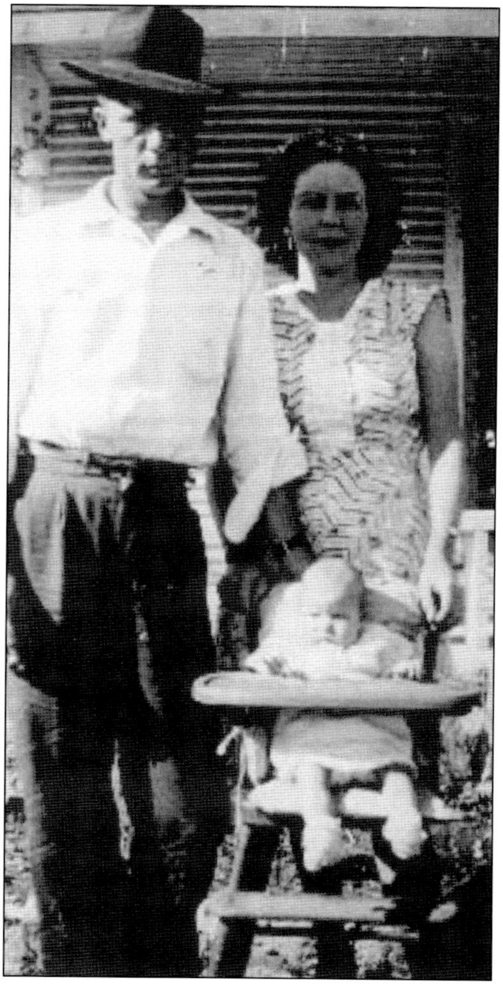

Joe and Junie Belle Myers had a farm southwest of Krum. They also had seven children, four of whom are shown here. They are, from left to right, Earl, Junie, Jack, and George. Junie married Howell Knox. Earl and his wife, Mary, owned the Krum Drug Store for several years.

Jack Wilkins and his wife, Edna, stand behind their daughter Deanna. Edna and Jack lived in a home formerly owned by the Rucker family.

Six

THE MILITARY

Krum is very proud of its men and women who have served in the nation's armed forces. An entire wall in the Krum Heritage Museum is devoted to remembering their patriotic service. Beginning with World War I, it is estimated that approximately 140 persons from the Krum area have served. Space is not available in this book to acknowledge the service of all of these individuals; therefore, this chapter will focus on those who made the ultimate sacrifice by giving their lives in service of the nation so that freedom and the American way of life can be preserved. One exception will be made, however, to honor the two Koiner brothers who became the highest-ranking officers to serve from Krum. The authors had hoped to include photographs of all the servicemen honored in this chapter, but unfortunately, print-quality photographs were not available in some cases.

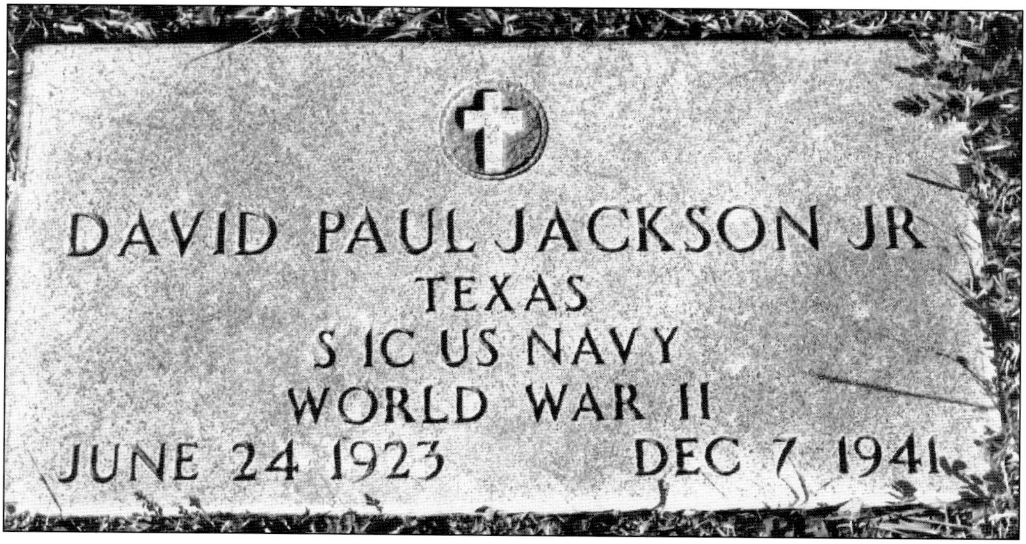

David Paul Jackson Jr., son of David P. Jackson and Mae Ethel Greene, was the first of Krum's servicemen to lose his life in one of America's conflicts. He was aboard the battleship *Arizona* at Pearl Harbor when he was killed during the Japanese attack on December 7, 1941. He was awarded the Purple Heart posthumously. It is said that, in 1940, Jackson walked 25 miles at night, after working all day, to enlist in the U.S. Navy. This tombstone in the Jackson Cemetery commemorates Jackson's life and death.

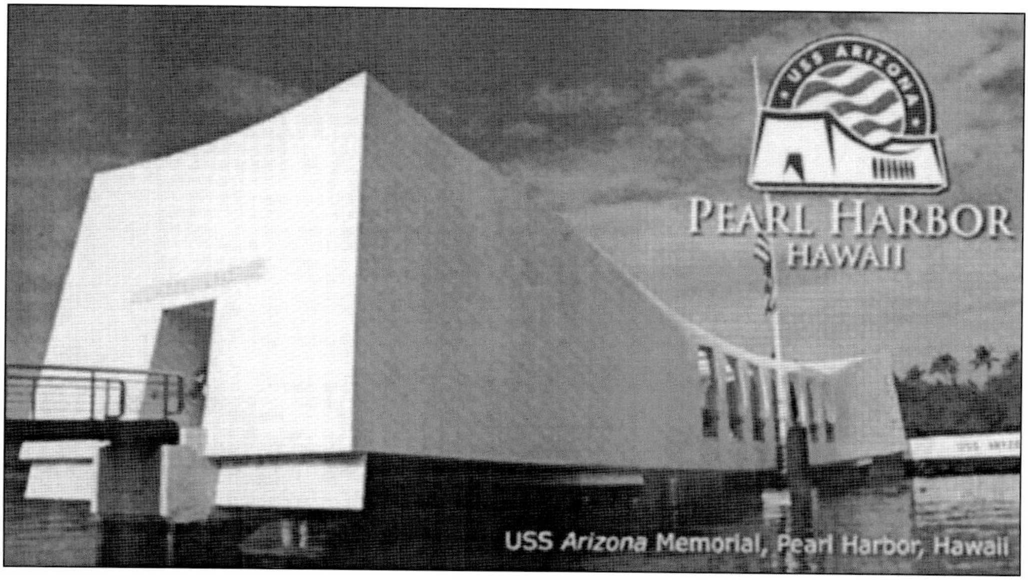

Pvt. William M. Mitchell, son of Willis Henry Mitchell and Mable Boyles, went overseas in November 1944, and a month later, he was reported missing in action in Germany. Among other decorations, he was awarded the Purple Heart posthumously.

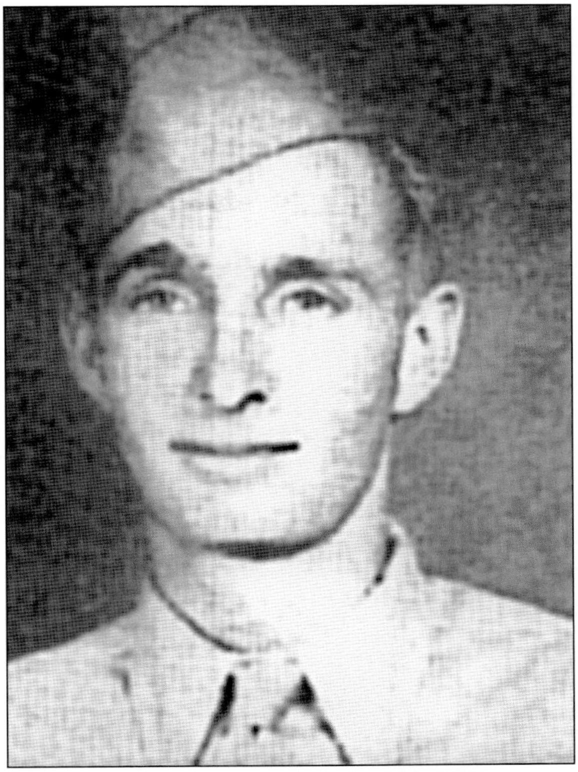

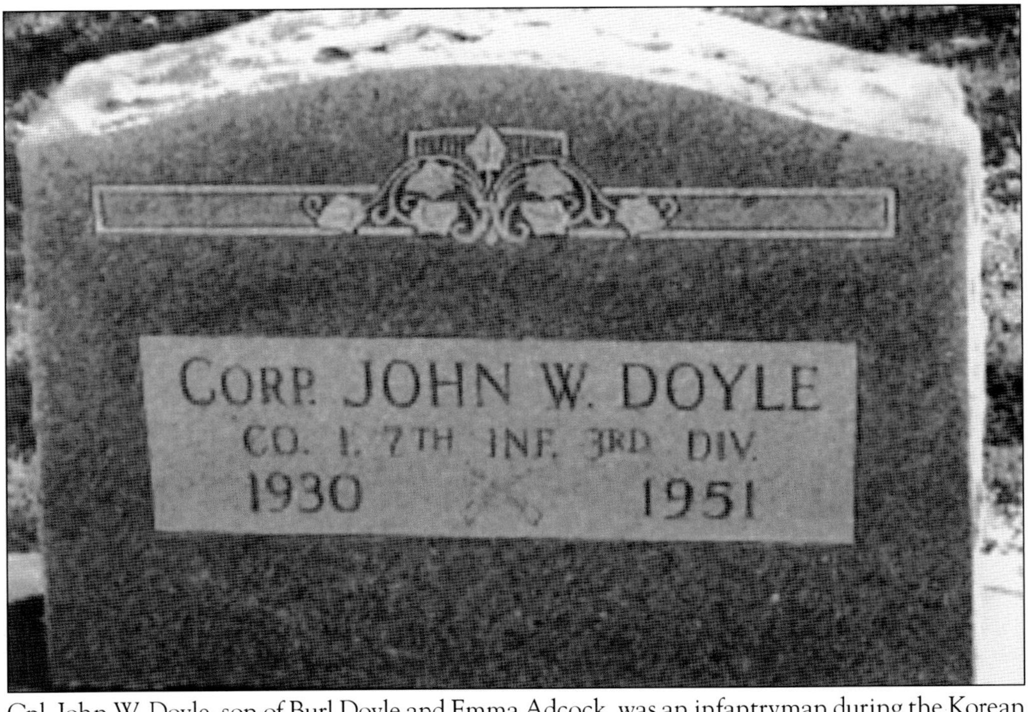

Cpl. John W. Doyle, son of Burl Doyle and Emma Adcock, was an infantryman during the Korean War and was killed in action on November 22, 1951. Corporal Doyle's brother, Pvt. Billy Doyle, also served in Korea and accompanied John's flag-draped coffin home.

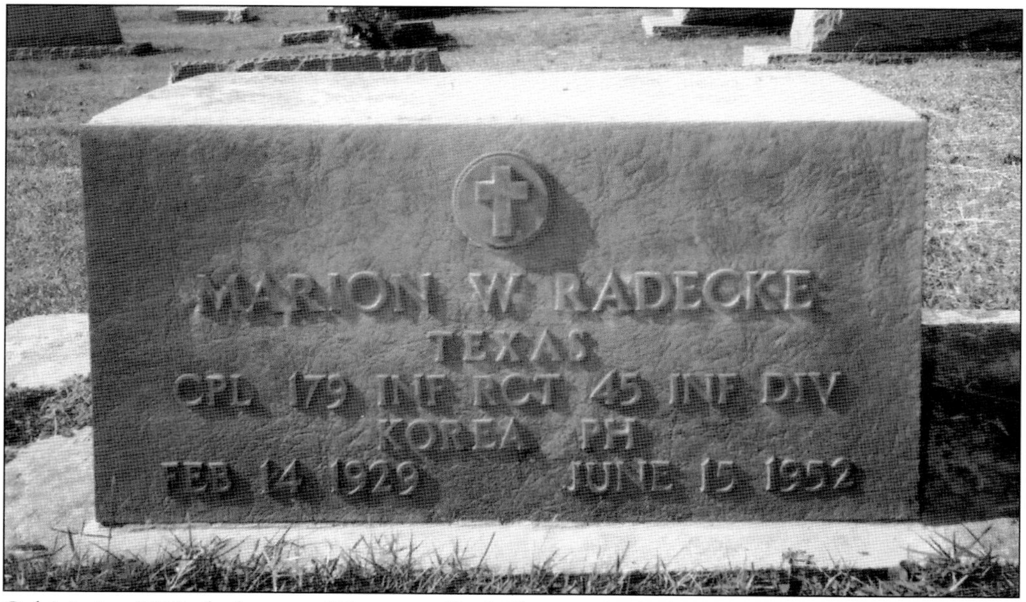

Cpl. Marion W. Radecke, son of Ernest and Icel Chestnut Radecke, served in Korea with the 179th Regiment, 45th Infantry Division. He was killed in action on June 15, 1952. Corporal Radecke was awarded the Purple Heart, Combat Infantryman's Badge, Korean Service Medal, United Nations Service Medal, National Defense Service Medal, and Korean War Service Medal.

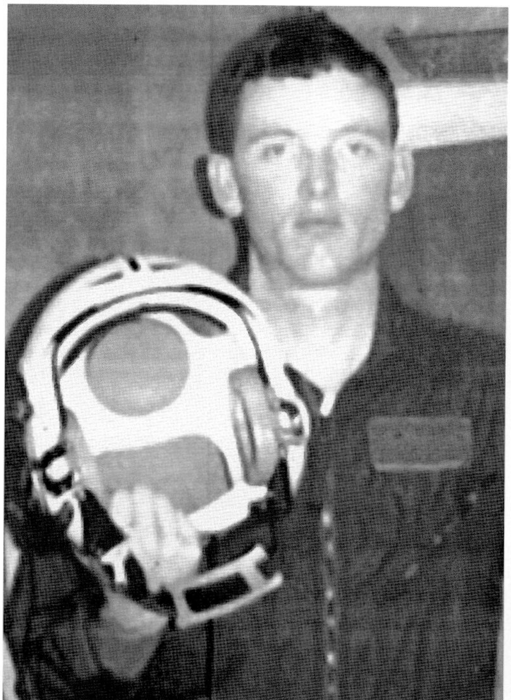

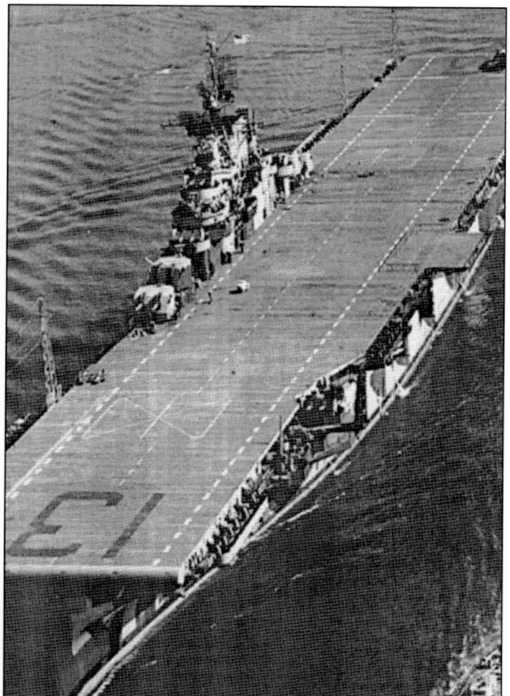

Ens. Joe Don Watson, son of George Edwell and Venita Jean Basye Watson, died on August 25, 1975, while trying to land an F-4 Phantom fighter jet on the flight deck of the USS *Franklin D. Roosevelt*. The plane landed on the flight deck and then crashed into the sea. A navy spokesman said that the gear designed to stop the plane malfunctioned.

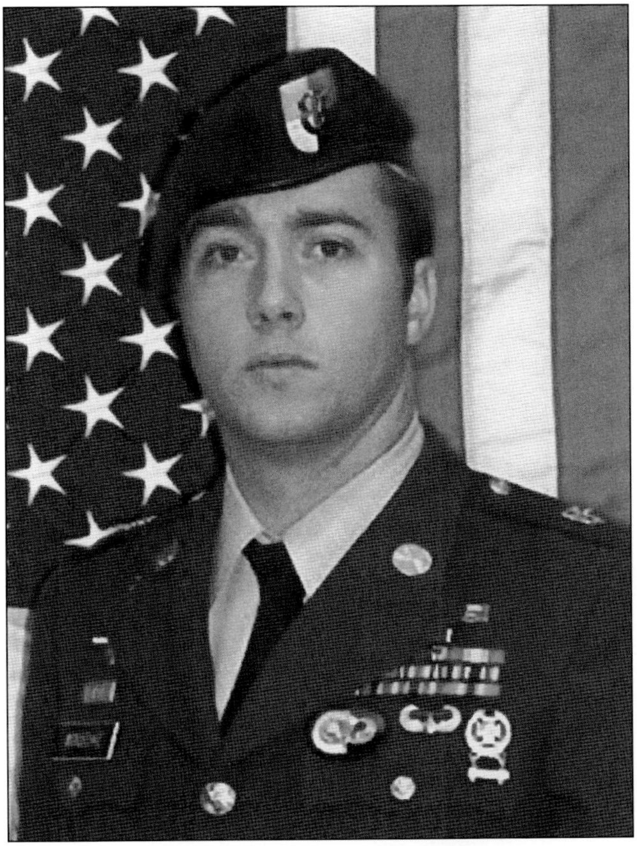

Sfc. Justin S. Monschke, son of Larry Monschke and Patty Forsythe, was killed on October 14, 2007, while serving with the U.S. Army Rangers, Special Forces, in Iraq. Sergeant Monschke earned a Silver Star, Bronze Star Medal, Meritorious Service Medal, Purple Heart, Army Forces Expeditionary Medal, Afghanistan Campaign Medal, Iraqi Campaign Medal, Global War on Terrorism Medal, Non-Commissioned Officer Professional Development Ribbon (third award), Army Service Ribbon, Special Forces Tab, Ranger Tab, Combat Infantry Badge, Expert Infantry Badge, Parachutist Badge, Air Assault Badge, and Russian Parachutist Badge.

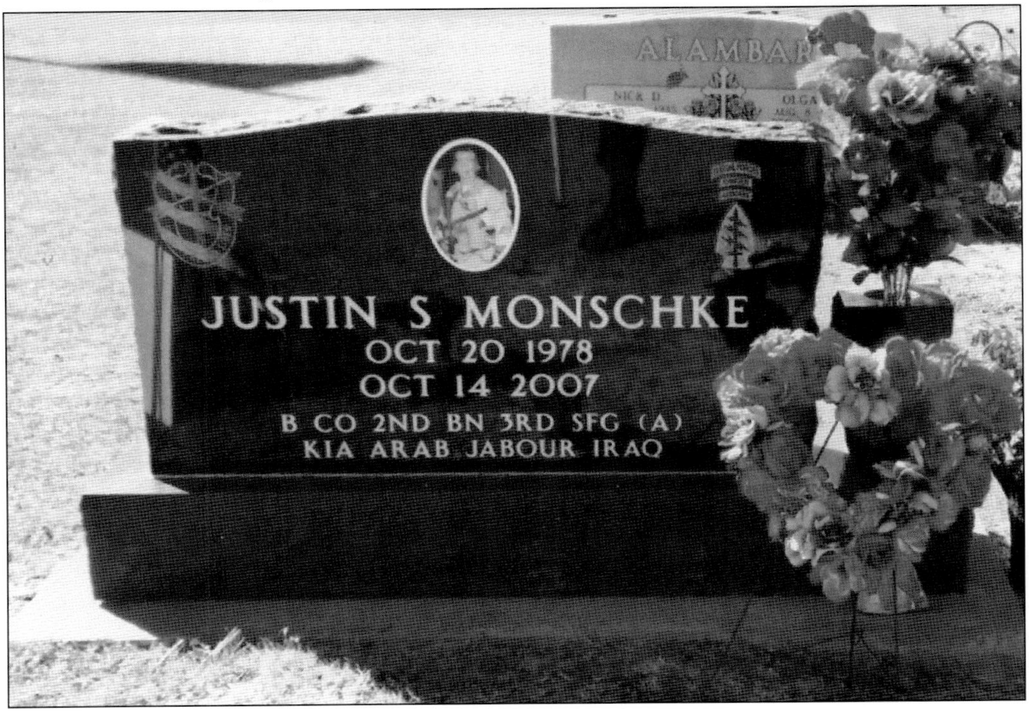

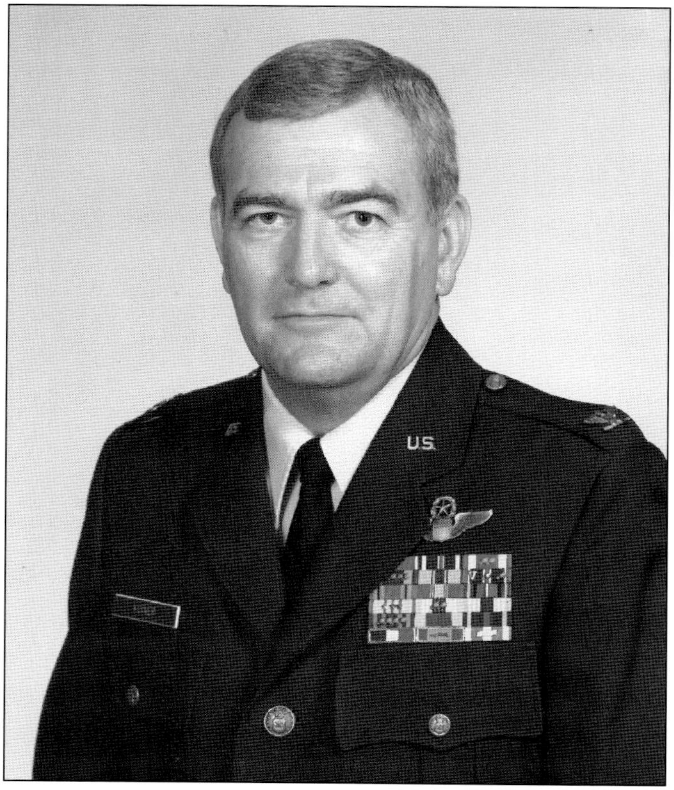

Col. Wylie J. Koiner served in the U.S. Air Force from 1966 to 1990. His areas of service included Southeast Asia, Vietnam, Korea, Japan, Taiwan, Germany, Italy, Egypt, Saudi Arabia, Oman, and "the ole USA."

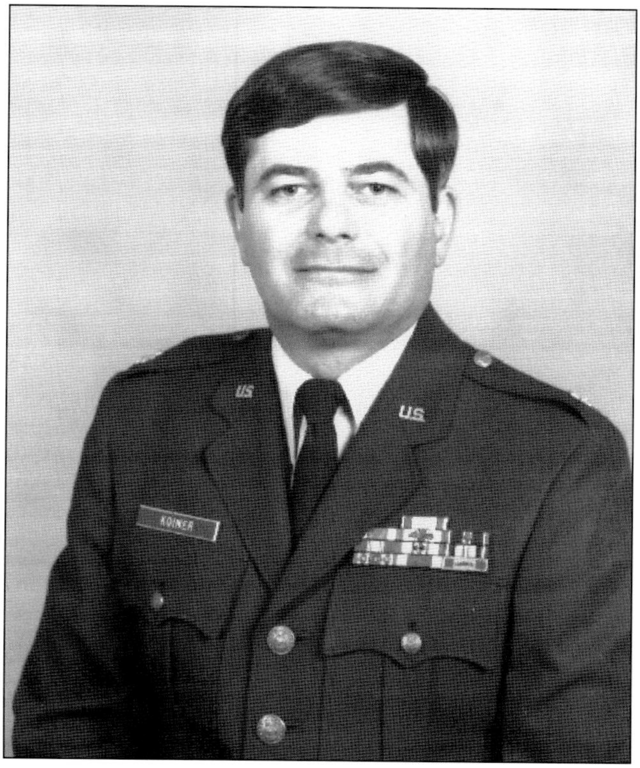

Lt. Col. John H. Koiner served in the U.S. Air Force from 1962 to 1982. He also served in all parts of the world, much of the time in Vietnam and Southeast Asia. It is a tribute to the Koiner family to have two sons serving with such distinction.

Seven

OUTLYING COMMUNITIES

Three smaller communities—Plainview, Hawkeye, and Stony—share Krum's heritage. Plainview is situated about 5 miles west of Krum. Prominent landmarks there were the school and the Baptist church. Organized in 1894, the church is still active as a place of worship and is recognized as a model country church. In 1898, a cemetery was created to the east of the church, and in 1907, Mrs. G. H. Fletcher donated 6 acres of land on which a parsonage was built. One condition of the donation was that the land be cultivated with its profits going into the church treasury. This policy is still being observed. A one-room school building was erected across the state highway (1173) from the church. In 1921, the original frame house was replaced with a brick building. It was an attractive and up-to-date structure with convenient, well ventilated, and correctly lighted recitation rooms, a spacious hall, and a large library and music hall. It was a source of genuine pride to the community.

The Hawkeye School, located about 5 miles north of Krum, was built in 1887 on land donated by pioneer John Koiner. The school also served as a community center. A literary society was organized there and met weekly. Occasionally the club issued a challenge to the Krum Literary Society for a debate or spelling match.

The Stony School was organized in 1884 with 31 students. In 1925, Stony had 10 grades. It was named for its stony location.

In 1934, a proposal from the Country School Board would "cut the Plainview School to seven grades if Krum will take one teacher of the present four, and if Krum will take the 8th and 9th grade students and furnish them with transportation." The board made the same proposal to the Hawkeye School. Both schools accepted the proposal, while continuing to operate their elementary schools. Then on December 16, 1946, the Krum School Board invited the Plainview, Hawkeye, and Stony Schools to consider consolidation, and the three outlying schools accepted the invitation. Half of the Stony students were absorbed into the Krum schools and the other half went to Ponder. The Hawkeye students were distributed equally to Krum and Sanger. All Plainview students came to Krum.

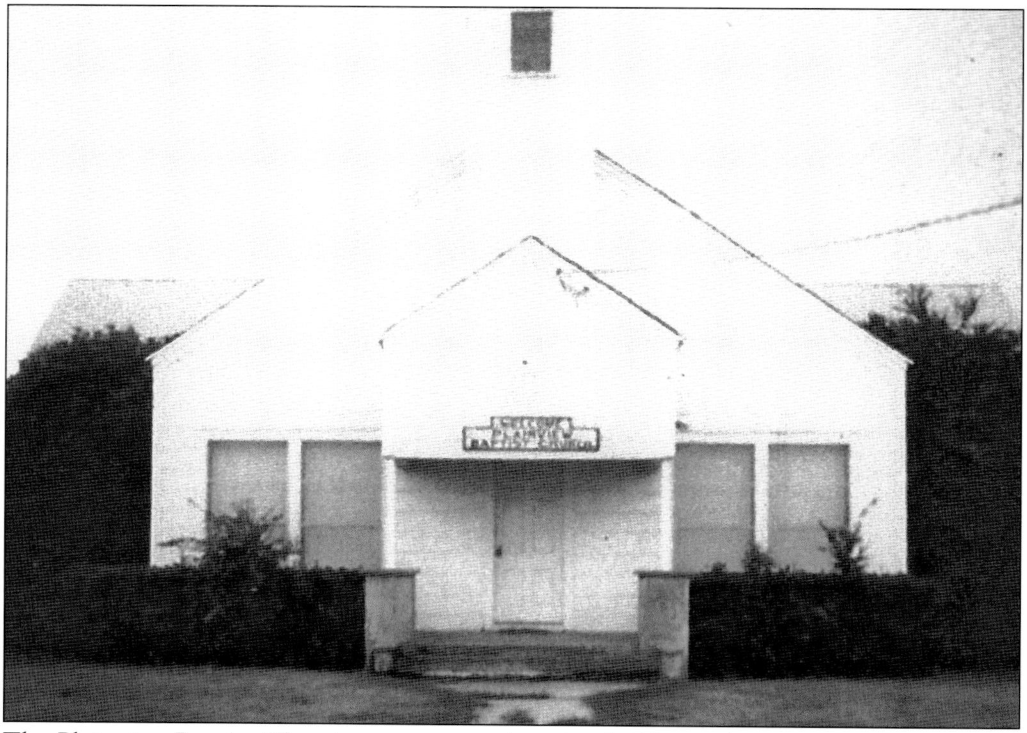

The Plainview Baptist Church was organized in April 1894 in the community's one-room schoolhouse, which was later replaced by the current church building. The church has maintained full-time services in the building, including Sunday school and mid-week prayer meetings, since it was founded.

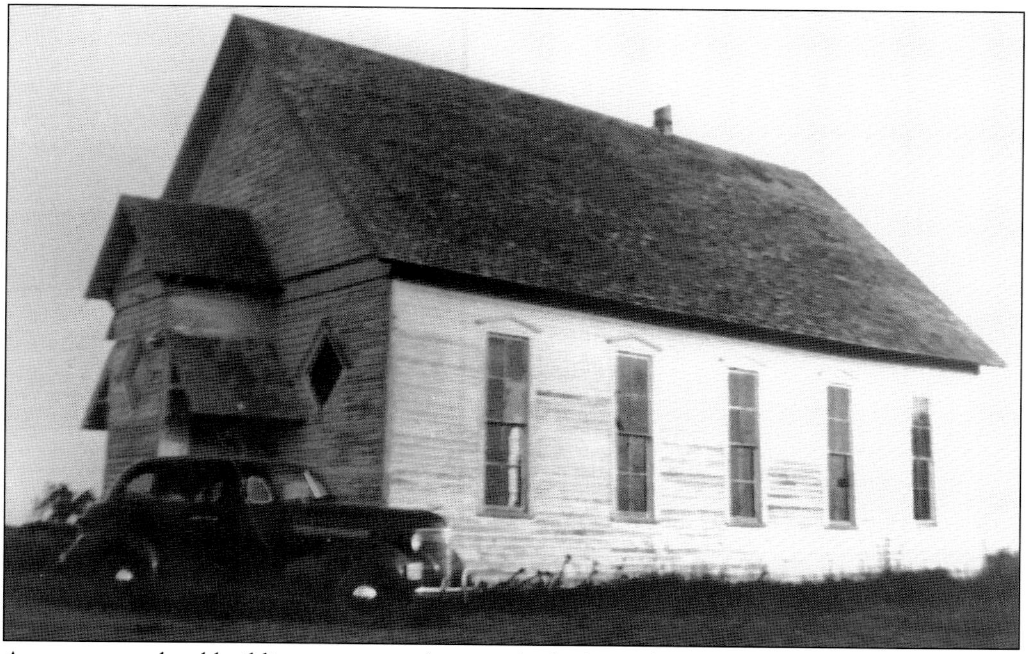

A one-room school building was erected across the highway (SH 1173) from the Baptist church. A large storm cellar, built for the safety of the pupils, is still on the lot.

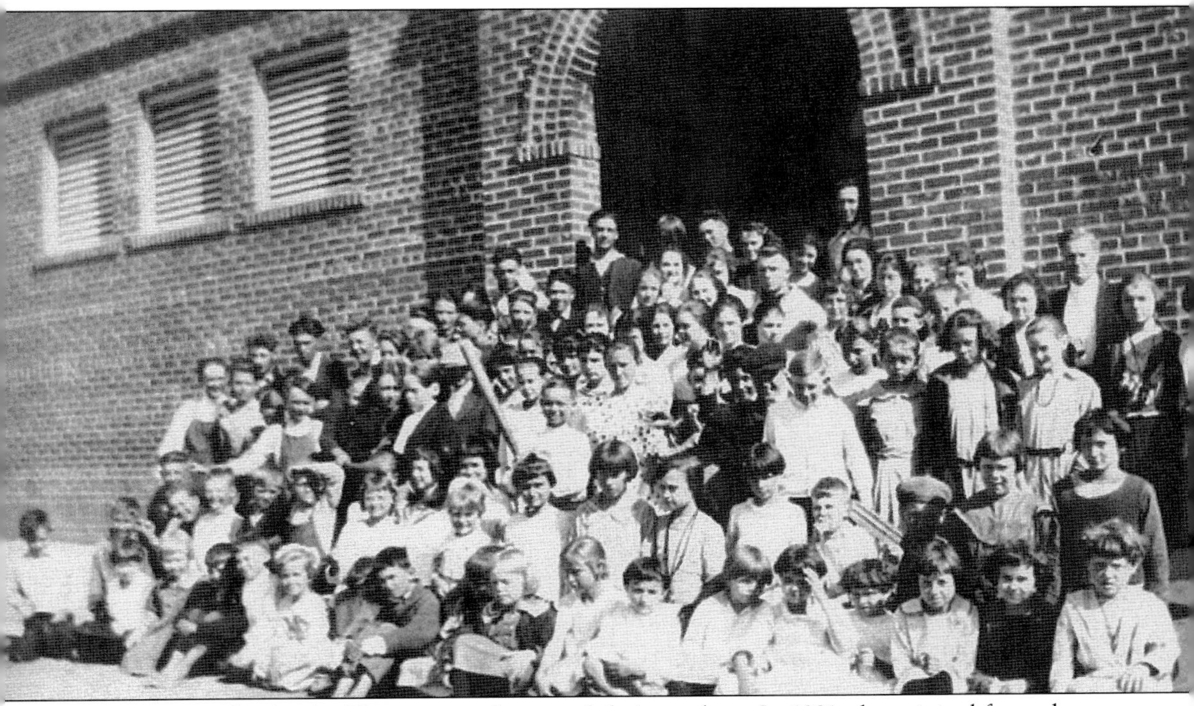

It is picture day for the Plainview students and their teachers. In 1921, the original frame house was replaced with a new brick building at a cost of $8,000. The school occupied this building until 1946, when the Plainview School District was discontinued. The building was later torn down. Many of these students still live in the area and have pleasant memories of their experiences in the Plainview School.

Course of Study
FOR THE
Plainview School
R. F. D. 1, Krum, Texas

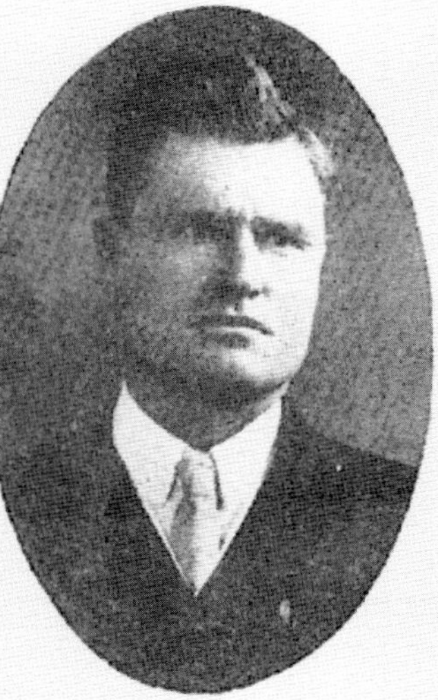

I. N. BURNETT, Superintendent
Twenty years experience, did degree work in Simmons College, Abilene.

1921-1922
WITH
Rules and Regulations
King's Messenger Print

Upon completion of the school's new brick building, Plainview's superintendent, I. N. Burnett, issued a new handbook to faculty members. The essence of the rules was that there would be no nonsense among students and that the new building and other school property would be well cared for.

teachers are:

1. All teachers must be in their respective rooms thirty minutes before the time for the opening exercises, require the pupils to be in their seats punctually at the appointed time, exercise a vigilant care over the conduct of their pupils in the school room, and, as far as possible, on the going and returning from school.

2. All teachers shall be subject to the Superintendent in the discharge of their duties, and shall do any additional work assigned to them by him.

3. The teachers shall not allow the pupils to play or romp in the halls or class room at noon or recess intermissions.

4. Teachers, though assigned to one grade, may afterwards be changed, or assigned to teach another, or part of others, as convenience or necessity may require.

5. Teachers shall hold pupils responsible for the neatness of their books and desks and around them, and shall not allow them to soil the floor in eating, or to scatter waste paper about the room. All marking, cutting, scratching or in any way defacing the walls, doors or furniture is positively forbidden, and teachers must punish the guilty.

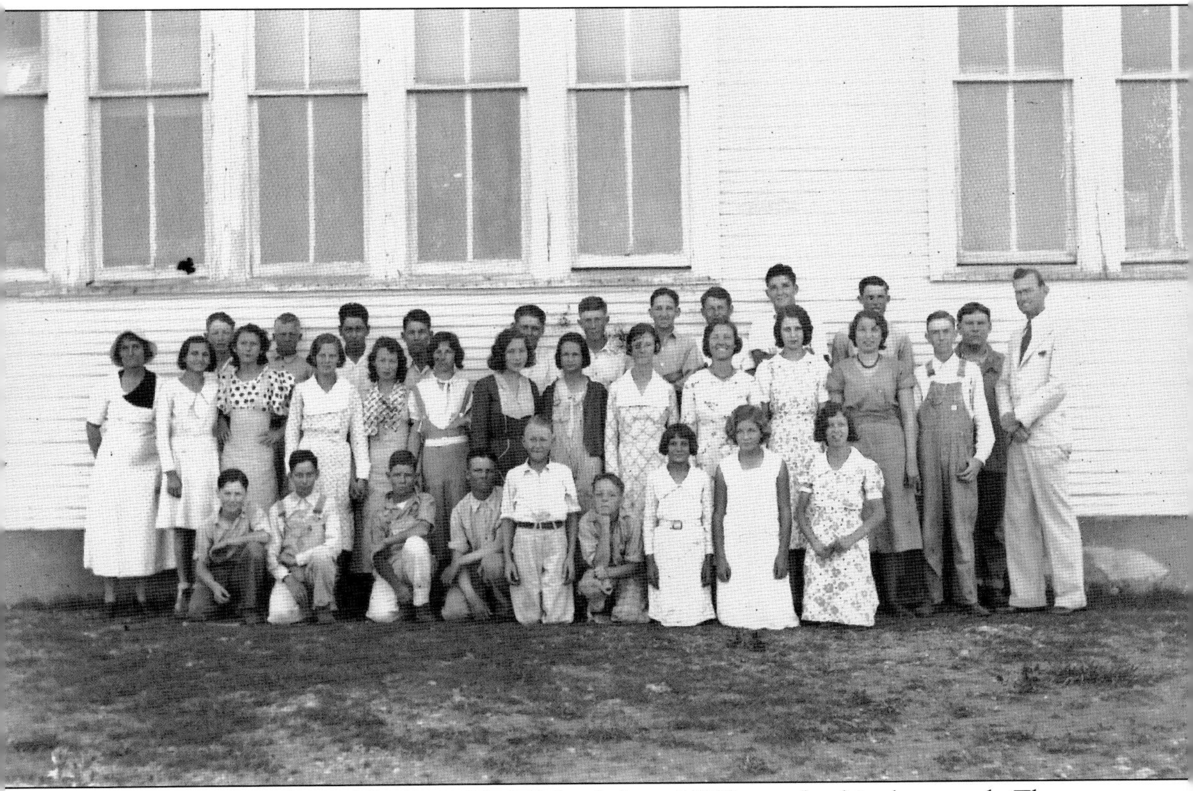

Students and teachers of the Stony High School class of 1932 pose for this photograph. They are, from left to right, (first row) Charles Smith, LeRoy Elmore, Mike Turner, Pat Coulter, Pierloyd O'Dell, Junior O'Dell, Doris Berstrom, and two unidentified; (second row) Mrs. Sparks, Francis Morin, Knovy Bunnell, Jane Thatcher, Ira May Bunnell, unidentified, Imogene Bottoms, Bernice Berstrom, Margaret Foster, Verna Mae Coulter, unidentified, Eula Coulter, Elvin Shifflett, and Jim Cox; (third row) two unidentified, Woody Snow, Richard Coulter, unidentified, T. B. Carroll, Duane Morin, Clarence Underwood, Joe Curtis Foster, A. J. Coulter, and Lonnie Riggs.

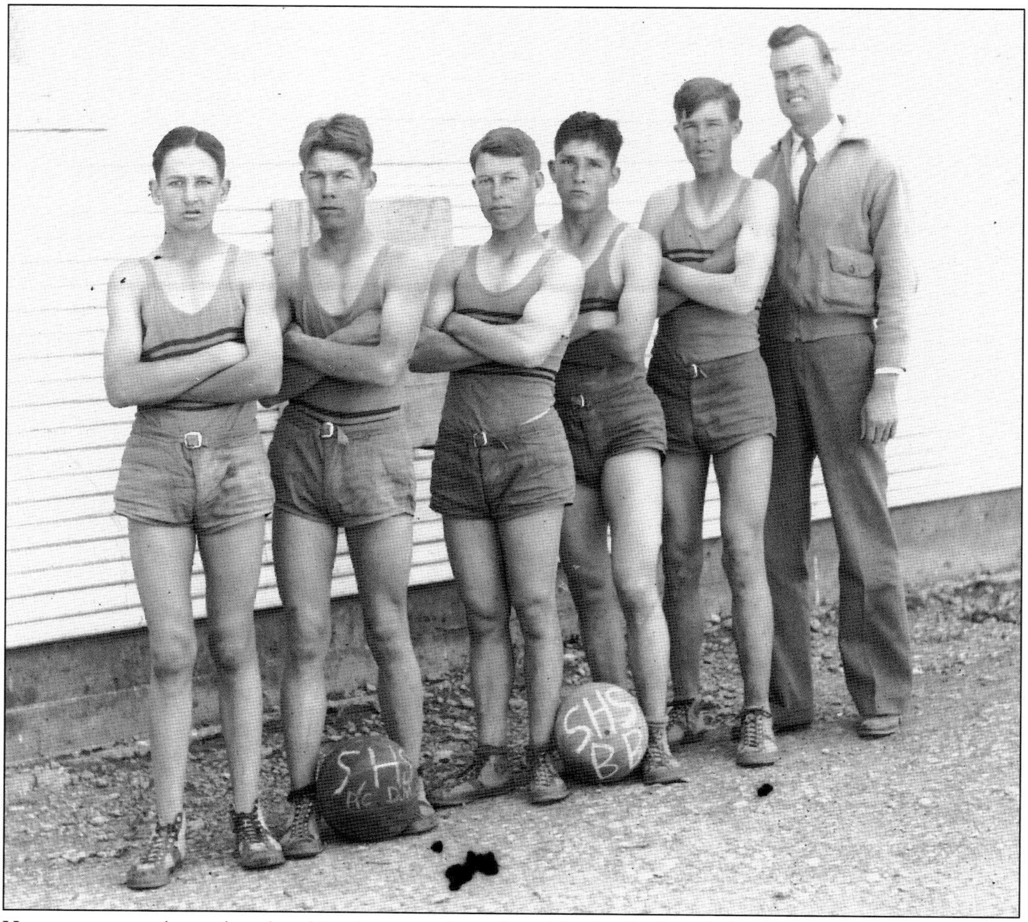

Krum was not the only school in the area that played basketball. While the Stony School existed, it also fielded a basketball team. Members of Stony's 1932 team are, from left to right, Duane Morin, Richard Coulter, Clarence Underwood, Joe C. Foster, A. J. Coulter, and coach Jim Cox.

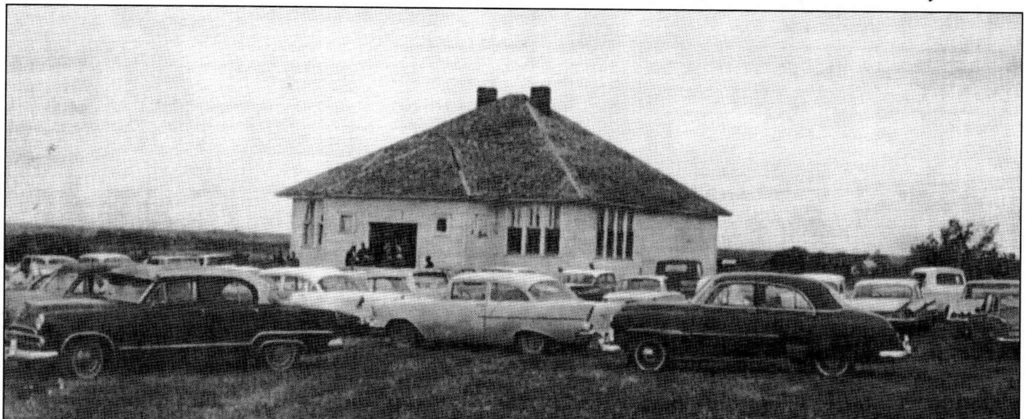

The number of cars in the picture indicates the high degree of interest for the 1965 homecoming of the Stony School. It was, and still is, a close-knit community. Today the building is used for homecomings, but it will always be the Stony School to all who attended.

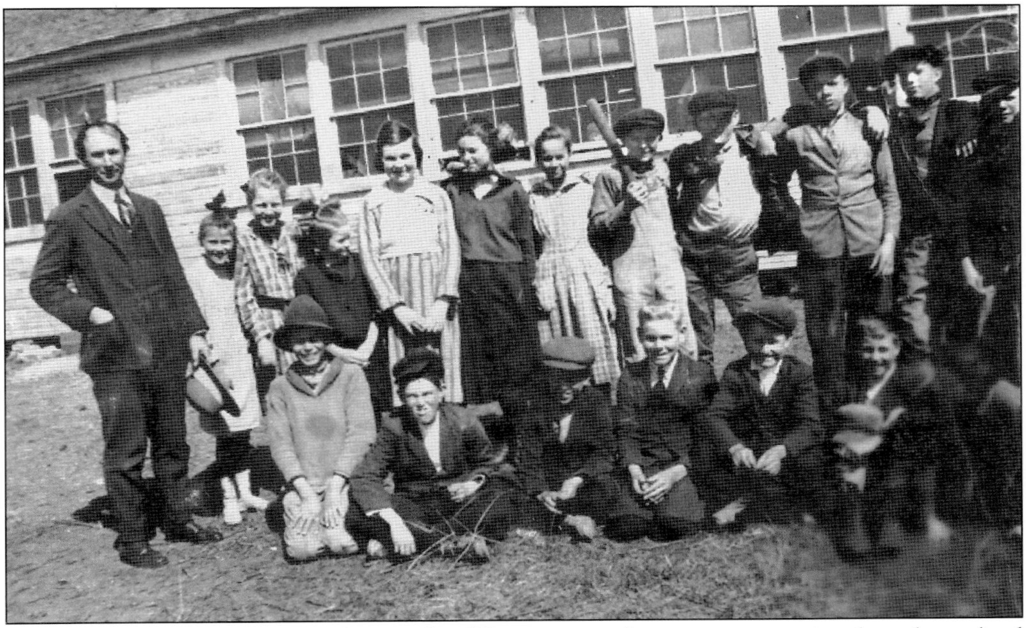

The Hawkeye area, about 5 miles north of Krum, was a farming community that also valued education. Although small in numbers, they built their own school in 1887, and it accommodated all elementary and secondary grade levels. When the school was discontinued in 1946, half of the students were absorbed into the Krum schools and half went to Sanger. The above photograph shows the Hawkeye students in 1919 with Professor Hudson, and in the image below, 1923 students are shown.

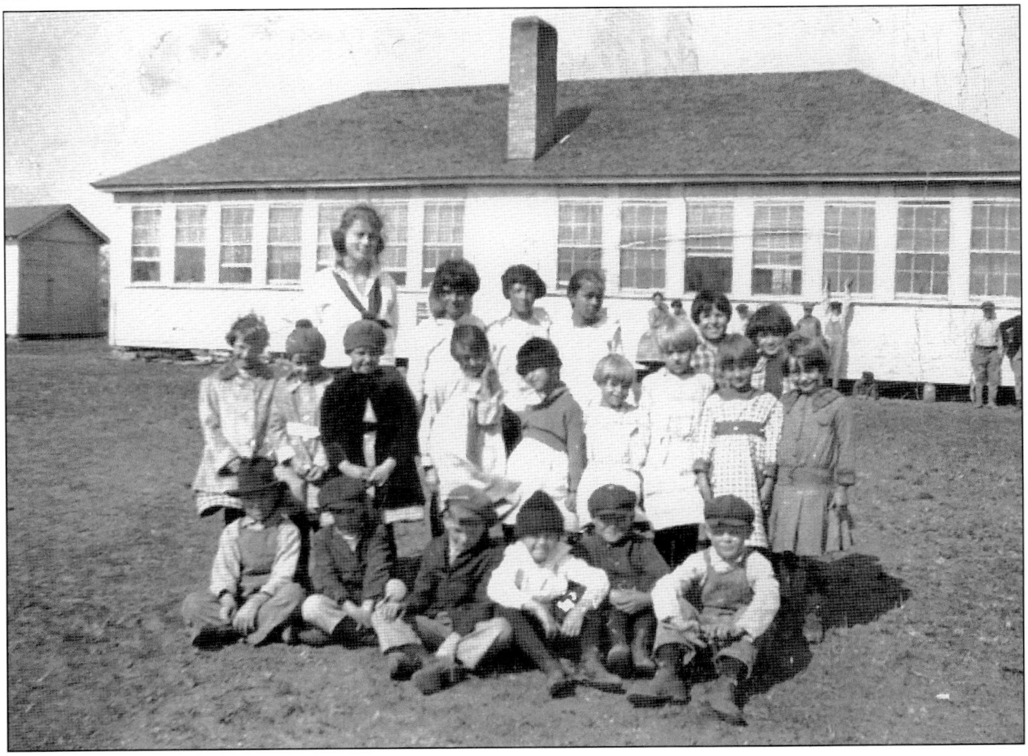

Consistent with our mission to preserve history on a local level, this book was printed in South Carolina on American-made paper and manufactured entirely in the United States. Products carrying the accredited Forest Stewardship Council (FSC) label are printed on 100 percent FSC-certified paper.

MADE IN THE USA